THE STORY OF THE BANNED BOOK

NAGUIB MAHFOUZ'S *CHILDREN OF THE ALLEY*

Mohamed
Shoair

Translated by
Humphrey Davies

The American University in Cairo Press
Cairo New York

First published in 2022 by
The American University in Cairo Press
113 Sharia Kasr el Aini, Cairo, Egypt
One Rockefeller Plaza, 10th Floor, New York, NY 10020
www.aucpress.com

First published in Arabic in 2018 as *Awlad haratina: sirat al-riwaya al-muharrama*

This translation is based on the third edition of *Awlad haratina: sirat al-riwaya al-muharrama* by Mohamed Shoair (Cairo: Dar al-'Ayn li-l-Nashr, also published in 2018). Divergences from the Arabic text reflect changes made by the author in anticipation of future editions.

ISBN 978 1 649 03085 6

Library of Congress Cataloging-in-Publication Data

Names: Shu'ayr, Muḥammad, author. | Davies, Humphrey, 1947- translator.
Title: The story of the banned book : Naguib Mahfouz's Children of the alley / Mohamed Shoair ; translated by Humphrey Davies.
Identifiers: LCCN 2021020079 | ISBN 9781649030856 (hardback)
Subjects: LCSH: Maḥfūẓ, Najīb, 1911-2006. Awlād ḥāratinā. | Maḥfūẓ, Najīb, 1911-2006--Criticism and interpretation. | Prohibited books--Egypt--History. | Prohibited books--Arab countries--History. | Arabic fiction--20th century--History and criticism.
Classification: LCC PJ7846.A46 A936513 2021 | DDC 892.7/3--dc23

1 2 3 4 5 26 25 24 23 22

Designed by Jon W. Stoy

To Taha Hussein and Nasr Abu Zayd

A donkey cart passed under the window, loaded with clapping singers.
Recite a prayer for the soldier boy.
He threw off his fez for a job as a saint!
Qassem smiled, remembering the night Yahya had sung this hymn stoned on hashish. Oh, if things would only straighten themselves out, all you'd have to do is sing, alley of mine!

Children of the Alley

"I'm a tourist in a museum where nothing belongs to me.
I'm merely a historian. I don't know where I stand."

Kamal 'Abd al-Gawad, in *Sugar Street*

CONTENTS

21 SEPTEMBER 1959

A sudden drop in temperature. The weather is almost cold. Autumn clouds cover Cairo's skies. The communists are sitting in prison at al-Mahariq but the campaigns against them continue. An unknown burglar breaks into "Ibn Hani's Vineyard" (the poet Ahmad Shawqi's house, on the banks of the Nile at Giza); among the stolen items are "a palm tree made of gold" (a gift from Bahrain's ruler, Hamad bin 'Isa, to Shawqi to celebrate Shawqi's installation as "the Prince of Poets" in April 1927), as well as a silver cup from the Feminist Union headed by Hoda Shaarawi.

The newspaper headlines speak of large demonstrations in Iraq against 'Abd al-Karim Qasim following the execution of a number of the leaders of the Shawwaf Uprising. The weekly *Akhbar al-yawm* leads the most violent of the attacks, vilifying Qasim as "the Nero of Baghdad." It also publishes a piece under the title "The Accursed Book," stating that Qasim is a follower of the ideas contained in it and claiming that the book, which attacks Islam, has been put together by Soviet intelligence sources. It then devotes a full-page spread to the popular proselytizer 'Abd al-Razzaq Nawfal refuting its ideas.

The main photograph in almost all the papers is of Abd al-Nasser, accompanied by 'Abd al-Hakim 'Amir, receiving the greetings of the masses from the window of the train on which they are returning from Rashid to Cairo. Two days previously, Abd al-Nasser had delivered a speech at Rashid as part of that city's celebrations of the victories over the British Army in 1807. The captions focus on the abolition of feudalism, the distribution of plots of land to farmers, and the launching of "Nasser's Project for Peasant Cattle Ownership." At the same celebration, Abd al-Nasser handed out the prizes to the winners of the "On the Road to Freedom" competition organized by the Higher Council for Arts and Literature, in which participants had been invited to complete the short story of that name about the Battle of Rashid that Nasser had begun as a high-school student but never finished. Three hundred forty-one stories have been submitted and the Council's Publications Committee has met fourteen times to select the three winners—Staff Officer Lt. Col. 'Abd al-Rahim Haggag and Captains 'Abd al-Rahman Fahmi and Faruq Hilmi. In an article titled "How to Complete the President's Story?," Yusuf al-Siba'i, the council's secretary-general, had complained at the exclusion of leading writers from the competition, resulting in a poor standard of contribution. The press had praised most highly the text by Haggag, even though it was the weakest artistically, perhaps because he was an officer and had used Abd al-Nasser as a character in his narrative and perhaps also because the story had been praised by Kamal al-Din Husayn, then minister of local government and president of the Higher Council for the Arts and Literature.

At the international level, the newspapers are occupied with the first visit by the Soviet leader to the USA, where Nikita Khrushchev has delivered a speech at the United Nations demanding "abolition of the armies of all the world's states, abolition of ministries of defense and military colleges, and limiting ourselves to small units for the maintenance of internal peace." For its part, *al-Ahram* maintains its coverage, which began two weeks previously, of the arrival of Russian rockets in space, thus launching a new era of science and knowledge.

A number of newspapers keep up their campaign against what they call "the disciples of James Dean," a small group of young Egyptian admirers of the American actor (1931–55), who shot to global stardom before completing his twenty-fourth year. His performance as Jim Stark in the film *Rebel Without a Cause* (1955) has made him a youth icon and his shocking demise in a car accident has lent him the glamor of legend, leading young people to imitate both his looks and his clothes. The press campaign accuses the same young people of rebelling against their fathers and their generation, of performing a wanton dance called the "cha-cha," of smoking cigarettes, and of letting their hair grow long and unkempt. Certain preachers in the mosques accuse them of corruption and decadence, while journalists and politicians demand that they be drafted into the army, to teach them manners and make men of them. All this uproar has found a willing ear in 'Abd al-Hakim 'Amir, who has stepped in to deal with the phenomenon, ordering his men of the military police, in his capacity as minister of defense, to stop and shave the head of anyone whom they find dancing the cha-cha in a public place or singing 'Abd al-Halim Hafiz's "Abu 'uyun jari'a" (The Boy with Bold Eyes).

In *al-Akhbar*, Nasir al-Din al-Nashashibi interviews Prof. Sten Friberg, a member of the administrative committee of the Nobel Prize in Literature, who pronounces that "it is the fault of the Arab universities that no Arab has been nominated for the Nobel Prize," while Ahmad Baha' al-Din writes from Stockholm about Jean-Paul Sartre's play *The Condemned of Altona*, which he regards as "the most significant work of literature since the end of the World War."

In Cairo, the National Theater is presenting *al-'Ashara al-tayyiba* (The Lucky Card) and the Rihani troupe's *Hikayat kull yawm* (An Everyday Story). The *Kitabi* (My Book) series is issuing an Arabic translation of Pasternak's *Doctor Zhivago* in two parts, and the series *Maktabat al-funun al-diramiya* (The Library of the Dramatic Arts) a translation of Tennessee Williams's play *Cat on a Hot Tin Roof*, while Riyad al-Sunbati has just finished setting to music "al-Hubb kida" (That's the Way Love Is), with which Umm Kulthum is about to open her new season. The cinemas are full, with posters for new films taking up much of the advertising space in the newspapers, and on that one day we can watch more than fifteen foreign films, including Sophia Loren's *The Millionairess*, Bob Hope's and Jane Russell's *The Paleface*, and *Tarzan's Greatest Adventure*, as well as approximately the same number of Egyptian movies, including *'Ashat li-l-hubb* (She Lived for Love) with Zubayda Sarwat, *al-Hubb al-akhir* (The Last Love) with Hind Rustum and Ahmad Mahir, and Isma'il Yasin's *al-Bulis al-sirri* (The Secret Police).

On that same day, *al-Ahram* newspaper began publication, on page 10, of the first installment of Naguib Mahfouz's new novel *Awlad haratina (Children of the Alley)*, an event announced on its front page a week earlier:

> *Al-Ahram* has agreed with the great writer Naguib Mahfouz to publish his new long work, in installments. Mahfouz is a writer who has proved himself capable of portraying Egyptian life with the hand of a creative and highly gifted artist; thus the appearance of a new work by him has always been a literary event of

> outstanding importance for the history of the intellectual revival of recent years. *Al-Ahram* has signed a contract for one thousand pounds with Naguib Mahfouz granting it the right to publish his new story in its newspaper. *Al-Ahram* does not mention this sum—the largest paid for a single story in the history of the Arabic press—out of pride or presumption but to mark the start of a new era of appreciation for literary production. (*al-Ahram*, 14 September 1959)

The large sum was not the only form in which *al-Ahram*'s celebration of Naguib Mahfouz manifested itself. The newspaper prepared for the event with what amounted to a publicity campaign, starting four days before publication with a long interview with the author by Inji Rushdi in which he spoke at length of his creative worlds, his experiences, his study of philosophy, and his love of music, and alluded briefly to the new novel (*al-Ahram*, 18 September 1959). And one day before, the following news item appeared: "Naguib Mahfouz in *al-Ahram* Tomorrow," accompanied by two portraits, one of Mahfouz and one of the painter al-Husayn Fawzi, who had drawn illustrations depicting the novel's characters.

Reality, it appears, is always interwoven—artistically, intellectually, and politically. Naguib Mahfouz was writing the screenplay for *Ihna al-talamza* (We the Students), based on a story by Tawfiq Salih and Kamil Yusuf. Publicity for the film (starring Omar Sharif, Shukri Sirhan, Yusuf Fakhr al-Din, and Karioka) focused on its being "a film for every young man and every young woman, every father and every mother, every family and every household, a film that combats effeminacy and calls for strength and positivity!" according to a sentence written in large letters on the poster and which would seem to be an extension of the campaign to discipline "the disciples of James Dean." People who knew Naguib Mahfouz and the ways of the cinema world thought it likely that the sentence had less to do with Mahfouz than with the producer, Hilmi Rafla, who spoke of the film, in the magazine *al-Jil* (The Generation) ("al-Sinima tu'addi risalataha nahw al-mujtama'," *al-Jil*, no 406 [5 October 1959], 17), as part of a mission "against the likes of James Dean, the manifestations of whose effeminacy have multiplied and the instances of whose perverseness have become so widespread that they have resulted in the intervention of the morals police, now that sexual frustration has driven these persons down the path of pain, the path of evil!" Rafla stated that he had chosen Naguib Mahfouz to write the screenplay because "he is known for the profundity with which he studies situations, the power with which he portrays characters, and the brilliance with which he gives expression to feelings and reactions."

Mahfouz was also writing the storyline for *Bayna al-sama' wa-l-ard* (Between Heaven and Earth), a film produced by Salah Abu Yusuf that appeared in theaters simultaneously with the publication of *Children of the Alley* and that marks a shift in Mahfouz's cinema work away from realism and toward an openness to the symbol, just as in *Children of the Alley*, where he abandons the "naked realism" that had reached its apogee with *al-Thulathiya: Bayn al-qasrayn*, *Qasr al-shawq*, and *al-Sukkariya (The Cairo Trilogy: Palace Walk*, *Palace of Desire*, and *Sugar Street)*. The film poses philosophical questions whose answers divide, multiply, and are left hanging—like its heroes in their broken elevator—between heaven and earth.

Mahfouz's thumbprint as scriptwriter, and one seeking creative solutions to the restrictions on the space available to him in the film, is clear. It was an artistic dilemma that Mahfouz had already succeeded in overcoming as a novelist. Indeed, he had excelled at exploiting it for his dramatic purposes in both *Zuqaq al-midaq (Midaq Alley)*, a novel whose events take place in a narrow alley, and in *Tharthara fawq al-Nil (Adrift on the Nile)*, most of whose action occurs on a houseboat on the Nile. Throughout *Bayna al-sama' wa-l-ard*, and despite the restricted space (out of which, even so, emerge worlds pulsing with life), Mahfouz poses questions about the limits of truth and fiction, death and life, sanity and madness, reality and the cinema. On release, the film met with little acclaim from either the critics or the public; years later Mahfouz explained its failure by saying that it was "an experiment in terms of the Egyptian cinema of the time, and its success may have come after the premiere. People weren't used to that kind of film." Referring to the source of his inspiration for this important experiment, he added, "They had made a film of the same type in America that was meant to be a nod to Hitler. Its hero tyrannizes people in a closed apartment, and the film did very well in the West" (Yusuf al-Qa'id, *Naguib Mahfouz in haka*, 28).

Some months previously, Salah al-Bitar, minister of culture and national guidance of the central government of the Egyptian–Syrian union (at the time, Sarwat 'Ukasha was the minister in the Southern Regional, that is, Egyptian, government) had made a statement that had set literary circles in an uproar. The minister had said that "our literature does not sufficiently express the Arab-nationalist aspirations of the Arabs"("Hal hunaka adab wihda wa-adab tajzi'a?," *al-Gumhuriya*, 5 March 1959). When *al-Gumhuriya* (The Republic) newspaper confronted the world of literature with the minister's words, Naguib Mahfouz commented that "the movement for the revitalization of the Arab literary legacy and its study according to new programmatic principles, as undertaken by Taha Hussein, al-'Aqqad, and others, is a part of the Arab Nationalist intellectual project. At the same time, any literature that is not actually against Arab unity must be counted as being for it" (*Sabah al-khayr*, 26 March 1959). Strangely, the poet Ahmad 'Abd al-Mu'ti Higazi, in his comment, adopted a similar position to al-Bitar's, considering that "the men of letters of the Southern Region [Egypt] are the Arab literary figures most accepted by and best known to the Arab masses. Despite this, they have fallen short in giving expression to the broad aspirations with which the emotional life of those masses pulses." Higazi poured scorn on the excuses put forward by other writers (Naguib Mahfouz, Yusuf Idris, Yusuf al-Siba'i, Amin Yusuf Ghurab, 'Ali Ahmad Ba Kathir) in response to *al-Gumhuriya*'s investigation and called for "workshops to be held for the writers of the Northern and Southern regions at which Arab Nationalist ideas could be expounded and promoted," going on to recommend

> the conversion of the National Unity committees into cultural and intellectual schools where the People could be educated in the truth of the Nationalist creed, a creed that President Gamal Abd al-Nasser had been the first politician and intellectual to place, with great firmness and faith, before the Arab People in Egypt, it being the duty of youth to follow the path set by their leader until such time as it becomes a living reality and the very breath of every citizen.

At this point, according to the minister, the man of letters would find himself propelled, without volition on his part, to give it expression (*Sabah al-khayr*, 26 March 1959).

NO TABOOS IN LITERATURE

As Ahmad 'Abd al-Mu'ti Higazi claimed, Naguib Mahfouz had never written of the causes dear to Arab Nationalism. His preoccupation was with other ideas. In *al-Akhbar*, Mahfouz spoke to Anis Mansur of the strict regime he had set himself and of his extreme hatred of travel, because it "made a mess" of his life (*al-Akhbar*, 4 November 1958). Mansur asked him, "Imagine, Naguib, you're asleep, and ideas and insights come thronging to you and you have to write them down immediately or they'll be lost—what do you do?" Mahfouz replied, "You mean inspiration? In the first place, I never interrupt my sleep because if I did so I'd arrive at work exhausted and unable to do my job, or I'd be obliged to go back to sleep after recording those inspirations and that would complicate my life. I would, therefore, go on sleeping and pay no attention to them." Anis Mansur called Mahfouz "the Train." He wrote, "Naguib Mahfouz looks around him, and I realize that the station bell has rung and the Train is on its way home to eat, sleep, wake up, and start writing the first page of a long novel that he will finish after precisely two years and whose name will be *Children of the Alley*." It was in this way that the press revealed, for the first time, the existence of a new novel by Mahfouz, and that he had started work on it.

Four months later, on his assumption of his new post as director for literary works at the Censorship Authority, *al-Ahram* asked Mahfouz, "What do you hope for?" to which Mahfouz responded, "I hope to be able to continue working on my novel *Children of the Alley*, which I've started" (*al-Ahram*, 11 February 1959). This was the first time that Mahfouz himself spoke of his novel, seven months before its publication.

Four days after Mahfouz's interview with *al-Ahram*, *al-Bulis* (The Police) magazine published an extensive report on the new novel, which the magazine expected to cause a major sensation as soon as it appeared:

> Naguib Mahfouz is currently writing a new novel, titled *Children of the Alley*, despite his earlier decision to give up writing altogether. Until this point he has completed seventy pages of the new novel, which will cause a major sensation when it appears. Naguib has never ceased writing for an instant. He is now forty-seven years of age, unmarried, and lives a modest and disciplined life. He leaves his government job at two in the afternoon, then he takes lunch at home and rests for a little. Afterward he reads and writes, daily, until 10 p.m. Then he goes to sleep, like clockwork, at 10 p.m. He is a great artist but, at the same time, a government employee who observes working hours and never ever arrives later than eight or whatever the official time may be. Naguib exudes vivacity, modesty, intelligence, and kindheartedness. There is a long history of such men in the world of talent and genius, and his like can never, under any circumstances, cease to produce art. And soon we shall be reading *Children of the Alley*. (*al-Bulis*, 15 February 1959)

References by other magazines and newspapers to the long-awaited novel followed. The editor of *al-Jil* asked him (20 March 1959):

> "What are you working on now?"
> "A novel called *Children of the Alley* that I started in October 1958 and of which I've written 150 foolscap pages. It will be about 300 pages."
> "What is the subject of the novel?"
> "Please don't press me to answer that question."
> "Never mind the subject. What kind of novel is it?"
> "And that too. It's a novel of a new kind, unlike anything I've written before. So I'm scared. Very scared."

Three weeks later, the magazine returned to Mahfouz and asked him what prayer he would utter on the Night of Power. He answered:

"O Lord, help me to finish *Children of the Alley*, which I started last October! O Lord, let a ban on atomic weapons be agreed so that we can live to realize our hopes for our country and ourselves! O Lord, let the war in Algeria end with victory for the Arabs!" (*al-Jil*, 6 April 1959)

Sabah al-khayr (Good Morning) magazine published an item describing the new novel as containing a new view of life on Mahfouz's part and stating that he had put into it a set of ideas that would surprise everyone who followed his work (*Sabah al-khayr*, 16 April 1959).

Kuwait's *al-'Arabi* (The Arab) magazine, less than two months before the novel's publication, asked, "What are you writing now?" to which he replied, "The screenplay for a film about Saladin and my forthcoming novel, which I'm calling *Children of the Alley*" (*al-'Arabi*, August 1959).

During the same interview, the interviewer asked him, "What is your opinion of 'explicit' literature?"

Mahfouz replied, "I believe in good literature, by which I mean profound, all-encompassing, humanistic literature that deals with the problems of mankind seriously and sincerely. Candor in such literature is comparable to candor in medicine and the law, since its very nature is to guide the reader toward reflection and the sublime, not decadence and vulgarity, and one can find such things in the Torah and the Qur'an. It may be that the fear of what is called 'explicit literature' may come not so much from its explicitness as from its superficiality and triviality, which has no purpose other than to titillate and sell copies."

This led the magazine to give the interview the title "No Taboos in Religion—or Literature!"

Every response given by Mahfouz in every interview that preceded the novel's publication indicates that he submitted the novel for publication immediately on finishing it. Mahfouz's writing year ran from September to April, after which he would stop for the four summer months because of an eye allergy that first afflicted him when he was a student at the university. This means that Mahfouz finished writing the novel in April of the same year, before taking his "holiday for contemplation, cogitation, and relaxation," as he called it.

At first, the attention of the press was focused not on the new novel itself but on the fact that Mahfouz had started writing again, after a long gap during which he had more than once announced his retirement from literature, for which silence, or pause, he had offered numerous justifications.

Mahfouz wrote nothing during the five years from 1952 to 1957, years that he named "the menopause" or "the drought." When he finished his *Trilogy*, his publisher, Sa'id Guda al-Sahhar, had refused to publish it because of its length. Some, however, believe that al-Sahhar's rejection of the novel had nothing to do with its size and that the true reason may be deduced from Mahfouz's comments to Gamal al-Ghitani:

> I made a big mistake, one I never committed again. During this period, I talked a lot about that kind of novel and expounded at great length my ideas and my intention to write something of the sort some day. A writer who had been listening to me went off and set about writing a novel of the same type, that is, a novel of generations, publishing it in six months. (Gamal al-Ghitani, *Naguib Mahfouz yatadhakkar*, 63)

Mahfouz does not mention the name of the writer in whose presence he had spoken of his idea, but his close friends knew that he meant Sa'id Guda al-Sahhar's brother, the novelist 'Abd al-Hamid Guda al-Sahhar, and his novel *Fi qafilat al-zaman* (In the Caravan of Time). Mahfouz tells al-Ghitani, "I grieve when I think of the period following [Sa'id] al-Sahhar's refusal to publish the novel. It was a terrible blow. Indeed, it was a humiliation, especially as he asked me, the moment he saw it, 'What in hell's name is this?!'" (Gamal al-Ghitani, *Naguib Mahfouz yatadhakkar*, 61).

Sulayman Fayyad recounts the incident differently: "Mahfouz told ['Abd al-Hamid] al-Sahhar, 'I want to write a novel about Egypt.' Al-Sahhar liked the idea and bet Mahfouz that he too could write 'the story of Egypt.' So they agreed to meet after a year to see which of them had finished first." Al-Sahhar finished before the date set and sent his novel to be published, but Mahfouz took longer. Speaking of al-Sahhar's novel, he told Fayyad, "It's nice. If only though he'd been able to give it a bit more time and not been in such a rush!" (personal interview, June 2014).

Mahfouz's shock at ['Abd al-Hamid] al-Sahhar's deceit—especially when taken with the delay of five whole years in the publication of the *Trilogy*—caused him to stop writing. Additionally, in 1954, he married (the marriage remained a secret until revealed by *Sabah al-khayr* ten years later) and suddenly found himself responsible for three households—his mother's, his wife's, and that of his sister, whose husband had died leaving her with children to support. In such circumstances, as he says, "I had no choice but to find work from which I could obtain the additional income needed to face the responsibilities of marriage and my new family" (Raga' al-Naqqash, *Naguib Mahfouz: safahat min mudhakkaratihi wa-adwa' jadida 'ala adabihi wa-hayatihi*, 141). He therefore resorted to another art, that of the cinema, which gave him a reasonable income, writing, during this period, around twelve screenplays. He also wrote the occasional short story, as evidenced by the publication, in *al-Risala al-jadida* (The New Message) magazine, of *Laka ma tasha'* (Whatever You Wish Is Yours), a work not included in any of his subsequent short-story collections and to which no bibliography of his refers (*al-Risala al-jadida*, September 1958).

> When journalists or critics would ask Mahfouz about this pause in his output, he would justify his silence in a variety of ways. Sometimes he would say that he had "found himself to be exhausted" and his vision depleted by the writing of the *Trilogy*, other times that he had "understood life before the Revolution and lived it to the full, but the post-revolutionary period is a new stage in our lives, a stage that requires a different way of thinking and more time before the artist can depict it or express it in a well-grounded work of art, for the new society needs a new artist" (Gamal al-Ghitani, *Naguib Mahfouz yatadhakkar*, 101). Sometimes he would add, "The Revolution has achieved its goals, and society no longer holds issues that provoke me" or "the pre-revolutionary period is now a lifeless corpse and no longer worth writing about," or that the novels that he used to write "followed a traditional pattern suited to the fixed, stable society of its day with its clear landmarks and which no longer works for a society full of changes and transformations." (Husayn Eid, *Naguib Mahfouz: sira dhatiya wa-adabiya*, 224)

Mahfouz's responses confirming that "the revolution had killed his desire to write" multiplied, although, at his most frank with Gamal al-Ghitani, he told the latter: "The questions about my stopping writing had a political side, and the answer I gave was designed to keep suspicion at bay. My answer seemed to me reasonable but was it true? It was just an interpretation of the truth." "Perhaps," Mahfouz added, "the *Trilogy* was the reason, since you could say that my vision had been depleted by the writing of it but at the same time I couldn't take a final decision not to write. Screenplays were a limited consolation, but I was in the worst state I had ever been in—so much so that I longed for death!" (Gamal al-Ghitani, *Naguib Mahfouz yatadhakkar*, 101).

From the creative standpoint, we may perhaps find an explanation for Mahfouz's abandonment of writing during this period in his novel *al-Summan wa-l-kharif (Autumn Quail)*, which he published in 1962. The hero, Isa al-Dabbagh, is a member of the Wafd Party and belongs to the generation that came of age between the two revolutions. However, the revolution of July 1952 treated that generation as rivals and insisted on wiping them off the Egyptian political map, forcing them to choose one of two, and only two, options: "acknowledge that the revolution of 1952 was the beginning of the country's history and that everything that had gone before was nothing but corruption and betrayal (thus murdering their own history) or stay absolutely silent and withdraw from public life, placing padlocks on their mouths," as Salah 'Isa puts it in his *Shakhsiyat laha al-'ajab* (Characters to Wonder At, 541). Al-Dabbagh's friend, Samir 'Abd al-Baqi, says of the crisis of their generation, "We were the vanguard of a revolution and now we're the debris of one!" (*Autumn Quail*, 118). Al-Dabbagh's problem, according to Salah 'Isa, is that

> he hates the new era with his heart but cannot hate it with his head and even though he greets the news of the revolution's success in expelling the British from Egypt with satisfaction, he cannot escape a lack of enthusiasm, touched with anger, for no better reason than that it had not occurred at the hands of his own party. Thus al-Dabbagh and his generation remain captive to a sense of disappointment because they participated in the making of the revolution but, when it was victorious, it treated them, inexplicably, as enemies, and forced them to make an evil choice, between unreserved support and everlasting silence! (Salah 'Isa, *Shakhsiyat laha al-'ajab*, 541)

Al-Dabbagh's silence does not last long. One evening in 1957, while sitting under the statue of Saad Zaghloul in Alexandria, he encounters a young man he had interrogated in the past, when his party was in power, and a long conversation ensues. The youth invites him to discuss the affairs of the world, as a better alternative to sitting in the dark under Zaghloul's statue. Al-Dabbagh realizes that the young man is inviting him to shrug off the superfluous mantle of his sensitivity and to resume his struggle for his country and his people. Al-Dabbagh, though he hesitates briefly, then "jumped to his feet in a sudden drunken spurt of enthusiasm and started after the young man with long strides, leaving the seat behind him sunk in solitude and darkness" (*Autumn Quail*, 118).

True, one cannot establish a literal link between the real character Naguib Mahfouz and the fictional character al-Dabbagh, but there are similarities in that both belong to the same generation that the July 1952 revolution "forced to make an evil choice, between unreserved support and everlasting silence!" And both, in the end, abandoned their silence.

During his silence, Mahfouz was

> searching for a new kind of literary creation, or new sources of inspiration, different from *Midaq Alley*, *Khan al-Khalili*, and *Sugar Street*, and for new characters different from the effendis and master craftsmen that he had repeatedly presented in his stories. The problem with such literary renewals is that they require a similar renewal in the life of the writer. They require journeys and human discoveries beyond the borders of the café and the office of the Arts Authority and the home. (*Sabah al-khayr*, 27 March 1958)

It was this that made Mahfouz, when interviewed by *al-Idha'a* (Broadcasting) magazine, ask his interviewer to write a kind of proclamation in the lead-in to the interview.

> Naguib Mahfouz has asked me to publish an announcement on his behalf, as follows: "The writer of realism is fed up with realism. He is sick of people's pains and the unmediated manifestations of their lives and has nothing new to write about them. When he writes again, he will either write in a new way—one whose features have yet to fix themselves in his mind—or else abandon writing forever." ('Abd al-Tawwab 'Abd al-Hayy, *al-Idha'a*, 21 December 1957)

However many the responses given by Mahfouz for his failure to write and no matter how contradictory they may sometimes have been, there can be no doubt that his "silence" (as he referred to it in a number of press interviews) was not passive. Indeed, it took on philosophical and artistic dimensions and became in itself "a source of power exactly like writing" or "a contemplation of existence in order to broaden the capacity to investigate the meaning of reading and writing." It was, thus, the silence that grants the creative artist "the opportunity to rename things and words, so that he may protect his inner self and his culture" ('Ali ibn Tamim, *al-Nuqqad wa-Naguib Mahfouz*, 327).

The period of silence and abstention endured for a while, then Naguib Mahfouz suddenly began writing again. In 1957, he felt a strange tingling running through his body and, as he told Raga' al-Naqqash, "I found myself drawn once again to literature" (Raga' al-Naqqash, *Naguib Mahfouz: safahat min mudhakkaratihi*, 141). Mahfouz's own ideas about that period tended toward the religious, the Sufistic, and the philosophical: the idea for *Children of the Alley* was seen as coming to grant a rebirth in the writer within him that he believed had died. Mahfouz was guided to the title of his new novel by a song from his childhood: "Children of Gabalawi, Charm Our Snakes!"—a song to which he had alluded in his novel *Khan al-Khalili*, when Ahmad Akif leaves the Sakakini neighborhood for Khan al-Khalili, to escape the German and Italian air raids during the Second World War. Early on during his stay in the new district, Ahmad Akif opens the window and looks out onto the street. He finds it filled with groups of boys and girls shouting and laughing. They have divided themselves into teams, each of which is enthusiastically engaged in playing some game. "Dust flew up in the air and noise was everywhere. He realized that from now on an afternoon snooze was out of the question. He heard some amazing tunes too" (*Khan al-Khalili*, 20): "Hey There, Cameleer!" and "Children of Gabalawi, Charm Our Snakes"—the same song that the children chant in *Children of the Alley* in front of the café:

> *Children of Gabalawi, charm our snakes!*
> *Are you Christians or are you Jews?*
> *What do you eat? We eat dates.*
> *What do you drink? We drink coffee.*
> (*Children of the Alley*, 166)

Abd al-Nasser Asks a Question

Of all the news items about Mahfouz's return to writing with a new, and unusually interesting, novel, the most interesting and tantalizing was that published by *al-Idha'a*'s editor-in-chief Hilmi Sallam. It consisted of just a few lines in the "Literature and Men of Letters" section, as follows:

> *Al-Idha'a* is pleased to inform its readers that it has come to an agreement with Naguib Mahfouz for the publication of his new novel *Children of the Alley*. The magazine will commence publication in installments immediately following the summer vacation. (*al-Idha'a*, 2 May 1959)

Despite its announcement, *al-Idha'a* never did publish *Children of the Alley*: the novel went instead to *al-Ahram*. How, then, did it end up there?

We have many stories to choose from, including what Mahfouz himself said and what Muhammad Hasanayn Haykal said. The differences between these two versions are minor and may not change much.

According to Mahfouz's account, as related to Raga' al-Naqqash, Ihsan Abdel Kouddous put on a celebration for him on the occasion of his being awarded the State Prize in 1957, at Abdel Kouddous's house on Qasr al-'Ayni Street, which was attended by writers and journalists, the most illustrious of whom was Kamil al-Shinnawi. During the party, 'Ali Hamdi al-Gammal, managing editor of *al-Ahram*, approached Mahfouz and told him that he was speaking to him on behalf of Muhammad Hasanayn Haykal, the newspaper's editor-in-chief, who wanted a novel from him that he could publish in installments. Naguib recounted:

> I hadn't yet begun writing *Children of the Alley*, so I excused myself on the grounds that I didn't have a novel ready for publication. I promised Ali Hamdi al-Gammal that the next novel I wrote I would send to *al-Ahram*. When I finished writing *Children of the Alley*, I remembered my promise, contacted al-Gammal, and took him the typescript of the novel, which he read, liked, and declared he would publish without editorial intervention. It seems al-Gammal read it as an ordinary novel about an Egyptian alley where a conflict occurs between two gangs of local bullyboys. (Raga' al-Naqqash, *Naguib Mahfouz: safahat min mudhakkaratihi*, 143)

When I asked Haykal how the novel came to *al-Ahram*, he answered, "It came to 'Ali Hamdi al-Gammal, who got nervous and postponed publication without telling me. It seems Naguib complained to Husayn Fawzi, who told me about the novel, and I told Husayn Fawzi, 'We can't deny access to a novel by Mahfouz, however critical or acerbic, especially after we chased after him to write for *al-Ahram* and used Tawfiq al-Hakim as an intermediary more than once and even though Mahfouz asked us to wait until he had retired'" (personal interview, 25 January 2015).

Haykal continued:

> I asked al-Gammal to bring it to me immediately, took it home with me, and read it in a single evening. In the morning, I decided to publish it right away in daily installments, not weekly as had previously been the way with literary works. I took this decision for two reasons. First, it was a long novel and publishing it on a weekly basis might have taken a whole year, which was too long: it might give anyone who wanted to exploit the novel for religious purposes enough time to halt its publication. Second, I grasped the message of the novel and its enormous significance.

At first, publication proceeded extremely smoothly. After publication of installment number 17, however, according to Haykal, complaints started, and demands that al-Azhar take action to halt publication. News of all this found its way, naturally, to Abd al-Nasser, who asked Haykal, "What's going on?" Haykal explained all the factors involved, ending with the words, "Any novel written by Naguib Mahfouz has to be published, down to the last word." Abd al-Nasser agreed to let the novel be completed. However, as the outcry grew, Abd al-Nasser brought the matter up again with Haykal, who made the following proposal: "Have them form a committee of scholars of al-Azhar and let them look into the matter." Haykal explains his reasons for making this request as follows: "I wanted to gain enough time to complete publication of the rest of the novel. The committee did in fact decide to halt publication. This happened ten days from the end of the novel but publication continued until the end, and I took care to finish the final installment with the words 'The End.'"

Haykal seems to have had an intuition, from the start, of the political complications into which publication would drag him. One of these was a violent attack on the novel, part of which was directed at *al-Ahram* and which, in turn, led him to write a short article one week after the start of the publication of *Children of the Alley*, on page 6 of the newspaper, titled "Freedom of Expression." This was in effect the start of a counterattack in which Haykal put up a heated defense of literary freedom. Haykal made a further contribution to the developing battle by giving space on *al-Ahram*'s pages to articles and readers' letters that addressed society's problems and criticized the regime in a gentle, non-aggressive way. Notable in Haykal's short piece is his insistence that one of the most important issues facing society at the time was freedom of opinion. He writes:

> Freedom of opinion does not lie in angry, excited headlines directed against a particular person. It does not lie in campaigns launched with fury and ferocity in a search for scapegoats. Freedom of opinion is freedom to discuss. Liberated thought is a prerequisite, and the release of this thought as spoken discourse on the tongue, or silent discourse on paper, is a result. Without the prerequisite it is impossible to arrive at the result, and without the result, the prerequisite has no point. This is what we understand freedom of opinion to be. (*al-Ahram*, 28 September 1959)

Haykal stated that he did not himself delete a single word from the novel and denied absolutely that he would have asked Mahfouz to do so, stressing the incorrectness of the findings of the Swedish researcher Marina Stagh, in her book *The Limits of Freedom of Speech*—in which she relied on an article published in *al-Hilal* (The Crescent) magazine—concerning certain incidents during the crisis and her insistence that Haykal had demanded of Mahfouz that he censor his own work by deleting numerous passages that might add to the protesters' fury.

Haykal chose al-Husayn Fawzi to illustrate the novel as published by *al-Ahram*, the newspaper acclaiming the artist before publication in the same manner as it did Mahfouz: "The lines drawn by al-Husayn Fawzi emerge from the very core of our lives, the very same source from which Naguib Mahfouz also draws his feelings and emotions" (*al-Ahram*, 20 September 1959). Fawzi may have been chosen for this task because he had been born and raised in Cairo and was raised in the Hilmiya district, which had much in common with the environment that Mahfouz so loved to depict in his works. Al-Husayn drew one hundred illustrations for the novel. Describing his experience with the work, he recounted:

> When *Children of the Alley* reached me, I was running a fever. Despite this, I left my house in Giza to go to *al-Ahram* for a meeting with the editor-in-chief Muhammad Hasanayn Haykal. We exchanged thoughts and I got the idea. I started to read and understand the novel. I found it to be a living novel, powerful, that gave me the inspiration for my illustrations, then their actual form as published. (*al-Ahali*, 22 February 1989)

Al-Husayn Fawzi believes that the campaign against Mahfouz by men of religion led to "the poisoning of the atmosphere around the novel, which as a result was never allowed to fulfill the role that its author had hoped for it in terms of its meaning and deeper objectives." He adds,

> This collaboration created a movement in the arts, one that turned newspaper illustrations into something of value with which to enrich a literary work and give it a clear voice. Many readers who were my students at the Faculty of Fine Arts told me while it was being published that they would be holding on to their copies because of the drawings. Similarly, the drawings inspired some of the high school students who had collected them to enter the various fine arts faculties.

AN ANGRY MESSAGE

How did the problems begin?

Again, there are numerous answers to the question. Angry letters from readers reached *al-Ahram*, as Hasanayn Haykal recounts. Others went to the presidency of the republic directly.

Nevertheless, certain things are public knowledge while others unfolded on the sidelines and remain unknown. Naguib Mahfouz told Raga' al-Naqqash:

> The crisis began when *al-Gumhuriya*'s literature page published an item drawing attention to the fact that the serialized novel being published by *al-Ahram* contained allusions to the prophets. Following this provocative story, some people, including, unfortunately, certain writers, began sending petitions and complaints demanding a halt to publication of the novel and its subjection to trial. These people began inciting al-Azhar against me, on the basis that the novel was explicitly blasphemous and that the novel's characters symbolized the prophets. I learned these facts from a friend of mine, Prof. Mustafa Habib, who worked as a secretary to the Sheikh of al-Azhar and whose brother was a prosecutor. He told me that most of the petitions that reached the public prosecutor's office were sent by other writers. (Raga' al-Naqqash, *Naguib Mahfouz: safahat min mudhakkaratihi*, 143)

In an interview with 'Adil Hammuda in the presence of Haykal, published by *al-Ahram*, Mahfouz explains that "no one would have paid any attention to the novel had it not been for a leftist writer at *al-Gumhuriya*, perhaps Ahmad 'Abbas Salih or Sa'd al-Din Wahba, who told them, 'Listen, guys. This is no ordinary novel. This is a novel about the prophets!' That was when all hell broke loose" (*al-Ahram*, 13 January 2007).

Mahfouz's charge sheet is inaccurate in terms of where, when, and by whom the attack was launched. Salih and Wahba may have taken part in the battle but not at *al-Gumhuriya* and not at that time: it is an established fact that the first open attack on the novel was launched in *al-Musawwar* (The Illustrated) magazine, in a letter sent by a reader named Muhammad Amin to the poet Salih Gawdat, editor of the Literature and Arts section, on 18 December 1959; in other words, an entire week before completion of the publication of the novel. According to his statement in the letter, the reader in question chose Gawdat because he was "one of the few not competing in the marketplace of hypocrisy." The reader opines that Mahfouz, in his new novel, "deviates from and avoids every principle of the novel. His most recent piece of writing is simply symbolist; it is neither realist nor a product of the imagination. It does not fit into any known mold." The reader adds, "Mahfouz has set out to challenge deeply rooted beliefs. To present such ideas simply in a novel is necessarily a difficult task for anybody, even Mahfouz. Mahfouz's hiding behind symbols weakens his case in a society that, by its very nature, holds a deep respect for religion." Gawdat responded to the writer of the letter that "I cannot judge the most recent novel by Mahfouz, who is, without doubt, considered the vanguard novelist of the day. If he has taken a new path in his new novel, one with which we have not become familiar from his earlier masterpieces, then it is up to those who have read the novel to pass judgment." He adds, "The door is open to letters from readers who have read Mahfouz's novel."

Despite Mahfouz's claim to that effect, *al-Gumhuriya* did not in fact attack the novel. On the contrary, Yusuf al-Siba'i was one of the first to defend the writer, when he published an article in his daily column under the heading "Naguib Mahfouz and Our Readers' Criticism." This was on 29 December, or ten days after the attack in *al-Musawwar* and after completion of publication of the novel in *al-Ahram*. In his article, al-Siba'i attacks both the unknown reader and Salih Gawdat as publisher of the letter:

> We find that the letter launches a devastating attack on Naguib Mahfouz, despite the reader's professions of appreciation for him.

> Likewise, even though Mr. Salih Gawdat absolves himself of responsibility for the missive, and expresses his admiration and appreciation for Naguib Mahfouz, I can absolve him of responsibility for the contents of the letter only if he absolves me of responsibility if I should publish a letter from a reader who insults him. Readers have the right to abuse whom they like. It is impossible that every reader will like every book. There are always people who are displeased, annoyed, obscure. Any person can say whatever they like about any other person and think whatever they think, but they do not have the means to publish whatever they say and think to all and sundry when they are themselves one of the editors. If, then, the letter in question is from some unknown reader, that same editor becomes in effect its writer, in which case he should either confess that what he has written is his and publish it, or make no such confession and leave the responsibility for publication to the person who wrote it and have it published anywhere but the place for which he himself is responsible. It would have been more proper for the writer of the letter, if he did not intend to use it for the defamation in which our colleague Salih Gawdat assists, or, to be precise, of which he is the cornerstone—it would have been more proper for him to have sent the letter to Naguib Mahfouz himself, if his intention was to inform him of his opinion of his novel.

It was never al-Siba'i's intention, he asserts, to comment on the letter published by Gawdat, and he did so only when he heard that "some quarters thought that publication of the novel should be stopped." As a result, he felt that more than just a reader's letter was involved and that "we have to think more broadmindedly and welcome the novel with truly open arms. After all, it is not yet finished and we do not know what the writer is aiming to achieve through the events and characters of the story. By giving space to exasperated views we are simply rushing to judgment on something whose fundamental features are not yet fully visible." Al-Siba'i does not make clear in his article the nature of the quarters that were pressing for a halt to publication but he does state, and refute, their arguments.

> I shall accept the supposition of those readers who are exasperated that Naguib has used the alley to paint a portrait of humanity and that he tells the history of humanity through the alley; likewise that

> he uses some of the story's characters as symbols of certain prominent characters in the history of humanity, among them the prophets. This has led to attempts to match the characters whom Naguib has used as symbols of the prophets to the prophets themselves, a somewhat tendentious exercise in and of itself in that the symbol can never match the original in all its minutiae; if it could, there would be no need for the symbol . . . . Can we be so narrow-minded as to ask Naguib Mahfouz to make his symbolic inhabitants of the alley match the prophets in every one of their features and acts? Or should they possess the same characteristics as the rest of the inhabitants of the alley, just as we allow the lion and the eagle their natural characteristics? If we insist on this, why would Naguib not have spared himself the effort of writing the novel, of providing the symbols, and not just tell us the stories of the prophets as they have come down to us in divine scripture and as related by history?

After a few days of silence, Salih Gawdat resumed the initiative by publishing, over a period of more than six weeks, letters from readers to *al-Musawwar* containing comments some of which praised Mahfouz and his novel and some of which were violently opposed to it. Gawdat then wrote a reply to al-Siba'i's article, impelled, as he claimed, by a question posed to him by a friend, namely, "Is there really a critic called Muhammad Amin or did you use the name as a screen from behind which to criticize Mahfouz?"

> I hesitated before replying to my friend since it had never occurred to me that I might lack the courage to criticize anyone, no matter how close he might be to me, and whatever his status might be in people's eyes, when I believed that he deserved criticism. I leafed through the papers that had accumulated on my desk until I successfully located Muhammad Amin's letter. I looked for his address but all I could find was "Shibin al-Kom." But I have to be honest with you: these two words were not enough for me and I felt a certain doubt as to the real existence of Muhammad Amin and felt it not unlikely that some enemy of Naguib Mahfouz's might have written the letter, made up the name, and added these two words!

Gawdat's doubts did not last long. Suddenly, he writes, he received another letter from Muhammad Amin confirming his identity and providing his full address: 3, 'Abd al-'Aziz Habib Street, Shibin al-Kom. With the letter was another, which was "an identical copy of another letter sent by Amin to Yusuf al-Siba'i in which he responds to what the latter wrote in *al-Gumhuriya*." Amin writes to al-Siba'i at the end of this letter, according to Gawdat, that "this is the opinion of a peasant. I would now like to hear your response, on condition that you forget for a few moments that Naguib Mahfouz is your friend and that you are dealing with a nobody from the countryside, one whom you described, in a moment of bad temper, as 'obscure.'" Based on the contents of this letter, Gawdat proposes that al-Siba'i, in his capacity as secretary-general of the Higher Council for Arts and Literature, should sponsor an initiative to bring to light the talents lying wasted in the countryside. Gawdat's initiative later met with a warm welcome from "provincial writers," if we are to believe the readers' letters in praise of it. The campaign ended with a reference to an apology by Yusuf al-Siba'i to Amin for his use of the word "obscure" to characterize him in his article and where he describes the word as "a printing error—of the sort that we suffer from so often at the printers' hands!"

The career of Salih Gawdat was not devoid of other, similar, incidents, some of them likewise linked to Naguib Mahfouz, who would speak to Raga' al-Naqqash, years later, of the pain caused him by the violent campaign led by Salih Gawdat in the wake of Mahfouz's signing of Tawfiq al-Hakim's famous statement of 1972 in which the older generation of writers urged a group of then young writers to support the demands of the student protesters and those calling for democracy and an end to the state of "no-war no-peace." That same day, Anwar al-Sadat had banned all the signatories to the statement from writing for any newspaper or magazine. This punishment affected Mahfouz not only by banning him from writing in *al-Ahram* and appearing on television but also by banning his films from the cinema, while Gawdat, whom Mahfouz had considered a friend, led a rabid campaign against him. Mahfouz told Raga' al-Naqqash:

> My relationship with him had solidified during our visit to Yemen, when we shared a single room on the ship on which we traveled for fifteen days—a week out and a week back. At the time when he (Gawdat) was blacklisted under Abd al-Nasser, his friends had abandoned him and avoided mentioning his name in their pieces in the press, on radio, or on television. I could see no justification

> for ignoring him in this way and insisted, for my part, on mentioning his name whenever appropriate without fearing the wrath of the authorities. When this occurred and I mentioned him in my public talks to the media, he would call me immediately on the telephone, extremely moved and grateful for what I had done. (Raga' al-Naqqash. *Naguib Mahfouz: safahat min mudhakkaratihi*, 136)

Gawdat's inconsistencies were a spur to Mahfouz's mockery. He would refer to him as "the bright-green poet" and said that he was "a person I was forced to know in spite of myself." Mahfouz seems to have taken belated revenge on Gawdat. In a conversation with Yusuf al-Qa'id he spoke sarcastically of his companionship with Gawdat during the journey to Yemen.

> We talked a lot, though we hadn't mixed socially before, so we got to know one another well. He told me he had diabetes, which created a further bond. However, I noticed that they would send us tea to the cabin. I used to drink a cup without sugar but he would produce sugary fruits from his trunk and eat two or three. I asked him, "My dear Gawdat, is your problem too much sugar or too little?" and we laughed. (Yusuf al-Qa'id, *Naguib Mahfouz in haka*, 53)

Mahfouz's words imply that he became acquainted with Gawdat only on the trip to Yemen, or that their relationship only became established then. Oddly, however, Mahfouz had in fact participated with Gawdat and 'Abd al-Hamid Guda al-Sahhar in writing a joint story titled *'Ala al-bilaj* (On the Beach) published in *al-Qissa* (The Story) magazine in August 1950, or before they became acquainted.

A few years later, Salih Gawdat's name would appear in connection with another ban. After Nizar Qabbani published in Beirut's *al-Adab* (The Humanities, July–August 1967 issue) magazine his celebrated poem "Hawamish 'ala daftar al-Naksa" (Notes in the Margins of the Naksa) in the wake of the June 1967 defeat, and even though that issue of the magazine came out in Egypt, Salih Gawdat called in *al-Kawakib* (The Planets) magazine (12 September 1967) for "a ban on the songs of Nizar Qabbani" on the radio. In his article he asserts, "Nizar is finished as a poet, finished as an Arab, and finished as a human being." The following week, Gawdat demanded that Qabbani be blacklisted because he "shatters the morale of his people with such poems" (*al-Kawakib*, 19 September 1967). On the other hand, Raga' al-Naqqash led, also in *al-Musawwar*, a campaign in defense of Nizar, stating that "Nizar has the right to write what he feels" (*al-Musawwar*, 29 September 1967). In the end, however, it was Gawdat's point of view that prevailed, with an absolute ban being imposed on Nizar's entering Egypt, while the radio stopped broadcasting his poems and songs. The poet was then left with no choice but to send a letter to Abd al-Nasser (this was later published after Abd al-Nasser's death, in *al-Hilal*).

> It pains me, Your Excellency, that my poem should have been banned from Egypt and an official embargo placed on my name and my verse at the United Arab Republic's broadcasting service and in its press. . . . The issue is not the banning of a poet. The issue is whether any poet should be trampled under the hooves of mob-thinking for giving voice to the truth. All I demand, Your Excellency, is freedom of discussion. I have been insulted in Egypt without anyone knowing why I have been insulted and I have seen my patriotism and my honor impugned because I wrote a poem of which no one has read a word . . . . Your Excellency, I cannot believe that one such as yourself would punish the wounded for their wounds . . . . I cannot believe that such a thing could happen in your era. (*al-Hilal*, November 1970)

The letter achieved its purpose. Abd al-Nasser issued a decree lifting the ban on Nizar and his poems, and in 1969 Umm Kulthum sang his first poem hailing the armed Palestinian resistance, "Asbaha 'indi al-an bunduqiya" (I Have a Rifle Now) to music by Muhammad 'Abd al-Wahhab.

Ghali Shukri, in his *al-Arshif al-sirri li-l-thaqafa al-misriya* (The Secret Archives of Egyptian Culture, 110), gives further details of Gawdat's role in the attack on "metered free verse" and on *al-Shi'r* (Poetry) magazine (first issue 1964), whose editor-in-chief was Dr. 'Abd al-Qadir al-Qutt.

> It was a war with no quarter in which he referred to the modernist poets as "cochineals" because cochineal beetles are bright red and in his book everything red was communist. At the time, 'Abd al-Qadir Hatim had ordered the High Council for the Arts and Literature to take a stand against these poets, and the poetry committee immediately met at the council and issued a declaration that

> was not devoid of the influence of Salih Gawdat. This declaration stated that "those who call themselves 'the new poets' are simply poisoned spearheads pointed at the breast of Islam, for they allow themselves to use references and symbols inspired by non-monotheistic religions. This wave of poets is not simply hostile to Islam, it is against Arabism as well, for it demolishes the foundations of the language and prosody that we have inherited from our fathers, grandfathers, and great-grandfathers. Their imaginations have run wild in their return to past regional glories. They are neo-'Anti-Arabs' who have no problem with the intermittent use of the vernacular language or the repeated severing of the very spinal cord of Arab poetics."

Was there ever, though, in reality, a reader, or a provincial litterateur, who wrote poetry and lived at the address mentioned by Salih Gawdat in his article?

Shibin al-Kom's 'Abd al-'Aziz Habib Street (where the writer of the letter criticizing Naguib Mahfouz and published by Salih Gawdat resided) is off Gamal Abd al-Nasser Street. It is a short street. Most of its houses, which date back to the 1940s, are empty. They are of the architectural style known as "classical," and are, for the most part, villas that have been abandoned by their inhabitants and left to fall into disrepair. Some houses have been demolished and the land taken over by apartment blocks. I went to No. 3, where Muhammad Amin supposedly resides. It was uninhabited, but a woman selling tea had set her stall up opposite. I asked, "Did anyone live in the building previously who wrote poetry or stories?" She referred me to her husband, a man of over sixty who knew, as he informed me, all the inhabitants of the street, old and new. According to him, "Mr. 'Abd al-'Aziz Zayn al-Din was a poet. He died in 2002. He was well known. Journalists were always visiting him. He used to go to the Culture Palace and poetry evenings were held in his honor."

And what of Muhammad Amin?

He replied, "You mean Muhammad *al-Amin*, not *Amin*?" Then he pointed to the next-door house, which bore the number "6." "He used to live in that house, but he didn't have anything to with writing or literature. He was a wrestler and worked as a trainer. He died several years ago too but I never heard anything about him being a writer or having any interest in literature."

"Do you know any members of his family?" I asked. "They emigrated to Italy," he told me.

Al-Gumhuriya did not, then, participate in the attack on Mahfouz, or at least not directly, and it continued to publish news stories about him, whether related to his screenplay *Bayna al-sama' wa-l-ard* or "the return of the Hoodlums to writing" (in reference to Naguib Mahfouz and to Muhamad 'Afifi and Adel Kamel, two of the coterie around Mahfouz who referred to themselves as "the Hoodlums") after a long gap ("al-Harafish ya'udun li-l-kitaba," *al-Gumhuriya*, 13 December 1959, 8). At the same time, however, *al-Gumhuriya* wanted to challenge *al-Ahram* by also publishing a novel, and by a writer who could compete with Mahfouz. It chose *al-Bayda'* (The White-skinned Woman) by Yusuf Idris, a novel that violently criticizes Egypt's underground communist organizations. Publication began twelve days after the beginning of the publication of Mahfouz's *Children of the Alley*. In her book *The Limits of Freedom of Speech*, Marina Stagh reports Yusuf Idris's comment that he published *al-Bayda'* in *al-Gumhuriya* at the urging of Salah Salim, one of the Free Officers. Salim had oversight of *al-Gumhuriya* at that time and wanted to challenge *al-Ahram*. Idris's novel met with no serious critical response, however, during that period. Sulayman Fayyad, in an article published in *al-Shahr* (The Month, February 1960) magazine, whose editor-in-chief at the time was Sa'd al-Din Wahba, noted the irony of the outcry caused by the publication of *Children of the Alley* when compared with the complete disregard for Yusuf Idris's *al-Bayda'* in *al-Gumhuriya*, despite the fact that they appeared simultaneously. He attributed this to the fact that "Naguib Mahfouz only published his novel in *al-Ahram* after he had written the last line and the last word, while Yusuf Idris embarked on the publication of his novel before he had written more than a few pages, or so it is claimed, and it was published daily, Yusuf writing pages of his novel and throwing them into the maw of the printing machines one day after another. Maybe that is why *al-Bayda'* left no trace and created no outcry of the sort stirred up by the interest of the readers and some critics in *Children of the Alley*" (*al-Shahr*, February 1960).

Writer and journalist Muhammad al-'Izabi has shown that Idris's novel was never published in full in *al-Gumhuriya* "because he was always late in delivering it and the editorial secretary was at his wits' end for a solution . . . . So he wrote 'The End,' after the last line was received but before the novel was complete, which put paid to the matter!" (Muhammad al-'Izabi, *al-Misri al-yawm*, 19 March 2018).

Yusuf Idris had previously asked Muhammad Hasanayn Haykal, in an interview in *al-Gumhuriya* (30 January 1960), about the experiment of publishing novels as serials in daily newspapers. Haykal replied, "It's been highly successful, as witness our publication of Naguib Mahfouz's *Children of the Alley*." Idris followed up with the question, "And what do you think of *Children of the Alley*?" but Haykal cut the exchange short by saying, "Didn't I just tell you I liked it and published it?"

Further evidence may be found that Naguib Mahfouz was wrong in thinking that the attack on *Children of the Alley* began with *al-Gumhuriya*. A few days before the end of publication of the novel, *al-Masa'* (The Evening) newspaper, which belongs to the same al-Tahrir Publishing Company that puts out *al-Gumhuriya*, published a short news story, written by the newspaper's literary editor, in which he states that "in a few days' time, Mahfouz will complete publication of his serialized novel in *al-Ahram*. Literary circles expect the novel, when complete, to inspire heated discussion with regard to its style and form" (*al-Masa'*, 21 December 1959). The story postdates the outcry. Mahfouz's indication to 'Adil Hammuda, in the presence of Haykal, to the effect that the attack was started by 'Abbas Salih is not entirely accurate either, since the latter wrote no attack on the novel during the crisis. On the other hand, he did not appear to be enthusiastic about the novel when it was published and may perhaps have attacked it at Mahfouz's weekly literary discussion group. He did not set out his position in writing until later, however, in an article published in the *al-Sharq al-Awsat* (The Middle East) newspaper, in which he declared his discomfort with its publication:

> It was, in my opinion, an artistic borrowing from the Marxist vision, which claims that history passes through five stages, culminating in the dominion of science and its technologies, with the novel trying to reconcile the religious and the scientific visions. Generally speaking, the issue of science and religion belongs to the twenties of the last century. It may be that Egyptian intellectuals had read Nietzsche, and Darwin, and perhaps had been made anxious by Nietzsche's words to the effect that religion was dead and that Superman, who bases his knowledge of the world on science and its research methods, would lead and develop the world with no need of religion and its cultures.

Enumerating his reasons for not liking the novel, he says:

> Personally, I was averse to such formulations, which are overly concerned with symbols. I believed that art takes refuge in symbols only when the area to be explored is closed to the rational mind and normal experience and the only means available to access that mysterious world is the symbol . . . . It follows that *Children of the Alley* adds nothing new aside from the aforementioned reconciliation of religion and science, which is an idea already innate in Hegelian philosophy, which I do not believe Mahfouz had read well. (*al-Sharq al-Awsat*, 14 December 2002)

Elsewhere, *al-Idha'a* had not forgotten how it had been "cheated" by Mahfouz's choice of *al-Ahram* for the publication of *Children of the Alley*, despite the magazine's announcement that he had agreed to publish it with them. It too, therefore, joined the attack. During publication of *Children of the Alley*, Hilmi Sallam, the editor-in-chief, wrote an article titled "Cause for Suspicion" that contained a scathing attack on Mahfouz for having announced that he would never write a screenplay for the cinema as long as he held the post of director of censorship, in order to distance himself from any cause for suspicion. Sallam asked, "What do you have to say about the numerous film posters we see these days, all carrying the name of Naguib Mahfouz either as author of the original book or of the screenplay or of the dialogue?" (*al-Idha'a*, 26 December 1959). In the next issue of the magazine, Mahfouz sent an extensive rebuttal of Sallam's article.

> When Sarwat Abaza, minister of culture and guidance, was gracious enough to offer me this sensitive post, I presented him with a list of the cinematic works that I had completed, or had signed contracts for, before the minister had been so kind as to offer me the post of director of film censorship. I also made it clear to the minister that, once I had assumed the responsibilities of the post, I would be unable to continue my work in the cinema, since to do so would place me in a difficult position, in which it would be impossible for me to reconcile the two jobs and which would expose me to matters to which I did not care to be exposed.

Mahfouz continues:

> The minister was generous enough to take into consideration the material losses to which I would be subject as a result of this decision of mine, whose object was to protect my name and my post from any suspicions that might be created around them. The minister was generous enough in his appreciation of this situation to promise to compensate me for those losses by putting me in charge of the cinematic works that the Ministry of Culture and Guidance was planning to undertake or which it was currently involved in. I thanked the minister for this generous stance of his but stuck to my decision. I have not therefore signed any contracts or written a single new word for the cinema beyond the scope of the list that is in the minister's possession and which contains a statement of the cinematic works that I completed before taking on the sensitive post that I now occupy. And the cinematic works that are being advertised these days, and which bear my name, and likewise those that will be announced over the coming months of the new year, are simply those contained in the list to which I have alluded. I have signed no other contracts. (*al-Idha'a*, 2 January 1960)

Mahfouz's statement provided no balm for the magazine, which did not halt its attack. On the contrary, the nods and winks reappeared from time to time, against his films, his position, and his writings. This was not just because Mahfouz had gone back on his commitment to publish his novel in it but because, despite its being an arts magazine, *al-Idha'a* had a traditional conservative take on many of the topics it dealt with. During the same period, for example, Sallam mounted an attack on another arts magazine for publishing a photograph of the artist Kamil al-Shinnawi that showed, in the background, "an in-house bar," when it would have been more appropriate, according to Sallam in his introduction, for the magazine in question "to have presented its readers with a photograph of the Muslim Arab artist painting one of his canvases, for example, or reading from one of the many books he has read."

HOW DO SHEIKHS READ LITERATURE?

Sulayman Fayyad was one of the first to write about *Children of the Alley*, in February 1960. In an article that he published in *al-Shahr* (February 1960), he stated his opinion that the outcry over the novel "was not a matter of literary criticism. It took place in houses, streets, and the provinces, as well as at the seminars of critics and writers, but it never went beyond the spoken word to become written discourse among the latter in newspapers and magazines." Fayyad attributes this to two reasons: that the novel had not yet been published in book form, leading to a lack of confidence that it had indeed, as Naguib Mahfouz claimed, been published in full in *al-Ahram*, plus the fact that few critics and litterateurs had actually followed it in *al-Ahram*. It followed, according to Fayyad, that "any attempt to comment on *Children of the Alley* now would be premature, especially given the atmosphere of mistrust that exists among the critics, *al-Ahram*, and Naguib Mahfouz himself." Fayyad ends by asserting that Naguib Mahfouz

> was, up until *Sugar Street*, "a mountain without a summit," to use the expression of his friend Adel Kamel. Now he has finally found that summit with *Children of the Alley*—a splendid, icy, towering summit. He has finally found his way to that modern novelistic style that is the upshot of what the great writers of our age have arrived at, and abandoned the classical style of the novel that has prevailed for the past two centuries. His new style is manifested,

> above all, in its reliance on dialogue and action, focused description, the compression of the romantic language of the monologue that distinguished him in his second stage as a novelist, and his awareness of the value of the symbol in the narrative work—the symbol as character, as situation, and as incident, for the symbol is the cloak and weapon of the artist in the land of the word.

What Fayyad wrote was only one dimension of his experience with *Children of the Alley*. When I met with him at his home in January 2015, one month before his death, he told me of his relationship with Sheikh Muhammad al-Ghazali, to whom he was related. When Fayyad was a student at al-Azhar, al-Ghazali had promised to have him appointed upon graduation as an imam at the mosque of Sayyida Zaynab but Fayyad had refused, despite the sheikh's attempts to convince him by mentioning the income that would come to him from the offerings box (23,000 Egyptian pounds at the time) and that he could not possibly turn the place down, as it was the dream of every established, never mind newly graduated, sheikh—"a mosque," as al-Ghazali put it, "for which people would give their right arms." Sulayman persisted in his refusal: "The preacher's mantle was too big for me. I wanted my freedom, nothing else. I wanted to be a novelist." Following his graduation, Fayyad worked as a journalist, with Sa'd al-Din Wahba, on *al-Shahr*, editing a permanent feature titled "Monthly Roundup." He was paid by the piece. Then he worked for *al-Gumhuriya* but left it in 1959. Broke, he was at his wits' end but, recalling Sheikh al-Ghazali's offer, went to pay him a visit. The visit ended with the sheikh suggesting that he take the necessary steps to get Fayyad appointed as a secretary in the office of the minister of religious endowments.

During the period that followed, Fayyad attended a meeting of what was called the Committee for the Defense of Islam, a committee put together by two sheikhs, Sayyid Sabiq and Muhammad al-Ghazali, with the goal of "being on guard against the slanders of the Orientalists against Islam and responding to them." Both sheikhs were sometime members of the Muslim Brotherhood. Sheikh Sayyid in particular had been responsible for giving Brotherhood youth members lessons in religious law, to prepare them for entry into the group's special military wing; a picture of him giving weapons-training had appeared prominently on the cover of an issue of *al-Ikhwan al-Muslimun* (The Muslim Brotherhood) magazine. He had also ruled that the killing of Prime Minister Nuqrashi Basha in 1948 was legal and was therefore known as "the Blood Mufti." He was detained, along with many other members of the group, in the prison at Tur but continued to play a role in preserving the core of the organization through teaching and tutoring of group members in its organizational principles and ideas up to the moment of the clash with the Free Officers in 1954. Thereafter, the sheikh, along with al-Ghazali, distanced himself from the organization as its larger part fell victim to either the gallows or prison. Now, in late 1959, the two sheikhs had become useful to the authorities as they entered the great battle against "communism," in Egypt and several other countries, notably Iraq, and their role had begun to grow. Not only were they high-level officials in the Ministry of Religious Endowments, they had made efforts to rally the energies of other sheikhs through the Committee for the Defense of Islam, which was headed by Sheikh Sabiq and included among its members twelve leading clerics.

At one meeting, the committee's main focus of attention was a discussion of "how to oppose the novel *Children of the Alley*." Fayyad happened to be present and remembers it thus: "I was taking the minutes. When discussion of *Children of the Alley* began, Sheikh al-Ghazali attacked the novel fiercely, saying it was 'atheism, and a mockery of the history of religion.' The pen shook in my hand, and al-Ghazali looked at me. He knew that I wrote novels, and he ordered me not to write down any of the committee's discussions, saying that he would do that." Fayyad obtained two copies of the final report, which included sharp criticism and condemnation of Mahfouz. At Mahfouz's weekly discussion group, he gave Mahfouz a copy of the report. Fayyad states: "When Mahfouz read the sheet, his color changed. He turned as yellow as a lemon."

I asked him about the other copy. Fayyad replied, "Ghali Shukri got hold of it." I asked him, "Do you think the committee was acting on the government's orders?" He replied, "I don't think so. Those people were sleeper cells belonging to the Brotherhood. They worked in secret to spread its ideology among the imams and in the mosques." He added, "Naguib Mahfouz didn't just critique religion and political authority in *Children of the Alley* but the Arab cultural system in its entirety, and that was unacceptable to everybody." I asked him, "Most of the members of the Committee for the Defense of Islam were former members of the Muslim Brotherhood. How had they managed to reach such influential positions within the state bureaucracy?" He answered, "Al-Ghazali and Sabiq belonged to the Brotherhood faction at al-Azhar. They hated Sayyid Qutb and agreed to work with the state after this faction had duped the security apparatus into thinking it had changed. They never abandoned the ideas of the Brotherhood at all. The only one to quit the Brotherhood and reject its ideas was al-Baquri." Fayyad fell silent, then added, "They were sleeper cells belonging to the Brotherhood inside the state, and the security apparatuses were unaware of them. They worked behind Abd al-Nasser's back and spread the ideas of the Brotherhood among the imams and weren't arrested." Fayyad remembered the only meeting he had with Sayyid Qutb, who lived in Helwan at the time, in a house on a half-acre plot, half of which was a flowerless garden. The house had been the property of Helwan's marriage registrar, and Qutb had bought it for two thousand Egyptian pounds. At their meeting, many things were discussed but Fayyad remembered one thing Qutb told him that day: "My dear Sulayman, there are wild beasts and wolves among us, and nothing makes people bolder in facing up to the wolves than religion."

A PRISONER OF SYMBOLISM?

Throughout the period of the novel's publication, which came to an end on 25 December 1959, Mahfouz maintained total silence. On that day, however, he went to the weekly discussion group at the Casino Opera. Usually, he left at 1:30 a.m., but that evening the discussion of the new novel was so heated he stayed until 3:30 a.m. Objections to the novel were led by a literature teacher from the faculty of humanities and a critic from one of the daily newspapers, neither of whose names is given by *al-Masa'*, which covered the event in detail. Mahfouz revealed, for the first time, his overall point of view on the novel. He stated that he had wanted to uncover the basic goal of humanity, namely, the search for the meaning of existence; for humanity to uncover that secret, it needed to be both free to do so and ready to do so—things it could achieve only by putting an end to the exploitation of the poor by the rich and the internecine struggle for a crust of bread. He added:

> The novel portrays the bitter struggle led by the prophets and messengers of God in defense of the poor and to make a prosperous life available to all, so as to free them for the greatest pursuit of all. No sooner, however, does one prophetic mission end than the rich once more seize the reins of power and the battle to attain justice and a decent standard of living for all is resumed. Then, with the end of the prophetic missions, science intervenes to adopt the same objective, namely to make people prosper. The exploiters,

> however, again set science to work for their own interests and they murder the character who symbolizes it in the novel. However, another person is able to flee with the secrets of the modern scientific inventions and resume the fight to put an end to the struggle for a crust of bread, leaving humanity free to discover the secret of life. (*al-Masa'*, 31 December 1959)

The unnamed critic objected to Mahfouz's words, stating that "the novel adds nothing new. It's an old idea, simply a chronicling of the history of humanity with nothing new added by the writer, who has not tried to extract from that history any new general signification or specific intellectual position. Moreover, he has made science sanctify itself with the oil of the occult, although in reality it has always rejected such things."

A little less than a week after the completion of the novel, Ahmad Hamrush conducted a lengthy interview with Mahfouz, published in *al-Gumhuriya* (2 January 1960). During the interview, Mahfouz spoke of his amazement at the outcry against the novel and repeated his earlier words about his intentions:

> I intended this novel to be the story of humanity . . . and nothing was further from my mind than setting the lives of the prophets in an alley. However, I did want to communicate to the common man that, even if his life is in an alley, circumstances require him to emulate the actions of the prophet . . . any prophet.

Hamrush asks, "But I heard, Naguib (and I haven't yet read the novel myself), that you present the character who represents our prophet, Muhammad, smoking hashish?"

Mahfouz answers:

> That character is not Muhammad in person and he is not the prophet whose religion we follow. He is "humanity" in the alley . . . or are you going to tell me we have to burn *Kalila and Dimna* and the animals in it that represent humans? The dog in that book represents loyalty, even though it barks and is a dog.

During the interview, Mahfouz speaks of the end of the traditional, realist, stage of his creative output:

> This isn't the outcome of my thinking about art but of a personal change. In the past, I was concerned with people and objects . . . but objects have lost their importance for me. Their place has been taken by ideas and meanings, and I believe this is a natural development for a writer as he ages. Today, I am concerned with what lies behind reality.

Hamrush expressed his view that this was a "new philosophy" but Mahfouz objected to its characterization as a "philosophy."

> Not a philosophy, I beg you. I am not a philosopher. But I dream, and these are my dreams. I look forward to a kind of life that we might call "socialist Sufism."

Mahfouz then clarified what he meant by the term.

> It's keeping our eyes on God, and humanity can only experience this if its life rises to a level that is clean and devoid of evil and wickedness. As long as one person exists who exploits others, the evil and wickedness remain. The exploiter is wicked and the exploited is wretched. There will be malice and hatred in their relationships with one another. Peering through the wickedness and the wretchedness, I train my eyes on God.

Mahfouz added:

> I train my eyes on a humane way of life, on people's relationships being based on love and cooperation until they can make their way to God. This is the socialism I desire.

Hamrush asked him, "Are your recent novels in harmony with your new ideas?" Mahfouz replied, "I believe so."

Not long after, on 9 April 1960, *al-Gumhuriya* also published another interview with Mahfouz, titled "A Journey inside Naguib Mahfouz's Head," in which Ibrahim al-Wardani asked him, "Why did you lock yourself, and your readers along with you, inside the prison of symbolism?" Mahfouz answered:

> Listen. Everyone has his own idea about this universe in which we live. I just felt that I wanted to express my idea in the way that I did. Even now, I don't know why I wrote it that way, and to be honest, I sometimes think about it to myself and say that it's a call for socialism and the advancement of science via religion. Why, indeed, shouldn't science be sacred, like religion? Or—and why shouldn't I be frank with you?—it may be that there is some personal intellectual development of mine within this novel that isn't clear to me even now.

The ideas within the novel, and the questions Mahfouz poses in the text, were not the only things preoccupying cultural circles at that time. Some asked an important question: Was the novel published in full in *al-Ahram*, or had passages been cut? Were these the supposed cuts to which Sulayman Fayyad had alluded earlier in his article in *al-Shahr*? In an interview with Mahfouz for *al-Masa'* (26 October 1960), Malak Isma'il asked him, "Why didn't you continue the publication of your recent novel *Children of the Alley*, which came out in *al-Ahram*, to the end?" Mahfouz was silent for a while, then smiled before replying, "How can you say that? I published it in full to the end, but the readers didn't understand. When it comes out as a book, and they read it to one another, it will seem stronger, and they will know for sure that I published every word of it in *al-Ahram*."

Mahfouz continued to defend his novel, and cultural and press circles continued to show interest in it. *Al-Idha'a* magazine questioned Mahfouz yet again in a survey piece titled "What I Want to Achieve Now," in which a large number of writers and artists participated, among them Muhammad 'Abd al-Wahhab, Amina Rizq, and Salah Jahin. Naguib Mahfouz stated, "My dream is to leave literature and live without care on a farm where I can work far from the din of the city and its people." The magazine's editor, however, kept doggedly after Mahfouz, going far beyond the topic of the survey, by asking him, "In all your earlier novels and stories you proceeded like an ordinary realist, describing and analyzing. Then suddenly your last novel, *Children of the Alley*, appeared and your style was completely different from the realism to which we'd become accustomed in all your other novels. *Children of the Alley* was a symbolist novel in which you took small persons and used them to symbolize extremely important persons. Did you mean to do so?" (*al-Idha'a*, 12 November 1960).

Mahfouz responded:

> Not at all. I never intended to symbolize big persons; my intention was to use those little persons to symbolize big ideas. I used some characters to symbolize religious thinking and others scientific thinking, so that I could portray the ideas of the age in which we live, whose anxieties we experience—and I am only too familiar with the period of angst and fear that the artist suffers before embarking on the investigation of a new idea or a new dream. As to the new thing that I want to write after *Children of the Alley*, please, old chap! Stop giving me a hard time!

Debate over the novel continued for approximately sixty years, with Naguib Mahfouz expressing his point of view from time to time in newspaper interviews or critical pieces. His clearest and most internally consistent interpretations are to be found in what he wrote for *al-Katib* (The Writer) magazine under the title "My New Direction and the Future of the Novel" (February 1964; see the appendix for the full text). The article was a commentary on the statement of French novelist Alain Robbe-Grillet to the effect that the novel has exhausted its usefulness and the only thing left to the novelist is form. Despite Mahfouz's agreement with Robbe-Grillet that the novel "has touched on every conceivable field. It has dealt with the individual, society, and the family. It has dealt with streets and cities, and even with continents" and indeed has gone beyond continents entirely "and . . . ascended to the stars" and that "there is, likewise, no human emotion that has not been the repeated subject of the novel, and over long periods," he nonetheless believes that we should not adopt Robbe-Grillet's view since, "if we take these opinions as an excuse to bury the novel, we shall have to bury all literature—nay, all the other arts—along with it," given that they also have covered every possible topic. It follows, in the opinion of Naguib Mahfouz, that art should not be judged according to its originality but according to the role that it plays in "deepening and enriching life through experience" and by the "pleasure and benefit" that it brings into being and which emerge as a set of criteria through which the entire artistic heritage of humanity may be viewed.

He goes on to say that the search for new techniques for the novel may be important for European writers, given the conditions of the age, but that he personally always has strived to balance technique, the preoccupations of society, and philosophy.

> When I was preoccupied with life and its meaning, the most appropriate style for me was realism, and it was in this style that, for many long years, I presented my works. The details, whether of the social environment, the characters, or the events, were extremely important . . . . Now, though, that abstract ideas and a sensitivity to them have started to preoccupy me, neither settings nor persons nor events are called for per se. Characters are closer to being exemplars or symbols, and settings no longer need to be presented in detail; in fact, they have become something closer to décor, and one's choice of events depends on the need to crystallize the main ideas.

There was no justification, therefore, from Naguib Mahfouz's perspective, for talking about the "crisis of the novel": if the European experience of the novel had been affected negatively by the collapse of values, "the many countries of the world that possess a philosophy of life and a humanistic creed" might still find in it a field of endeavor and an artistic outlet capable of forging visions, desires, and ambitions (Naguib Mahfouz, "Ittijahi al-jadid wa-mustaqbal al-riwaya" [My New Direction and the Future of the Novel], *al-Katib* magazine, February 1964; see the appendix for the full text).

These are the concepts that lie behind *Children of the Alley*, which chronicles, despite its small size, "the entirety of human history" and reflects his thinking on the crisis of the modern age. He writes:

> In this novel, Science (Arafa) thinks that he has no need of Gabalawi, so he kills him. This outcome leads Arafa to a sense of emptiness and of the bitterness of life. It is the same conclusion that Albert Camus reached when he decided that life has no meaning and only absurdity is meaningful . . . . Despite this, the novel in general has not stood idly by, observing the new situation. It has changed its approach and discovered a new technique, which explains the new experiments in the contemporary novel. When novels concerned themselves with life in and of itself, the traditional narrative was the style most appropriate, with the human character appearing with all its details. But when life itself becomes a problem, the human being is no longer a specific person but rather a mere human. He is not a person in and of him- or herself distinguished from other people by his or her peculiar and specific details . . . . It follows that

> details disappear, narrative disappears, and discussion takes precedence over all the other elements. *Children of the Alley*, for example, even though it chronicles the entire history of humanity, is shorter than any one part of a novel such as the *Trilogy*.

He then draws a significant comparison between the characters of 'Abd al-Gawad in the *Trilogy* and Arafa in *Children of the Alley*.

> When mankind finds itself face to face with its destiny, details lose their value. This is the difference between Arafa, hero of *Children of the Alley*, and Kamal Ahmad 'Abd al-Gawad, hero of the *Trilogy*. However, if the novel should try to renew itself after the fashion described by Robbe-Grillet, it certainly will cease to exist. The strange thing is that Robbe-Grillet does not believe in anything, even science.

This is how Mahfouz presented his interpretation of the novel, an interpretation he was careful to repeat throughout the 1960s. Even though it is perfectly possible to give the novel a political interpretation unconnected to any religious or metaphysical dimensions, Mahfouz never offered such an interpretation during that period. The religious explanation was, it seems, less dangerous than the political. But could the novel in fact bear the political interpretation that Mahfouz was so afraid to mention?

THE MORAL EDUCATION OF THE CITIZEN

Children of the Alley was part of a larger battle being waged at that time, the battle by the regime for religious, political, and cultural hegemony over society. Individual encounters took place within the context of an ongoing struggle between the newly arrived Islamists and the non-communist secularists. The latter, who would soon become the regime's leftwing intellectuals, fought an unceasing series of duels with the clerics against their demand for a degree of immunity and inviolability for themselves and their profession.

In his book *Nida' al-sha'b: tarikh naqdi li-l-idiyulujia al-nasiriya* (The Cry of the People: A History of Nasserite Ideology), Sharif Yunus examines a number of encounters that shed light on the skirmishes of the struggle.

> Ahmad Baha' al-Din attacked the exploitation of mosque pulpits to attack liberals, or those demanding women's rights, and decided that preachers, as employees of the state, should not be allowed to exploit their pulpits to put forward ideas that others found objectionable. He also rejected the notion of "religious government" that was being called for at that time by Jordan's Liberation Party, asserting that Islamic states had, over the past thousand years, embraced hideous examples of injustice, depravity, and abuse and that not all Islamic caliphs had been like 'Umar ibn al-Khattab. Baha' al-Din also attacked *al-Masajid* (The Mosques) magazine,

> issued by the Ministry of Religious Endowments, for showing hostility to the endeavors of the state through its rejection of the idea of life and property insurance and other concepts associated with modernity." (Sharif Yunus, *Nida' al-sha'b*, 370)

For his part, Sheikh Muhammad Abu Zahra accused Baha' al-Din of spinelessness for his defense of the equality of men and women. Baha' al-Din responded so violently that Salah Disuqi, a Free Officer, had to intervene to restrain him.

Simultaneously, Fathi Ghanim denounced the celebration of Abu Hamid al-Ghazali, describing him as "a cleric opposed to socialism and the mind," to which Sheikh al-Sharabasi countered that religion could not be opposed to "the mind" and that efforts, overt and covert, to demolish religion and mock its adherents were ongoing; al-Sharabasi called for the publication of books opposed to this point of view to be halted and the books confiscated. Ghanim denounced al-Sharabasi's calls for confiscation and the banning of opposing views, accusing him of "thinking with the mentality of a Public Security employee." Sharif Yunus asserts that "the battle was not simply one between journalists and sheikhs: journalists faithful to the dominance of the conservative values defended by the clerics also emerged. Campaigns, encouraged by Kamal al-Din Husayn, were waged in the press against 'loose songs' and the like."

In this atmosphere of conflict, *Children of the Alley* took on the aspect of a political treasure trove to be fought over by all political forces, each seeking to use it for its own ends—an open conflict, with the sheikhs allying themselves with the rightwing political forces within the Nasserite regime. Naguib Mahfouz thus found himself in a position similar to that of the narrator in *Children of the Alley*, who becomes a professional writer "despite the problems this brought him." The novel brought its author many problems, especially with the regime's attempts to "mobilize art and culture in the struggle against colonialism and communism," or in other words, the social and political engineering of society from above. In the wake of the publication of *Children of the Alley*, the National Guidance Committee issued a "Covenant of Honor for Literature, Science, and Art" that proclaimed "its members' ongoing role in national guidance and their mobilization of all the artistic and scientific energies they possessed in the building of a cooperative democratic socialist society; they would also safeguard artistic and intellectual production from destructive and deviant elements and work to make that production a positive agent for change and to raise its status." Specifically, this mobilization aimed at "the enlistment of all branches of art and literature, including, above all, the Islamic religious establishment, as propaganda tools for the regime" (Sharif Yunus, *Nida' al-sha'b*, 360). In the midst of all these measures for guidance and mobilization, the regime found itself at a loss as to what do about Naguib Mahfouz and *Children of the Alley*.

At the political level, the then minister of the economy, Hasan 'Abbas Zaki, led a campaign in parliament against the minister of culture, Sarwat 'Ukasha, for having entrusted the task of censorship to "a man with questionable religious beliefs." Zaki, known for his Sufi tendencies and who became, after leaving his post, a member of the Islamic Research Academy, also published in *al-Ahram*, two days after completion of publication of the novel, an article titled "The Art We Want" (*al-Ahram*, 27 December 1959). He followed this with twenty more articles published partly in *al-Ahram* and partly in *al-Akhbar* in which he discussed his theory of "Islamic socialism" and stressed that "what makes Egyptian society sick is the weakness of its spiritual dimensions," proposing the deployment of all resources, including art, in the service of the sound moral education of the citizen: "We have the right to ask of him (the artist) that his work should be oriented toward the ideas that the state has set down for our lives. Freedom of expression must not be a means to undermine or mislead, or a wellspring for deviation from our beliefs."

In contrast to Salih Gawdat and Hasan 'Abbas Zaki, who played overt roles in fomenting anger against Naguib Mahfouz, Kamal al-Din Husayn, a member of the new regime's Revolutionary Leadership Council, played an influential role but in the shadows, via his multiple posts within the regime at that time. His office manager contacted Naguib Mahfouz by telephone to tell him that the minister was angry that he had agreed to turn *Children of the Alley* into a play, which Mahfouz denied doing, explaining that the play in question was taken from his novel *Bidaya wa nihaya (The Beginning and the End)* and not from *Children of the Alley*. The minister was not, however, convinced. Sheikh Muhammad Abu Zahra, a member of the Popular Council for the Governorate of Cairo at the time, had objected to the staging of *The Beginning and the End* (adapted by Anwar Fathallah and directed by 'Abd al-Rahim al-Zurqani for the National Theater), declaring at a meeting of the Council, "Now they're showing *Children of the Alley* under a new name! And where? At the State Theater! *The Beginning and the End* are 'the beginning and the end of the universe,' and this is *Children of the Alley*, not as a book this time but dressed up in the costumes of actors and actresses!" (Ghali Shukri, *al-Qahira* magazine, issue no. 157, 15 December 1995).

All the same, Naguib Mahfouz fared better than another novelist, Fathi Ghanim, who published his novel *al-Barid wa-l-sakhin* (The Hot and the Cold) simultaneously with *Children of the Alley*. Ghanim was surprised to find himself called in by the morals police following a complaint from Kamal al-Din Husayn himself, accusing Ghanim of spreading depravity and debauchery. Husayn also wrote to the presidency of the republic, protesting the granting to the novel of a publishing license. Yusuf al-Siba'i intervened too at the time, asking his brother, Mahmud al-Siba'i, head of the morals police, to stay the investigation. Ghanim says, "I asked Yusuf al-Siba'i, 'What have the morals police got to do with the novel, or Kamal al-Din Husayn for that matter?' Al-Siba'i responded sarcastically, 'You're responsible for corrupting minds and seducing hearts!,'" an allusion to *Sabah al-khayr* magazine's slogan, "For youthful hearts and liberated minds!" Yusuf al-Siba'i told Ghanim to forget the matter, as the crisis was nothing more than an attempt to "exploit the novel to achieve a political goal in some conflict or other" (Rashad Kamil, *Rose al-Yusuf*, 24 March 2014).

The matter was not, however, over, for Ghanim received a phone call from Hasan Sabri al-Kholi, director of printed materials censorship, asking for a meeting. Ghanim went to his office, "and there al-Kholi pulled out of a drawer a copy of *al-Barid wa-l-sakhin*." Ghanim continued, "He showed me pages where passages had been underlined angrily in red ink. Then he said, 'Kamal al-Din Husayn couldn't stomach this description of a relationship between a man and a married woman.'" He advised Ghanim, "You'd better let the whole thing die down and not stir up these political currents."

Many writers of this period regard Kamal al-Din Husayn as representing the extreme rightwing within Abd al-Nasser's regime. He was extremely conservative at the religious, social, and cultural levels. During the 1940s, he had been linked, both as a sympathizer and organizationally, with the Muslim Brotherhood; he had even been a member of the Brotherhood's covert operations apparatus. He held the post of minister of education during the early days of the revolution. During the deliberations of the National Preparatory Committee for the Conference on Popular Powers in 1961, he had expressed the thought that *The Charter*—a document put together by a group close to Abd al-Nasser—bore a Marxist stamp and that it ought, rather, to be an expression of Arab Socialism, which believed in God and His apostles and in religious and moral values. With this in mind, he created a committee that wrote a report on *The Charter* that emphasized that laws must derive from the *shari'a* and that the values and culture of the society must be founded on religion. The report also alluded to the necessity of preserving family and social values. According to Kamal al-Din Husayn, as quoted in Sami Gohar's *al-Samitun yatakallamun* (The Silent Speak, 152), 'Abd al-Hakim 'Amir accused him of handing out copies of Sayyid Qutb's *Ma'alim fi-l-tariq* (Signposts on the Road) to visitors, to which Husayn responded that he had given out the copies in question because their contents were in line with his views, adding, "I never have hesitated and never will hesitate to express those views openly." On 14 October 1965, a decree was issued restricting his and his wife's right of residence to a government rest house in the Pyramids area.

The name of Hasan Sabri al-Kholi, as director of printed materials censorship, would also crop up in connection with many similar incidents. In September 1958, a year before the publication of *Children of the Alley*, Ihsan Abdel Kouddous began publishing his short-story collection *al-Banat wa-l-sayf* (Girls and the Summer) in *Sabah al-khayr* magazine. After publication was completed, he received an unexpected visit from Muhammad Hasanayn Haykal, who informed him of Abd al-Nasser's anger at the publication of the collection; Hasan Sabri al-Kholi likewise passed this opinion on to him. Abdel Kouddous detailed what had happened in a letter to Abd al-Nasser that he published as an introduction to his short-story collection *Asif lam a'ud astati'* (Sorry, I Can't Go On), although he does not state there whether he in fact sent the letter or whether Abd al-Nasser actually read it.

Ihsan Abdel Kouddous wrote:

> My respected friend Haykal has informed me of Your Excellency's opinion of the story collection that I published recently under the title *al-Banat wa-l-sayf*. Mr. Hasan Sabri al-Kholi, director of censorship, had earlier informed me of the same, and I had agreed with him that I would modify the trajectory of my stories. My friend Haykal informed me that Your Excellency had been taken aback when you read in one of these, in *al-Banat wa-l-sayf*, of the things that sometimes happen in the bathing huts of the beaches of Alexandria. The things I recorded in my stories, Mr. President, really do happen, and worse. The morals police will never be able to stop them from happening and the law will never get in their

way. These are not "individual cases" as you have stated. It is the society, a society in collapse. And the only thing that can set this society to rights is a call, an idea, one that erupts out of the anger of the people just as did the revolution of 23rd July 1952. And that is why I write my stories.

In his letter, Abdel Kouddous presents examples of writers from all over the world who "through their stories paved the way for social reform" or who "exposed the social blemishes within society" and in so doing had to suffer the wrath of the people. The letter also alluded to the articles of Mustafa Mahmud, which Abdel Kouddous used to publish in *Sabah al-khayr*.

This said, there remains the claim of atheism made in *Rose al-Yusuf*, and the articles published by Mustafa Mahmud. I have stopped publication of Mustafa Mahmud's articles dealing with the philosophy of religion. I would, however, like to bring my own views on this subject to Your Excellency's attention, so that I can feel I have been completely frank with you. I believe in God, Mr. President. I am not an atheist and, though you may not be aware of this fact, I pray. I do not pray only for outward show or out of hypocrisy. The outward appearance of my life may not indicate that I pray, but I pray, because I derive psychological comfort from doing so. Despite this, I believe that our religion has fallen under the sway of a great deal of superstition and has accumulated over the ages much dust—foolish interpretations that clerics seek to use to keep people in mental darkness so that these same clerics can exploit people and rule over them. At the same time, if our religion were to be purified of these superstitions and shake off the said dust, it would right itself, along with our minds and our souls, and it would be an easy matter for Your Excellency to lead the people along the path that you have laid out for it.

What was new in the *al-Banat wa-l-sayf* incident was the appearance of the name of Abd al-Nasser himself, not that of officials of the state, in connection with the demand for confiscation of the work. What was strange, even astonishing, is that the attack on Abdel Kouddous began with a letter from a reader in the readers' mail column in just the same way that the *Children of the Alley* crisis had begun with a reader's letter to the readers' column of *al-Musawwar*. This letter was, likewise, sent to *Rose al-Yusuf* by a reader from Alexandria called Ahmad al-'Aris, and demanded that Ihsan Abdel Kouddous "desist from writing stories about dissolute women and write for us about such immortal females as Khawla bint al-Azwar or al-Khansa' as she sent her sons off to fight the holy struggle . . . etc." (signed) Ahmad al-'Aris, Alexandria. The column's editor responded sarcastically that "Ihsan likes to keep things up to date."

It was in this atmosphere that Sarwat 'Ukasha, minister of culture, asked Mahfouz to quit the post of director of the office for the censorship of literary works and take over that for film censorship, a new office tasked with assisting the Cineastes' Union and supporting festival prizes.

Mahfouz had assumed his responsibilities as censor of literary works seven months before the start of publication of *Children of the Alley*, in February 1959. The move surprised many, for how could a man who called for freedom and had taken democracy as his avowed motto agree to keep watch over the arts and to limit the freedom of artists?

Mahfouz explained his position to Raga' al-Naqqash.

> The role of the censor, as I understand it, is not an artistic one and is not at odds with the arts or their value. The role of the censor is, quite simply, to protect the state's higher policy and to prevent it becoming involved in religious issues that might lead to confessional strife. In addition, it must pay attention, within reasonable limits, to public mores and the values and traditions of society. Other than that, the artist has the right to say whatever he likes and express himself in any way he sees appropriate.

He added:

> Censorship is not a shackle for the artist and the censor should be the artist's friend, not his enemy, bearing in mind that what is fundamental in art is "openness," while "restriction" is like divorce—permitted but not welcomed. Throughout my time at the censorship office, I was a partisan of the arts, despite the hostility to them that was in the air. I never felt for one second that I was betraying myself, as a man of letters or as an artist. (Raga' al-Naqqash, *Naguib Mahfouz: safahat min mudhakkaratihi*, 115)

Historically speaking, Mahfouz was not the first intellectual to be tasked with responsibility for censorship. He had been preceded by 'Abbas al-'Aqqad, who held the position of censor for printed materials throughout the Second World War. Al-'Aqqad announced that he had accepted the post in order to ban propaganda books from Nazi, fascist, and other similarly totalitarian regimes. In a discussion with Mahfouz about kissing, Mahfouz said that, as censor, he allowed every kind of kiss except one—the kiss on the neck, especially if the screen time was more than a minute. In a press interview he was asked, "So much for the screen. What about real life? What would Naguib Mahfouz the human being do if he were to see a boy and a girl snatching a kiss in the street?" He replied, "Nothing at all! I'd turn my face in the other direction." Then he smiled and added, "If only!" (*al-Kawakib*, 15 January 1960). The last screenplay Naguib Mahfouz wrote before accepting the post of censor was an Egyptianization of Emmanuel Roblès's play *Monserrat*. Mahfouz chose the 1919 revolution as the period most appropriate to an Egyptianization of the events. Tawfiq Salih was slated for director. The film did not, however, see the light of day until 1967, when it was directed by Nur al-Dimardash, with dramatic treatment by Mahfouz, dialogue by Lutfi al-Kholi, and screenplay by Tulba Radwan.

Mahfouz remained in the post of literary censor for one year. After he quit, he refused to go to battle to defend his novel *al-Qahira al-jadida (Cairo Modern)*, which the censor who replaced him, 'Abd al-Rahim Surur, refused to allow to be made into a film. Mahfouz believed that such battles were the concern of the director and screenwriter and that he had no right to get involved. The censor's rejection of *Cairo Modern*, and also of his novel *al-Sarab (The Mirage)*, continued for years, though literature won in the end.

The matter did not end with Mahfouz's leaving his post for another that, to all appearances, was simply honorific. During the same period, he was called in by Public Security for questioning about the novel. Mahfouz told Raga' al-Naqqash:

> I remember that the actor Farid Shawqi had pitched the idea of a film set in an intelligence services environment to Dr. Sarwat 'Ukasha and asked him to intervene with the intelligence services to get them to share in the financing. Dr. 'Ukasha agreed and entrusted me with the task of writing the screenplay. When I finished, he invited me to a meeting in his office, where he asked me to go to

> the Public Security building, meet with the officials there, get their opinion of the screenplay, and find out how willing they were to share in the financing of the film. I didn't know where the intelligence services building was, so he told me and I went. I met with the deputy head of intelligence, Tal'at Khayri, who specialized in things of this sort . . . . As I entered the deputy head's office, I noticed an individual who stared at me and then rose as if to leave, but Khayri asked him to stay, as the conversation would be about the cinema and this person might be of use to our discussion. The individual never introduced himself to me but started a long conversation with me about the *Trilogy*. Then he spoke to me about *Children of the Alley* and the issues that had arisen around it. He asked me what I'd been trying to convey and how true were the reports of its defamations of religion. The meeting ended and I left. Months later, on the front page of *al-Ahram*, I saw a photo of President Abd al-Nasser during one of his African tours and my attention was caught by the picture of someone standing behind the president. It was the same person who'd talked to me in Tal'at Khayri's office. I was astonished to learn that it was the head of intelligence, Salah Nasr. (Raga' al-Naqqash, *Naguib Mahfouz: safahat min mudhakkaratihi*, 135)

It immediately occurred to Mahfouz that the meeting had been a set-up and that arrangements had been made in advance of his visit to the intelligence services building. He indicated that many friends of his had told him that the intelligence services thought that the novel might be directed against the regime and smelled a conspiracy; others believed that the crisis stirred up against the novel by al-Azhar had been cooked up by the intelligence services themselves. He noticed during the same period that he was under surveillance and it was this sensation that made him feel like Mahmud Amin Sulayman, the man who specialized in robbing the villas of the rich and was famously caught while trying to rob Umm Kulthum's villa, a sensation that drove him later to write *al-Liss wa-l-kilab (The Thief and the Dogs)*. Hasan Sabri al-Kholi's niece, a leading participant in Mahfouz's weekly discussion sessions, had informed Mahfouz that "a vehicle loaded with privates accompanied by a high-ranking officer had gone to his house to arrest him but they'd received orders to return without completing their mission"; this is the version Mahfouz recounted to Raga' al-Naqqash in *Naguib Mahfouz: safahat min mudhakkaratihi* (p. 132) as having taken place immediately following the publication of *Children of the Alley*. However, the novelist Muhammad Sulayman, relying on what Sami Sharaf, Abd al-Nasser's information secretary, told him, tells the story as though it occurred after *Adrift on the Nile*: "In his novel *Adrift on the Nile*, Mahfouz exposed the inefficacy of 'security' solutions and the 'centers of power.'" 'Abd al-Hakim 'Amir became enraged and issued a decree for the arrest of Naguib Mahfouz, and the force tasked to do so indeed set off. Sami Sharaf told me that he had been by the president's side during a conversation with 'Abd al-Hakim 'Amir in which he angrily asked the latter to halt the procedures for Mahfouz's arrest. 'Abd al-Hakim told him that the force had actually set off and was on its way to his house to arrest him. Abd al-Nasser said one thing to him: "You sent it out, you can bring it back. How many Naguib Mahfouzes do you think we have?" (*al-Ahram*, 28 August 2015).

I asked Sami Sharaf, in a telephone call, whether this was true, and he confirmed that orders for Mahfouz's arrest had been issued after both *Children of the Alley* and *Adrift on the Nile* but that Abd al-Nasser had put a stop to the measures taken. I asked him about what had been going on behind the scenes during the crisis, and he replied, "Abd al-Nasser read the novel while it was being serialized in *al-Ahram* and it was he who gave instructions for it to be published all the way to the end despite the anger of all the people who sent him notes protesting against it." I asked him whether the protesters had been clerics exclusively, and he stated clearly, "No. There were cultural figures and politicians. They sent protest notes and reports against the novel, and these reports still exist, in the presidential archives in Abdin Palace. Field Marshal 'Abd al-Hakim 'Amir was angry about the novel too, but Abd al-Nasser refused to take any measures against Mahfouz because of it."

I asked him, "But didn't Muhammad Hasanayn Haykal take on the risk of publishing the novel to the end on his own responsibility?" He replied, "Haykal did nothing off his own bat. No one wrote for *al-Ahram* without Abd al-Nasser's assent and on his instructions. Even the members of the opposition who wrote for *al-Ahram* did so with permission from Abd al-Nasser. *Al-Tali'a* (The Vanguard) magazine was Abd al-Nasser's idea and it was he who gave permission for Naguib Mahfouz to write for *al-Ahram* and have a permanent office there, because he was an avid reader of all his works."

Before he published the novel, Haykal had had no expectation of the extent the crisis would reach. He had been mildly anxious. I asked him,

"Did you expect the novel to be exploited politically as well as religiously?" He answered, "Mahfouz's attack on the regime was obvious, but I had one clear principle at *al-Ahram* that no regime can be without critics, and if it can't take criticism, it loses its reason for existence as a regime and turns into a prison cell. Secondly, there are writers on whom no one, not even the editor-in-chief, can impose any censorship or admonition, among them Naguib Mahfouz, a man of great experience who took full responsibility before public opinion for what he wrote."

Haykal recalled that Mahfouz's was not the only novel published in *al-Ahram* to stir up debate: there was Tawfiq al-Hakim's experimental work *Bank al-qalaq* (The Anxiety Bank) too. 'Abd al-Hakim 'Amir protested against it fiercely and the disagreement between 'Amir and Haykal reached the level of a heated discussion in the presence of Abd al-Nasser, who quietly settled the matter by saying, "If al-Hakim could write his novel *Yawmiyat na'ib fi al-aryaf (The Maze of Justice)* during the former feudal period and give his views on social conditions in Egypt at that time and have no one try to stop him, how can we reasonably try to stop him when he criticizes certain conditions following the revolution?"

I asked him, "Was the attack on *Children of the Alley* directed at Naguib Mahfouz or at Muhammad Hasanayn Haykal?" Haykal smiled and said, "The target was *al-Ahram*, not me personally and not Mahfouz. There were people in the regime who were upset by *al-Ahram*'s success. We weren't under the National Union (or the Socialist Union, as it came to be called) or the government, and we didn't ask for handouts from them. On the contrary, we made a profit, which is why when 'Ali Sabri complained about *al-Ahram* to Abd al-Nasser, he told him, "I swear to God, Haykal never asks me for anything and not one penny of the state's money has gone into *al-Ahram*, not even at the beginning, unlike *al-Gumhuriya*, which was always asking for aid."

I asked Haykal, "So the Nasserite regime wasn't just one coordinated phalanx, but two, one of the Right and the other with leanings to the Left?" He replied, "It was multiple phalanxes! It wasn't just the Socialist Union that was against *al-Ahram* but the government too, and I remember that Sa'd Zayid, the governor of Cairo at the time, slighted one of the editors of *al-Ahram* in a public meeting, and I issued an order that no news was to be published about him in *al-Ahram* until he apologized. He complained about me to Abd al-Nasser but I stuck to my guns and in the end he apologized. It's a paradox that *al-Ahram*, whose editorial and administrative chief

I was and at a time when I was the person closest to Abd al-Nasser, was subject to regular attacks unlike those suffered by any other newspaper. There were those at the time who found themselves inconvenienced by *al-Ahram*'s role, which is why a number of its editors were imprisoned. I was a part of all that and at the same time close to Gamal Abd al-Nasser."

The aftereffects of *Children of the Alley* cast their shadows over discussions of the *Charter* of 1962. A celebrated battle unfolded on the pages of *al-Ahram*, between Sheikh al-Ghazali and Salah Jahin. During the discussions in question, Sheikh al-Ghazali called for the liberation of Egyptian law from its dependence on foreign norms, as well as the creation of a standardized form of dress for Egyptians. These were ideas that Jahin considered out of touch with the spirit of the age, and he devoted cartoons to a rebuttal of al-Ghazali's ideas. The first cartoon of the sheikh showed him preaching to the masses and saying, "We have to rid our country of all laws coming from outside—like the civil law, and the law of gravity!" (*al-Ahram*, 29 May 1962; 30 May 1962; 1 June 1962). Al-Ghazali was furious and attacked Jahin at the sessions of the conference devoted to the *Charter*: "Assaults like this on our white turbans will mean that scholars of religion go bareheaded, if their turbans cannot be protected!" adding, "This conference gives each individual the right to speak his mind honestly and freely, something that cannot be met with children's songs in daily newspapers that ought to have more self-respect!" (*al-Ahram*, 31 May 1962). Al-Ghazali's attack provoked Haykal into writing in the column *Kalimat al-Ahram* (*al-Ahram* Has Its Say) that, while *al-Ahram* respected religion, "We reject Sheikh al-Ghazali's attempt to turn the difference of opinion between him and the paper's cartoonist, Salah Jahin, into a religious issue" and that "*al-Ahram* believes in freedom of opinion and it is out of respect for al-Ghazali's right to express his opinion that we publish his speech, however much it may differ from that of the newspaper. At the same time, we give Salah Jahin the same right to express his opinion of what the sheikh says" (*al-Ahram*, 1 June 1962). Salah Jahin published further cartoons, with the caption "Sheikh al-Ghazali's Clothes Don't Give His Opinions Immunity from Criticism!" Jahin also wrote poetry critical of the sheikh.

Thus spake Abu Zayd al-Ghazali Salama,
His eyes, and his glasses, spitting fire:
"I'm the one who vanquished the ladies and made them wear

headscarves!
I'm the one who brought the roofs down on the cinema-goers in my ire!
If the sun comes up, I say, 'It's the moon!'
And if someone objects, I say 'An infidel and a liar!'
And you'd better watch it if I say, 'He's betrayed his faith!'—
Stoning is what you require.
You'd better cry 'Amen' to whatever I say,
Even if it's 'That's not a rose, it's a briar!'"

The battle, in the form of an attack on Salah Jahin and *al-Ahram*, had moved to the pulpits, with even Kamal al-Din Husayn intervening to ask Haykal to move on from the topic of *al-Ahram*'s differences with Sheikh al-Ghazali to a discussion of the *Charter*, stressing that respect and veneration for religion was something all should observe. The Jahin–al-Ghazali–Haykal battle was an aftershock of the *Children of the Alley* earthquake, which had paralyzed the regime and left it in a quandary over Naguib Mahfouz and his novel, which was published despite all directives and campaigns.

Naguib Mahfouz met Hasan Sabri al-Kholi in the elevator. "He was working in the same building with me," recounted Naguib Mahfouz, who was then head of film censorship while al-Kholi was head of the General Organization for Information and, as such, responsible for censorship of printed matter and the press; he was not, at that time, Abd al-Nasser's personal envoy, although Mahfouz indicates in one of his interviews that he was known as "the president's representative" (Raga' al-Naqqash, *Naguib Mahfouz: safahat min mudhakkaratihi*, 143). A conversation took place between them around *Children of the Alley*, and al-Kholi proposed that he set up a meeting between Mahfouz and a number of sheikhs from al-Azhar who had objected to the publication of the novel, among them the three who had written reports recommending that it be banned. These were Sheikh Muhammad al-Ghazali, Sheikh Muhammad Abu Zahra, and Sheikh Ahmad al-Sharabasi. Mahfouz went to al-Kholi's office at the appointed time but the sheikhs, perhaps fearing the encounter, failed to show, and a discussion ensued between Mahfouz and al-Kholi that ended with a gentleman's agreement that Mahfouz could publish the novel in any Arab country he wished except Egypt, unless he obtained the consent of al-Azhar. "We don't want to get involved in problems with al-Azhar," al-Kholi said. In an interview with *Paris Review* magazine (1992), Mahfouz stated that what Hasan Sabri al-Kholi, the censor for printed matter and the press, put forward was merely "advice" to the effect that the novel should not be printed in Egypt (Charlotte El Shabrawy, "Naguib Mahfouz, The Art of Fiction No. 129"), along with his undertaking that the novel would not be attacked in the Egyptian press (*al-Musawwar*, 21 October 1988, 63). Mahfouz accepted this advice and stuck to the agreement, expressing his view that the novel contained a message that had not yet been understood: "I felt my message hadn't been understood, so I made no effort to defend it or publish it" (*Rose al-Yusuf*, 5 May 2001).

The message referred to by Mahfouz was a political one, at least in one respect, but "the problems that accompanied it and the interpretations given to it caused many to ignore these background issues," as Raga' al-Naqqash puts it (*Naguib Mahfouz: safahat min mudhakkaratihi*, 142). Similarly, John Rodenbeck, in his foreword to the English translation of the novel *al-Shahhadh (The Beggar)*, notes that *Children of the Alley* "suggested that the new regime would ultimately not be much different from the old ones; and did so with a passionate, darting intelligence that seemed to have turned political disappointment—even despair—into a new freedom of expression." It is noteworthy that Mahfouz, having avoided any allusions to the social dimensions of the novel during the 1960s, or to its being banned for political reasons, was more daring in making such references following Abd al-Nasser's death, saying in an interview with Kuwait's *al-Qabas* (The Torch) newspaper:

> I write only when a split has developed between me and society, meaning when I have some form of anxiety and dissatisfaction. I had begun to feel that the revolution that had brought comfort and tranquillity had begun to go astray and reveal its shortcomings. Lots of disquieting contradictions had begun to appear, and I had begun to feel that there were major and disquieting shortcomings and mistakes, especially in the form of terrorist operations, torture, and imprisonment. I began the writing of my major novel *Children of the Alley*, which portrays the struggle between prophets and bullyboys, with this as my point of departure. I was asking the revolutionaries, "Do you want to take the path of the prophets or of the bullyboys?" (*al-Qabas*, December 1975)

I AM NOT A PHILOSOPHER

Interest in the crisis over the novel was not limited to Egypt. It spread throughout the Arab world via the correspondents of Arabic-language magazines based in Cairo. Muhyi al-Din Muhammad, correspondent of the Beirut magazine *al-Adab*, reported on the outcry accompanying the publication of *Children of the Alley*, even though "it was not published in book form. It was read in installments in a daily newspaper, with all that this leads to by way of loss of plot outline, timeline, focus, and the main thread that links the characters and gives them their living, human stamp" (*al-Adab*, February 1960).

He also revealed that "The outcry was not limited to the sheikhs of al-Azhar but extended to certain critics in the national press and at seminars who associated the characters of the novel with great men of history, such as the prophets." He explained further that

> al-Azhar's attack is based on what it calls the novelist's insolence toward everything held sacred by the Arab nation, be they Muslims or Christians, and its rejection of the way he has painted the Prophet in "shallow" colors that indicate nothing other than a desire to mock religion. The critics' attack is based on a more mature and sophisticated approach. Some have perceived a similarity to others like it in the West, driven to this conclusion by Naguib Mahfouz's personal desire to be a writer in the manner of

> a novelist of universal human relevance such as Thomas Mann and to abandon once and for all the unadorned, literal portrayal of the life of the city's middle class.

Having reported the causes of the attack, Muhyi al-Din Muhammad defends Mahfouz as follows: "Mahfouz has not abandoned his class. He has not taken his work on a leap to the level of human universality. He remains, still, mired in the mud of our Arab East, trying to treat its diseases, cure its ulcers. The naiveté of the thinking of some of these critics is due to their having been fooled by the novel's use of symbols and their rushing to draw conclusions." The writer adds, "The novelist's use of historical characters should not be understood as an attempt at narrative so much as an attempt to present, in condensed form, the mistaken measures by which the East has destroyed a number of the prophets, apostles, and reformers who have appeared during its history. The response has to be of the age and scientific to the extreme . . . . He has taken the Arab on a leap to ultimate self-liberation and freedom from slavery." In conclusion, Muhyi al-Din Muhammad calls on Mahfouz's critics and attackers not to rush to judgment but to wait until "the novel comes out in full as a book."

Similarly, Ghali Shukri, correspondent of Lebanon's *Hiwar* (Dialogue) magazine, interviewed Mahfouz about the novel, which Shukri describes as adding nothing to world philosophy; what is new is the addition of this particular genre to Arabic literature. Mahfouz commented quietly:

> *Children of the Alley* adds nothing to world philosophy, that is true. But when did I claim to be a philosopher in the true sense of the word? A philosopher is one who adds something new to world philosophy; a philosophical writer is one who gives artistic expression to what he has taken from that philosophy. In so doing, he benefits philosophy because he transforms it into a living experience dwelling in the human soul, when before it was a mental equation of concern only to philosophers and their disciples. What did Shakespeare or Goethe or Ibsen or Shaw add to world philosophy? Nothing. Literature does not create philosophies, but it concerns itself with them. If any literature has added something new to thought, it is because the author is both a philosopher and a writer at the same time, like Sartre.

Mahfouz goes on to try to present his view of the genre that he chose as the framework for his ideas in the novel by saying, "But to what genre does *Children of the Alley* belong? Perhaps—I say perhaps—it is the opposite of what Jonathan Swift did in his famous *Gulliver's Travels*, in that he used myth to critique reality. In my case, I use reality to critique myth. I have dressed myth in the garments of reality to make reality more understandable and hopeful."

The debate went on. Although Mahfouz published other works, journalists remained preoccupied with the question of why *Children of the Alley* had not been issued as a book. Sa'd Kamil, editor at *Akhir sa'a* (Stop Press), asked him, "Why have you so far not published *Children of the Alley* as a book? Mahfouz answered, "It wasn't published so originally because I wasn't able to obtain a license to publish from the then book censorship department. Even though that department has now been abolished, any publisher would be afraid to put it out for fear of opposition from al-Azhar." The interviewer asked him, "So what will be its fate?" Mahfouz replied, "Lebanon has tried to obtain printing rights but I have put them off, hoping it can be published in Egypt first, after the misunderstandings stirred up by al-Azhar, and all the fuss over it, have died down" (Sa'd Kamil, "al-Raqaba wa Naguib Mahfouz," *Akir sa'a*, 15 May 1963).

This was the first time Mahfouz had referred to an official ban on the novel inside Egypt, its failure to obtain a license from the censor, and publishers' consequent fear of issuing it. More than two years after this interview, the novelist Muhammad Gabril again raised the question, "When will *Children of the Alley* come out as a book?" (*al-Masa'*, 26 June 1965).

Gabril presents numerous details confirming Mahfouz's publisher's reluctance to print *Children of the Alley* and how the publisher would content himself with announcing, on the last page of each new book by Naguib Mahfouz, that *Children of the Alley* was "forthcoming" without actually taking any steps to have it printed. Gabril adds: "The publisher may have intended *Children of the Alley* to remain 'forthcoming' forever, indicating that no order banning its printing had been issued; otherwise he would not have insisted on announcing, at the end of each book, that it was about to appear. Does not 'forthcoming' mean that the book is about to appear?" Gabril suggested the following solution:

> that a public publishing house, meaning one such as al-Dar al-Misriya li-l-Ta'lif wa-l-Tarjama or al-Dar al-Qawmiya, and so on, which

> belong to the public sector, should take on the responsibility of publishing *Children of the Alley*, since it is unreasonable to ask Mahfouz to refuse an attractive offer from a Beirut publishing house and insist that the novel come out, like the rest of his works, in Cairo. It is also unreasonable, given that this is the position in which the author finds himself, that one of the public-sector publishing houses should not perform the first of their duties, which is to remove the obstacles to publication encountered by writers and other artists, among whom our writer is no cipher but rather a shining example of the development of our modern Arabic literature. (*al-Masa'*, 26 June 1965)

Mahfouz hesitated for a long time—more than seven years—before accepting the offer of Beirut's Dar al-Adab publishing house in December of 1967. Sulayman Fayyad recounts that he met Mahfouz at his weekly discussion group at the Café Riche and asked him what was happening with the publication of the novel in book form. Mahfouz responded, "It seems [Sa'id] al-Sahhar is hesitant about publishing it, and I don't think it will be published in Egypt." Fayyad continued, "In any case, I have a publisher, if an Egyptian publisher refuses to publish the novel." "Who is that?" Mahfouz asked him. "Dar al-Adab in Beirut," Fayyad answered. Mahfouz had no objection, so Fayyad phoned Suhayl Idris, who said, "For that novel, I'll be in Cairo within the week." And indeed, Idris came and made an agreement with Mahfouz for the publication of the novel, which *al-Adab* magazine promoted with a publicity campaign under the slogan "The Novel We Have Been Awaiting So Long!" (*al-Adab*, December 1967, 22).

During those years of waiting, no official written decision existed banning publication of the novel in Egypt. The censors neither rejected nor accepted it, since no one took steps to print it. During these years the outcry also died down a little, and Mahfouz busied himself with his other works.

From time to time, newspapers here and there would publish a study of the controversial novel, but on 12 May 1968, five months after its appearance in Beirut, the Islamic Research Academy, headed by its then president Mahmud Hubballah, issued the first-ever official report calling for the banning of the book. The report reviewed the events and characters of the novel and observed:

> These are the aspects of the story that demand censure, and the fact that real events and characters have been transferred into

> indicative events and symbolic characters in no way lessens the seriousness of that censure; none of that hides the true face of each event and character. Nor is the seriousness of these charges lessened by the fact that what the writer has given us is—all beliefs and sacred matters aside—an excellent work of art, and that it would have been within the writer's power to keep his work, as art, away from the depths to which it descends. It is therefore recommended that the story not be published in written, audio, or video form. (See the appendix for the full text)

Why was this report issued at that time? We have no clear answer, but some have concluded that copies of the Beirut edition must have made their way clandestinely to Cairo, that the Islamic Research Academy was afraid that someone would seek to distribute it in Egypt, and that the Academy issued the report to preempt any such attempt.

In his *Naguib Mahfouz: sadaqat jilayn* (Naguib Mahfouz: A Friendship of Two Generations), the novelist Muhammad Gabril mentions that copies of the novel had made their way into the country after it had been issued in Beirut. Muhammad Fayiq had therefore telephoned Naguib Mahfouz and informed him that the order prohibiting publication was still in force and that it would not be a good idea to distribute the work in Egypt (*Naguib Mahfouz: sadaqat jilayn*, 248).

At an encounter on the margins of a public seminar (11 February 2017), I asked Fayiq whether Muhammad Gabril was correct, and he said, "I'm the one who gave the order for the adaptation of the novel into a radio serial." The serial was broadcast in 1970, under the original title, on the *Sawt al-'Arab* (Voice of the Arabs) radio channel (directed by Husayn Abu al-Makarim, screenplay by 'Abd al-Rahman Fahmi, with Samiha Ayyub, 'Abd Allah Ghayth, 'Abd al-Rahman Abu Zahra, Tawfiq al-Daqn, Karima Mukhtar, and Muhammad Rida). It passed without objection from anyone.

Fayiq had confessed earlier to Marina Stagh that minor changes had been made to the serial: "I suggested these personally to Naguib Mahfouz to avoid protests, and he agreed to them." He added, "The toughest censorship always comes as a result of religious protests. Religious–moral reasons were behind the difficulties faced by most books that were passed for publication first in newspapers and then published as books. Their publication in the newspapers meant that there was no political objection to them." I asked him, "Did you obtain Abd al-Nasser's consent before it was broadcast?" He said, "No . . . . The president wouldn't have objected." Fayiq may not have obtained the president's consent but he did obtain al-Azhar's, according to *Sabah al-khayr*'s 25 March 1968 announcement that *Sawt al-'Arab* had obtained the agreement of the office of the Sheikh of al-Azhar to the presentation of Naguib Mahfouz's novel *Children of the Alley* as a radio serial and that a written agreement to that effect had been concluded between Mahmud Hubballah, general secretary of the Islamic Research Academy, and Mahmud 'Aruq, director of *Sawt al-'Arab*. The serial was broadcast in full at that time and rebroadcast after Naguib Mahfouz won the Nobel Prize, but stopped after the second episode for no stated reason.

THE SEARCH FOR THE MANUSCRIPT

Where might we find the manuscript of Naguib Mahfouz's *Children of the Alley*?," I asked Philip Stewart, the first translator of the novel into English, to which he replied, jokingly, "Perhaps lying in a safe in a bank in Beirut!" (email dialogue with Philip Stewart, August 2016).

Why Beirut specifically? The story has to be told from the beginning. In March 1962, the young Philip Stewart (born London, 1939) arrived in Cairo after studying Arabic at the University of Oxford. He had been sent by the university to carry out research into "the novels of Naguib Mahfouz" for his doctorate. He did not have a great deal of time—just six months, after which he was to return to study forestry. He frequented the same café where Mahfouz sat every morning, where he met an Egyptian lawyer called Harvey, a friend of Mahfouz's and a leftist, who used to attend the latter's discussion groups. Harvey advised him not to waste his time on research but instead translate one of Naguib Mahfouz's novels. *Children of the Alley* was chosen. The translation was not to be made with publication in mind. On the contrary, it would be an academic translation undertaken with the sole purpose of obtaining an academic degree. Stewart was convinced by the idea.

In a conversation with me, Stewart said, "I had expected that the translation, plus an introduction and remarks, would be enough for a doctoral dissertation but the university rejected it." While working on the translation, Stewart obtained a copy of the novel, as published in *al-Ahram* in installments, and met Naguib Mahfouz on numerous occasions to ask him about things in the novel that he did not understand or words and phrases that had been missed in the *al-Ahram* edition. When Stewart asked Mahfouz about the manuscript of the novel, he replied, "I gave it to *al-Ahram* for them to use for the publication but it was never returned, so I concluded it must have been lost and didn't ask about it."

I assume, based on my knowledge of Mahfouz, that his reply was diplomatic, since he was speaking of a fair copy made for publication, not the drafts made during the writing of the novel, with their erasures and corrections. All the same, not everything that Stewart took away with him from Naguib Mahfouz was "diplomatic." He put numerous questions to him and raised with him numerous (especially religious and symbolic) issues. Mahfouz responded, indeed, to the biggest question of all: "What is it that angers public opinion so much about the novel?"

Stewart raised three points:

1. The representation of the prophets in the flesh in a novel.
2. The death of Gabalawi as a parallel to Nietzsche's "death of God."
3. Mimicry of the Qur'an, given that the novel is divided into 114 chapters (the same as the number of chapters in the Qur'an).

Mahfouz laughed and said:

> God forbid! I'll tell you what's going on. The novel plus introduction is 115 chapters. I didn't have that arrangement in mind when I was writing. What I had in mind was that the novel would consist of twenty-five main chapters, and the internal division of the chapters occurred after I'd finished the novel. I had used the numbers to divide the chapters into smaller sections, simply to make for easier reading. Also, the *suras* [chapters] of the Qur'an carry names, not numbers, not to mention that they are of varying length. As to the claim that I presented the prophets in the flesh, that is something unacceptable to most men of religion, and to most religions. Kazantzakis was subjected to violent attack because of his novel *Christ Recrucified*. They don't want to imagine that the prophets are humans like us, who eat and drink. My answer to them is from the Qur'an: *They also say, "What ails this Messenger that he eats food, and goes about in the markets?"* (al-Furqan 25:7). Despite this, I never

> had the prophets in mind in the novel. Qassem isn't the Prophet Muhammad. He's a young man from nineteenth-century Cairo, not a young man from Mecca in the seventh century. As far as Gabalawi goes, the Marxists imagine, in their critique, that I am calling for the death of God but Gabalawi is not, obviously, God the Immortal, the Absolute. He is just "God" in the minds of some people. I am not capable of representing God in any way because, as it says in the Qur'an, *nothing is like Him* (al-Shura 42:11).

Mahfouz ended his response to his translator by saying, "On the contrary, when I finished the novel, I felt I had recovered my faith."

Spiritual matters were never far from Mahfouz's mind. Even in *Midaq Alley*, published in 1947, we find, for example, the two main characters, Radwan al-Husayni, who "trod the sorrows of this world underfoot and flew with his heart to the heavens, dispensing love to all men" (*Midaq Alley*, 8), and Sheikh Darwish, who "left family, friends, and acquaintances for 'God's world'" (*Midaq Alley*, 13). In the works he published after 1959, Mahfouz returned time after time to the topics of illusion, hallucination, and Sufi enlightenment, and this was clearly manifested in the short story "Za'balawi," which may be regarded as the writer's working notes for the character of Gabalawi.

Stewart completed translation of the novel within that short period, submitted it to the university, married, and devoted himself to the study of forestry. In 1967, he went to Algeria for seven years as a researcher, returning to Oxford in 1975. At Oxford, he met the American Arabist Roger Allen. They spoke of Naguib Mahfouz, and Allen informed him that the American University in Cairo Press had acquired the translation rights to Naguib Mahfouz's novels. Stewart recounts that Allen asked him if he would agree to grant them rights to his translation. "I answered that Heinemann was thinking of an Arabic literature series and I'd granted them the right to publish my translation." Heinemann had sent the manuscript of the translation to the academic and translator Fatma Moussa for review. Stewart assumed the latter would compare the Arabic text with the English and correct anything he had misunderstood. However, he was surprised to find her correcting the English, changing "strongman," for example, to "strong man." "I rejected what she'd done and changed the translation of *futuwwa* from "strongman" to "chief," which was a major mistake on my part." Stewart added:

> The translation came out in 1981 with a small print run and sold only four hundred copies in the eight years before Naguib Mahfouz received the Nobel Prize. Six weeks before the announcement of the prize, the American University in Cairo Press asked Heinemann to sell it the rights, and Heinemann agreed. However, the Press forgot to buy the rights from Three Continents Press, which had asked me to give them the rights to publish the USA edition, and this gave me the opportunity to revise the text and correct some mistakes that had crept into it; in that edition, I used *futuwwa*, as in the Arabic, instead of "strongman," at the suggestion of Pierre Cachia. In 1996, I began comparing the Beirut edition with the *al-Ahram* text. At the beginning, I found the work boring and monotonous but, starting with Chapter 3, I discovered numerous sentences and words that had fallen from the *al-Ahram* edition, just as there were many sentences missing from the Beirut edition.

In his introduction to the English translation of *Children of the Alley*, Stewart explains that there were 961 differences between the text published by *al-Ahram* and that issued by Dar al-Adab and about 1,241 words were missing, in addition to numerous differences in punctuation. Stewart drew the conclusion that the Dar al-Adab edition was based on the original manuscript. "Maybe someone at *al-Ahram* sold it to Dar al-Adab," he says. "Because the *al-Ahram* text missed out many words during printing and because entire paragraphs are omitted from the Dar al-Adab edition, neither text can be considered complete." Mahfouz had expressed his anger at the Dar al-Adab edition, on the grounds that it was "incomplete and I took no part in the proofreading," according to the translator.

Given that it was not only compared with both the Arabic texts but also checked by Naguib Mahfouz himself, who in addition helped with the translation (of which he says, in a letter to Stewart, "You deserve great thanks, first for translating the novel in a style to whose excellence and beauty all its readers have attested and second, for writing this excellent introduction"), Philip Stewart's English translation may be the only complete text of the novel in existence.

Stewart's statements concerning the novel's manuscript led me to question Rana Idris, daughter of Suhayl Idris, founder of Dar al-Adab, as to the whereabouts of the manuscript, and she referred us to her mother, 'Ayda

Idris, who witnessed the publication of the novel at her husband's publishing house. 'Ayda Idris responded as follows:

> The novel was published on the basis of what Dr. Suhayl Idris put together from what was published in *al-Ahram* newspaper. We do not possess the original manuscript. The novel was published with the agreement of Naguib Mahfouz, who refused to sign a contract. We do, however, possess all his signed receipts attesting to the fact that he received his rights in full from the first edition published by Dar al-Adab.

I turned to the Information and Research department of *al-Ahram* and was able to contact someone who had worked there during that period, namely Abu al-Su'ud Ibrahim, former head of the department, who started worked at *al-Ahram* in 1965, or about six years after the publication of *Children of the Alley*. I thought he might have come across the manuscript in the archives, but when asked, he said, "Throughout my time working at the archives I never saw any manuscripts of novels by Naguib Mahfouz. Usually, the original went to the proofreading department, then back to the author himself, to give it a final check. None of the novels of Naguib Mahfouz came to the department while I was working there" (personal communication to the author).

Abu al-Su'ud also undertook the cataloging of Muhammad Hasanayn Haykal's personal library and had deep experience and knowledge of its contents in terms of documents and sources. It was therefore appropriate to ask him about the possibility of finding the manuscript in the possession of the owner of the library, that passionate collector of documents. However, Abu al-Su'ud affirmed that "Haykal's library contains no originals of the novels by Naguib Mahfouz that were published during his tenure as editor-in-chief of *al-Ahram*."

Could President Gamal Abd al-Nasser have obtained the manuscript, in order to read the novel as it was being serialized? I asked Sami Sharaf and he responded, "Abd al-Nasser took care to read everything Naguib Mahfouz wrote but he did not read the manuscript of the novel before it was published. He read it in serial form, as published in *al-Ahram*." In his book *al-Namima* (Gossip), novelist Sulayman Fayyad wrote of Adel Kamel, one of the Hoodlums, as follows: "I saw the manuscript of *Children of the Alley* in Kamel's library before it was published in *al-Ahram*." I consulted the painter Gamil Shafiq, one of the oldest of the Hoodlums, who denied that Mahfouz had ever given its members a look at any of his manuscripts before they were published or that he had ever spoken of his manuscripts: "He had his secrets and he kept them well."

I asked him, "Did the late Adel Kamel's library contain any of Mahfouz's manuscripts?" He replied, "When Adel decided to leave the country, he wrote me a special power of attorney covering his works. Based on this, I acquired all the manuscripts of the author of *Mallim al-akbar (The Magnificent Conman of Cairo)*, and Sulayman Fayyad asked me to give them to him, so I gave them to him. There was a complete unpublished novel by Adel, titled *Allah wa-l-jasad wa-l-shaytan* (God, the Body, and the Devil), but there were no manuscripts of Mahfouz's."

Philip Stewart was not the only Arabist to take an interest in the novel after its publication in *al-Ahram*. Another was Père Jacques Jomier, who wrote a study of the *Trilogy* in the 1960s, the first by a foreigner on the works of Naguib Mahfouz. Jomier followed the novel as it was published. When the novelist Gamal al-Ghitani asked him, "Do you think the novel bears a religious interpretation?" Jomier answered, "No. The thought never occurred to me, but when I spoke to my friend Yahya Hakki on the telephone, he told me, when I said how much I liked it, 'Watch out! Naguib is writing the history of religion and the prophets'" (*Akhbar al-adab*, 19 June 2005, 6–7). In an article in *al-Masa'* newspaper, Hakki had said, referring to the novel, "Of the novels by Naguib Mahfouz, we read, after the *Trilogy*, *Children of the Alley*. In my opinion, it is to be numbered among the works of his that will pass the test of time and for which his name will be forever remembered, because he has done something that other writers have failed to" (*al-Masa'*, 13 February 1963).

THE ULTIMATE ORIGIN

During a working session on the English translation of *Children of the Alley*, Naguib Mahfouz confessed to Philip Stewart that the sole work of literature with any connection to his novel was Bernard Shaw's *Back to Methuselah*. Later, too, in a personal letter to Stewart, Mahfouz wrote:

> I read your introduction (referring to the introduction to the English translation of *Children of the Alley*, first published in 1981) and admire the idea behind it. I found that it offers a way of accommodating both those who accuse my novel of atheism and those who describe it as a Sufi work. I am also impressed that you traced it back to its origin in Bernard Shaw, in tune with my own admiration for him and especially for his major work *Back to Methuselah*. Dr. Mandur is probably the only critic to have hinted at such an idea, when he said that I had conveyed a traditional concept of God without alluding to God himself. (Full text in the Appendix)

In *Back to Methuselah*, which consists of five short plays, Bernard Shaw jumps from age to age. The first play begins with Adam and Eve in Eden before their temptation by the serpent and ends with their exit from the garden, soon after which Eve tells her son Cain that "Man need not always live by bread alone. There is something else. We do not yet know what it is; but some day we shall find out; and then we will live on that alone; and there shall be no more digging nor spinning, nor fighting nor killing" (Bernard Shaw, *Back to Methuselah*, 869). Events unfold, until we reach man's attempt to realize the dream of longevity, so that he can become like Methuselah—a character from the Old Testament, grandfather of Noah, who lived until he was 969 years old—and the play ends in the future, when science has succeeded in realizing that dream. The critics categorized Shaw's work as "science fiction" but Shaw himself rejected this description, stating that his concerns were political, not scientific, in that he discusses the evolutions through which humans must pass if they are to rule themselves and no longer need governments to organize their lives. Naguib Mahfouz read Shaw's play very early on, before publishing any of his novels; he even wrote a critical review of it in *al-Ma'rifa* (Knowledge) magazine. Mahfouz begins his exposition of Shaw's play as follows:

> Methuselah is a patriarch. It is said that he lived so long he passed the nine-hundred-year mark by half a century or so. To go back to him is, therefore, to take humanity back to the long lifespans of old, the point being to introduce the pivotal concept that underlies the plot and which will be revealed to the reader later. In a word, the writer aims to write a history of so-called Creative Evolution. He begins with the story of Adam and Eve and brings into the picture the eternal desire for the "philosopher's stone" that allows people to conquer death's sting. In addition, the defects of civilized life, and especially its political side, are acted out through the plot. (*al-Ma'rifa*, April–May 1934; full text in the appendix)

In his exposition of the play, Mahfouz alludes to humanity's dream of an extended lifespan, expressing the opinion that tyrannical politicians always die before reaching the age of discretion, so their lives ought to be extended so that they can attain wisdom and hopefully benefit from the experience of the past. Mahfouz translates extended passages of dialogue that throw light not so much on the main ideas of the play as on the ideas with which he himself was preoccupied. One of Shaw's characters does not believe in science. His belief in poetry is greater and he cites the myth of Eden as an example of the truthfulness of poetry. Then the character says, "Well, you remember, don't you, that in the Garden of Eden Adam and Eve were not created mortal, and that natural death, as we call it, was not a part of life, but a later and quite separate invention?" He adds:

> Adam and Eve were hung up between two frightful possibilities. One was the extinction of mankind by their accidental death. The other was the prospect of living forever. They could bear neither. They decided that they would just take a short turn of a thousand years, and meanwhile hand on their work to a new pair. Consequently, they had to invent natural birth and natural death, which are, after all, only modes of perpetuating life without putting on any single creature the terrible burden of immortality. (Bernard Shaw, *Back to Methuselah*, 885)

Did Mahfouz take his inspiration for his character Gabalawi from the Old Testament's Methuselah? And did Bernard Shaw's play inspire the ideas he expresses in *Children of the Alley*?

The 1930s were years of "intellectual anxiety" for Naguib Mahfouz, years of uncertainty and of delving into large ideas, and it was not until 1936 that he made his final choice between philosophy and literature. As he puts it:

> I was holding a book on philosophy in one hand and, in the other, one of Tawfiq al-Hakim's, or Yahya Hakki's, or Taha Hussein's novels, and the various philosophical schools were invading my mind from one side at the same moment that the stories' heroes were entering it from the other. I found myself caught up in a terrible struggle between literature and philosophy, a struggle of a kind that only those who have lived through it can imagine, and I had to make a decision or I would have gone insane. (*Akhir sa'a*, 12 December 1962)

Soon enough, however, Mahfouz made up his mind to devote himself exclusively to literature, although philosophy continued to make intrusions into his works. He published, in *al-Majalla al-jadida* (The New Magazine), a number of articles that reveal his philosophical concerns during that period, among them two with the title of "God in Philosophy" (January, March 1936), whose publication coincided with the start of Mahfouz's work on his first novel *'Abath al-aqdar (Khufu's Wisdom)*, published in 1939.

Khufu's Wisdom tells the story of a magician (*Khufu's Wisdom*, 8) who reads King Khufu's future and prophesies that none of his offspring will succeed him on the throne of Egypt and that the throne will be occupied after him by a recently born child, the son of the high priest of the temple at On (16). Khufu sets forth at the head of a military expedition to kill all the newborn children who could possibly threaten his throne, but he himself takes one of the children to the house of a high official and instructs him to raise it. The child lives to reach the highest rank and Khufu himself bestows on him the succession, after the crown prince is killed and his daughter marries. In Mahfouz's novel, the individual is a plaything in the hands of Fate, which sports with him as it wills.

Mahfouz recalls that he was inspired to write *Khufu's Wisdom* by "a pharaonic legend recounted by the Egyptians" (Gamal al-Ghitani, *Naguib Mahfuz yatadhakkar*, 44). On another occasion, Mahfouz says that "when he translated *Ancient Egypt*, he found a story about a fortuneteller who made a prophesy of some kind to Khufu but the story is incomplete because the final sheet of papyrus is missing, so he made up an ending for it in this novel" (Muhammad Bakr al-Buji, "Riwayat Naguib Mahfouz al-tarikhiya," *Majallat Jami'at al-Azhar* [Gaza] 11, no. 2 [December 2009]: 216).

By the "lost papyrus," Mahfouz meant the Westcar Papyrus, written by the priest Fayton, the first Egyptian historian. This contains five stories, some about priests who "split the sea," and a final, incomplete story that bears the name "The Story of the Birth of the Three Kings." The stories were published by James Baikie in *Ancient Egypt*, the book that Mahfouz himself translated, also in 1932. Baikie adheres to the text of the papyrus, in which the fortuneteller prophesies that "the three children, sons of the priest of Ra" will rule Egypt. A serving woman who was in the house of Ra hears about this and leaves angrily to tell King Khufu about the children. However, while she is walking beside the Nile, a crocodile suddenly appears, seizes her, and disappears with her beneath the water. Baikie says, "Here, unfortunately, the story ends and we do not know whether Khufu tried to kill the children or not, as the papyrus sheets are missing and no one knows anything about them" (Naguib Mahfouz, *Misr al-qadima*, 50).

This is the historical material that inspired Naguib Mahfouz's first novel, although he used both his imagination as a novelist and other sources to complete the story. Among the latter is the Islamic tale of the prophet Moses, which says that when Moses' mother becomes pregnant with him, she fears Pharaoh will kill him, so she conceals her pregnancy; when she gives birth to him, God tells her to put him in a chest and cast him onto the waters. She does that, the child is carried along by the waters, and Pharaoh's wife plucks him out and falls in love with him. He is taken into Pharaoh's court, where Pharaoh's wife asks to be allowed to keep him as her son, and she takes him into the palace and they name him Moses, meaning He Who Was Plucked out of the Water. The events of the novel may also be traced back to Sophocles's *Oedipus Rex*, where a fortuneteller prophesies to Laius, King of Thebes, that he will father a son who will kill him and marry his own mother. Laius is disturbed by this prophecy and avoids his wife, so that he will not father children. However, he has intercourse with her when he is drunk and the unwanted pregnancy occurs. The king, fearing the prophecy, waits until she comes to term and then gives the child to his guard, to kill. The guard takes the child, its feet bound, to the mountains but instead of leaving him on the ground there to die, he leaves him with a shepherd whom he meets. The shepherd feels pity for the child and takes him to the king and queen of Corinth, who have no children, and gives it to them. Laius believes that he has rid himself of his son and of the prophecy.

The intersections between Mahfouz's novel and the religious narrative appear to be far greater than its intersections with the legend of Oedipus. In other words, Mahfouz had been thinking from early on about how to give voice to, and exploit and build on, the religious tradition. And even though Mahfouz described his novel in later years as being no more than "childish," it is possible to observe within it numerous features that became a permanent part of his practice later on and which he worked to develop. This is especially true if we take into consideration that beginnings, according to Edward Said, possess "an obsessive persistence in the mind" (Edward Said, *Beginnings: Intention and Method*, 40). Indeed, it may be that *Khufu's Wisdom* forms the background from which Mahfouz's later novels, and specifically *Children of the Alley*, would eventually spring, not simply in the sense that both strive to make use of the religious tradition to express the crisis of contemporary humanity or both treat the present as though it was history; it is also a question of the idea, which preoccupied Mahfouz for so long, of the division of humanity into "bullyboys" and "riff-raff." In *Khufu's Wisdom*, the ordinary people are divided into "prisoners of war," who go and come "without any higher feelings, just as the bull pushes around the waterwheel without any reflection" (10), and Egyptians, who are "people with self-respect, pride, steadfastness, and faith. They are able to bear terrific torment, and to patiently tolerate overwhelming tragedies" and they strike at the rocks "with arms like thunderbolts, and with a determination like the Fates themselves, as they sing their rhythmic songs, and chant their poems." Similarly, in *Children of the Alley* humanity is divided into "bullyboys, who cannot be overcome," and the poor, "who live in the filth among the flies and lice, make do with crumbs, and strive to make a living with bodies that are barely clothed" (Dar al-Adab edition of *Awlad haratina*, 7). In this sense, might it be possible to regard *Khufu's Wisdom* as a trial run for *Children of the Alley*?

Mahfouz's interest in "the religious narrative" continued after the publication of *Khufu's Wisdom* and extended to all his works. In many of his interviews, he indicated that the narrative style of the Qur'an had provided him with an understanding of the novelist's art and that its impact ran through all his writings, although it was especially notable in *Hadith al-sabah wa-l-masa' (Morning and Evening Talk)*. He said, "When I read the Qur'an, I used to pay special attention to the stories in it because they enchanted me as elevated examples of the novelist's art, written like the most beautiful examples of elevated storytelling, and till now the human stories with the greatest impact on my sensibility continue to be those of the Qur'an. Which of us could come up with a story like that of Maryam, or of Our Master Moses?" (*al-Ahram*, "Conversations with Naguib Mahfouz," 5 June 2000).

He also indicated that the "stream of consciousness" that Europe became acquainted with at the hands of James Joyce and Marcel Proust was the very style that is used in the narration of the stories of the Qur'an: "The story of Maryam does not start, in *Surat Maryam*, at the beginning, and then proceed in a logical succession of events until it reaches the end, only for a new story, or a new *sura*, to start thereafter. We find instead that the story of Maryam is distributed among *suras* such as *al-Baqara*, *al-'Imran*, *al-Nisa'*, *al-Ma'ida*, *al-Tawba*, and *Maryam*, with a part of her story, or that of the Messiah, God keep him, occurring in each." This may explain Mahfouz's interest in Sayyid Qutb's book *al-Taswir al-fanni fi al-Qur'an* (Artistic Depiction in the Qur'an), in which Qutb deals with the esthetics of Qur'anic narration. Mahfouz offered a reading of the book on its appearance: addressing his words to Qutb he writes, "Our age is, from the esthetic standpoint, the age of music, painting, and the story. You have revealed to us, with power and inspiration, that our beloved book is music, painting, and story in the most sublime form to which revelation and creativity have ever risen" (*al-Risala*, April 1945).

When we speak of the distant origins of *Children of the Alley*, we cannot ignore the impact of Salama Musa on Mahfouz. The novel, in one of its aspects, is an expression of an idea that preoccupied Mahfouz greatly, and from early on, or more specifically from the early 1930s, when he met Musa for the first time. Mahfouz relates the details of this encounter in *Sugar Street*, when he has Ahmad Shawkat (a character who, like Kamal 'Abd al-Gawad in the same novel, is an avatar of a certain aspect of Naguib Mahfouz) meet with 'Adli Karim (who appears to be the artistic double in the novel of Salama Musa) so that she can work with him on his magazine *al-Insan al-jadid* (The New Human). 'Adli's advice to Shawkat is "Study literature as much as you want, but . . . don't forget modern science. In addition to Shakespeare and Schopenhauer, your library must contain Comte, Darwin, Freud, Marx, and Engels . . . and remember that each age has its prophets. The prophets of this era are the scientists" (*Sugar Street*, 88). Riyad Qaldas, also in *Sugar Street*, states the same idea in a different context: "Science provides mankind with its magic, light, guidance, and miracles. It's the religion of the future" (103).

Salama Musa was Naguib Mahfouz's spiritual father—the first reader of his first works, as well as his guide as to what he should read. Mahfouz's *Trilogy* reveals this clearly, as do his scattered interviews: "Salama Musa directed me toward two important things—science and socialism, and once they entered my brain, they never left it" (Fu'ad Dawwara, *Naguib Mahfouz min al-qawmiya ila al-'alamiya* [Naguib Mahfouz: From Nationalism to Internationalism], 219). It follows that the first seed of the idea was planted in him by Musa, who was "the foremost missionary among our generation of social justice, science, and the modern point of view. He was as much a moderate in political matters as he was an extremist in his proselytization for science, industry, and the freedom of women, and he never leant toward dictatorship, which is why I consider him the spiritual father of socialism and democracy." Mahfouz himself retained these ideas. He was truly preoccupied with the role of science in the life and progress of humanity. Less than a month before the publication of *Children of the Alley*, 'Abdallah Muhammad 'Abdallah conducted an interview with Mahfouz in *al-Idha'a* magazine and asked him what wisdom he had been able to glean from life. Mahfouz answered without hesitation, "Science is the foundation of sovereignty" (*al-Idha'a*, 22 August 1959). In numerous interviews, he repeated that "I hope the day will come on which we can all agree that science, rather than poetry, should be the supreme art of the Arabs" (*al-Ahram*, 17 March 1995).

13 OCTOBER 1988

Cairo is being boring: no fresh or exciting news today. Yasser Arafat, on a visit here, has announced that the Intifada will continue until all of occupied Palestine is liberated. The first of November has been fixed as the date for the start of the trial of members of Thawrat Misr (Egypt's Revolution), the organization led by Mahmud Nur al-Din and Khaled Abd al-Nasser; despite the obvious popular sympathy for the organization, Egypt's official press has tried to portray its members as "terrorists" and drug addicts, although this has failed to make a dent in that extraordinary sympathy, which will make itself clear throughout the trial. Zaki Badr, minister of the interior, announces at a seminar at the German Chamber of Commerce that "we will never abandon the rule of law and democracy." A few days before, the inauguration of the new opera house has taken place; the newspapers cover the event, along with the calls to Farouk Hosny, minister of culture, to review the ticket prices, which range from five to thirty Egyptian pounds, "so as to attract the masses to attend the sublime productions, raise their consciousness, and take them back to the traditions of the life of the arts" (*al-Akhbar*, 13 October 1988). The dollar is worth 231 piasters (which is something that, in a few hours, Egyptian writers will be obsessing over).

The literary sections of the newspapers speak of a delegation from Bavarian television headed by German orientalist Erdmute Heller, editor-in-chief of *Fikrun wa-fann* (Thought and Art) magazine, which is making a film about Naguib Mahfouz—his daily life, the places he has lived; the film is written by a Tunisian, Hassuna al-Misbahi. At the National Theater, Yahya al-Fakharani's production of *al-Bahlawan* by Yusuf Idris continues, while Faruq al-Fishawi is appearing in the play *Shabab imra'a* (Youth of a Woman), along with Fifi 'Abduh in her first performance as an actress. Cinemas are showing *Ightiyal mudarrisa* (Murder of a Teacher) and *Milaff Samya Sha'rawi* (The Samya Sha'rawi File).

At precisely one o'clock, the Permanent Secretary of the Swedish Academy, Sture Allén, emerges to announce that the Egyptian novelist Naguib Mahfouz has won the Nobel Prize in Literature, an achievement that transforms Cairo's quiet into clamorous joy.

Mahfouz had been sleeping, having returned from *al-Ahram* newspaper carrying with him green onions, which his friend the film director Tawfiq Salih had advised him were good for diabetes. He had eaten lunch and gone to his room to snatch his daily siesta. Then his wife received a call from Muhammad Basha, a journalist at *al-Ahram*, with the glad tidings that Mahfouz had won the Nobel Prize. She hurried to wake him, calling out the news, and as he got up he commented, "Enough with the dreams!" She, however, informed him that it was not a joke and he replied to the caller, in English, "Who is speaking?" although his wife told him that the caller was Egyptian. Mahfouz still did not believe it: "Someone whom I knew was always making practical jokes phoned, so I wouldn't believe the news, coming from him, and I told him, 'Let me sleep!'" (Raga' al-Naqqash, *Naguib Mahfouz: safahat min mudhakkaratihi*, 152). Suddenly, though, the parlor was filled with journalists, and suddenly too, the Swedish ambassador to Cairo arrived, at which point Mahfouz remembered the green onions and spent his time talking to the ambassador with his hand over his mouth throughout. But had the Nobel Prize really been a dream of Mahfouz's? And had he schemed to get it?

For thirty years, Naguib Mahfouz had been hearing the following question from journalists, as well as critics and friends who attended his various gatherings: "Do you dream of the Nobel Prize?"

His reply was always the same: "No!"

In 1958, *al-Kawakib* magazine had asked him, "Do you think a writer from our part of the world might one day win the Nobel Prize?"

Mahfouz answered, "It may happen one day, but our literature hasn't yet reached a standard worthy of the Nobel Prize. We haven't yet reached that international rank" (*al-Kawakib*, 29 July 1958).

In 1969, novelist Alaa Al Aswany asked him, during an interview for *Rose al-Yusuf*, to set aside his habitual diplomacy and talk to him frankly. Mahfouz agreed, joking to Al Aswany, "God protect us!" The interview touched on Russian literature, with Mahfouz speaking of the writers who had had the most important impact on him. Boris Pasternak he considered "a huge novelist but lacking in artistic vision and not deserving of the Nobel Prize." Al Aswany asked him, "Would you like to win the Nobel Prize?"

"No."

"Why?"

"I don't regard what I have offered as an addition to human heritage."

"I have read that Taha Hussein was nominated for the prize. Did Taha Hussein make an addition to human heritage deserving of the prize?"

"No. The only writer who could have been nominated was Tawfiq al-Hakim" (*Rose al-Yusuf*, May 1969).

In late 1987, during a conversation at the 'Ali Baba café on Tahrir Square, the critic Ghali Shukri asked him, "Why do you attack the Nobel Prize? Are you jealous?"

"Jealous?"

"Do you deny the greatness of most of the winners?"

"I deny nothing, although I do believe the Arabs are mistaken if they're dreaming of getting it."

"You've never dreamed of it?"

"No, I swear to God!"

"What do you dream of, then?"

"Why are you being such a pain this early in the day? Drink your coffee, if all you can dream about is what I'm dreaming about!" (Ghali Shukri, *Naguib Mahfouz: min al-Jamaliya ila Nubil*, 36–37).

A few days before Mahfouz was awarded the prize, the journalist As'ad Haydar asked him the same question in an interview for *al-Mustaqbal* (The Future) magazine. Mahfouz answered at length: "When the prize was being awarded to the traditional writers, meaning giants such as Bernard Shaw and Thomas Mann, it was never a dream of mine. After the age of the giants—writers like Jean-Paul Sartre and Albert Camus—came to an end, you know, the prize began to be given to ordinary, and I mean really ordinary, writers, so I didn't think about it any more. By the same token, I have no bitterness and I don't think I'll get it. It's not a prize for us. I don't have any desire for it and I have nothing to do with it" (As'ad Haydar, "Tharthara fawq al-Nil ma' Naguib Mahfouz," *al-Mustaqbal*, 22 October 1988). In the same interview, Mahfouz stated that he knew that a Swedish lady had come to Egypt four years before, in 1984, after visiting Syria, Lebanon, Tunisia, and Morocco in order to get to know the writers living in the East and had asked about writers who deserved the Nobel Prize. Sarcastically, he said, "She spent six months in each Arab capital, but she'd need sixty years to get to know this literature, not six months, plus she didn't know Arabic."

Despite Mahfouz's repeated denial that Arabic literature had not reached the level of world literature, many critics had placed his works, from early on, in a special category. When *Midaq Alley* came out, Muhammad Fahmi, critic at *al-Muqtataf* (The Digest) magazine, wrote:

> Let me (and I have no personal connection to this writer) clearly proclaim today what coming generations will confirm, namely that he has created a fictional literature of our own that is on a par with the Russian literature that, thanks to Dostoevsky, Chekhov, and Turgenev, has attracted the eyes of the world. Our fictional literature will stand tall among the literatures of the world, brimming with strength, life, and vibrancy. (*al-Muqtataf*, December 1947)

Sayyid Qutb said of the works of Mahfouz that they are "the true starting point of the creation of an authentic Arab novel, in which, for the first time, the flavor is local and the aroma national, in a literary work of a humanistic character whose artistry, at the same time, never falls below an acceptable standard in terms of its abstract literary qualities." Qutb added: "Today we can say that we have a long narrative, that is to say, a novel. We can also say that we are contributing a new dish to expand the global banquet of this art, one whose character is that of humanity in general but which exudes the flavor of the local. This is something that, until a few years ago, was missing" (*al-Fikr al-jadid*, 12 February 1948).

Taha Hussein considered that Naguib Mahfouz "has brought to the novel a degree of mastery, excellence, depth, precision, and near-magical impact that no Egyptian writer has before." He also considered that the novel *Palace Walk* "places the author on an equal footing with any world novelist you may wish to name in any of the languages people read in" (*al-Gumhuriya*, "*Bayn al-qasrayn*: qissa ra'i'a li-Naguib Mahfouz," 6 February 1957). On a trip to Morocco in 1958, Taha Hussein gave two lectures, the first on "The Status of Arabic Literature as a World Literature," the second on "Arabic Literature in Egypt, Ancient and Modern." Presenting Naguib Mahfouz to Moroccan readers, the dean of Arabic letters declared:

> If you have time to read some of the novels being published in Egypt now, I would like you to read the work of a young Egyptian of the new generation that has graduated from the Egyptian University. His name is Naguib Mahfouz, and he has written a bevy of novels that I consider the finest products of modern Egyptian literature. He has written novels in which he carefully chooses a street or a neighborhood of Cairo, then writes the history of one its families, thereby depicting the history of the neighborhood, the history of Cairo, and the history of the political events that have unfolded in Cairo. If you have time to read the series titled *Palace of Desire*, *Palace Walk*, and *Sugar Street*, you will find yourselves in the presence of novels that are authentic in the fullest sense of the word. (The lectures were published in *al-Ahram* with the title "*Al-Ahram* Publishes Taha Hussein's Unknown Moroccan Lectures," 6 July 2016)

When Naguib Mahfouz's winning of the Nobel Prize was announced, he said in most of the interviews he gave that al-'Aqqad had prophesied that he would win the prize during a television program in the 1960s. Al-'Aqqad had been commenting on the award of the prize to American writer John Steinbeck when he said, "We have a writer who deserves to win a Nobel. His name is Naguib Mahfouz." Al-'Aqqad then wrote a long article on John Steinbeck, in which he said:

> We really should point out that if it's about making the effort to do a thorough search, how come the search always stops short of the Arab countries, out of all the nations of the world? The committee does not find its way, nor does it seek to find its way, to any of their writers, and they are not few, those of this class. I may mention four writers of novels and plays, the same fields as Steinbeck's, this year's winner of the prize. These writers surpass him in certain respects and are no less great than he in others. They are Tawfiq al-Hakim, Mahmud Taymur, Naguib Mahfouz, and Mikhayil Nu'ayma. Naguib Mahfouz rivals, and perhaps exceeds, him in the depiction of his modern-day, traditional, naive, and primitive characters. (*al-Akhbar*, 31 October 1962)

Mahfouz's statement that al-'Aqqad was the first to nominate him for the prize was not entirely accurate: Louis Awad, who preceded al-'Aqqad in prophesying that he would be awarded the prize, had slipped his memory. This happened during an event put on by Muhammad Hasanayn Haykal at *al-Ahram* to celebrate Mahfouz's fiftieth birthday, which was attended by Umm Kulthum, Salah Jahin, Kamal al-Mallakh, and Husayn Fawzi. At this occasion, Fathi Radwan gave a speech praising Naguib Mahfouz. He was followed by Louis Awad, who said, addressing Mahfouz, "I look forward to your winning the Nobel Prize in the coming ten years." Mahfouz may have allowed Louis Awad to slip his memory on purpose, for he was, in Mahfouz's words, "a nitpicker as a critic and hypercritical when he nitpicks. As a critic, he's a fantasist, and he has issues that impact on his criticism" (*Rose al-Yusuf*, May 1969).

The Arabs paid no attention to the Nobel Prize in Literature when it was launched in 1901; it was assumed to be a prize for Europeans only. This assumption was strengthened by the fact that, for the first few rounds, the committee awarded the prize exclusively to Europeans. The Arabs first paid attention to the prize when it was awarded, in 1913, to the Indian poet Tagore. This marked the start of Arab ambitions for the award, which was suspended between 1914 and 1918 due to the World War.

At that period, there was no Arab writer more prominent than "the Prince of Poets," Ahmad Shawqi, who had returned from his exile in Andalusia in 1919. A campaign in support of his nomination for the prize was started. The first shot came in the form of a letter sent by a reader calling himself "an admirer of Shawqi" that was published in *al-Kashkul* (The Scrapbook) magazine under the title "The Poetry of Ahmad Shawqi and the Nobel Prize," which was republished in *Sarkis* magazine in December 1921. The anonymous letter writer begins with a question: "Is there no one in the East worthy of this prize? And if there is such a one among us, is there no one who can acquaint certain Westerners with our literary geniuses? Shawqi Bey has verse that the West must read. It is not going too far to request that he be proposed to the Nobel Prize committee. If our poet were to win the prize, it would be a win for us all and a source of pride for the writers of the East of our day. Who, then, will take on the task?"

The debate was renewed when Tagore visited Egypt in 1926. Surprisingly, Taha Hussein took a negative stand, expressing the view that Tagore was "a humanistic poet . . . lauded by the modern West just as he is by the ancient East" while, on the other hand, the poetry of Ahmad Shawqi and Hafiz or al-Barudi and Mutran lacked a "philosophy." In a letter to Muhammad Husayn Haykal he adds, "Tagore does not despise the mind and does not surrender himself totally to the imagination, whereas our friends do not seek for their poetry in the rational, real world but in the smoke that they expel from their mouths as they smoke their cigarettes or a waterpipe!" (Taha Hussein, *Hafiz wa Shawqi*, 99).

The question mark over Shawqi's worthiness of the prize remained even after his death. A reader from Iraq asks in *al-Hilal*, "Was not Shawqi a poet of genius? Was he not 'the Prince of Poets and of Eloquence'? Was he not a philosopher? Why then was he never considered for the Nobel Prize?" (March 1939). The editor of the "Between *al-Hilal* and Its Readers" column responded, "I believe there were many reasons, of which the foremost is that Shawqi's work was not translated into a European language known to the prize's decision-makers. As a result, they never heard of him."

The debate over the prize and whether any Egyptian writers deserved it continued. The magazine *Kull shay' wa-l-dunya* (Everything and the World) asked its readers, in 1930, "Who is the Egyptian writer most deserving of the Nobel Prize in Literature?" and offered a reward of 10,000 Egyptian pounds for the right answer. Not a single reader, however, sent in an answer to any of the magazine's subsequent issues.

In November 1932, *al-Hilal* published a survey with the title "Do Any of Our Writers Deserve the Nobel Prize?" that included the opinions of Muhammad Husayn Haykal, then editor-in-chief of *al-Hilal*, Anton al-Gumayyil, Ibrahim 'Abd al-Qadir al-Mazini, and Khalil Mutran.

Mutran states, "We have only recently been incorporated into the global family, we have no representative in the Swedish capital, and I do not believe our government is ready yet to draw the attention of the Swedes to our Arabic literature." He adds,

> I am well aware that in taking this stance I am acknowledging a painful truth, which is that the writer in our country is consigned to oblivion, unsung by the public and disregarded by the government, and that the means for destroying and impeding literary production are many, even though the life of the writer and poet should be made easy and productive. When this changes, we can think about winning the Nobel Prize, which is not something that we should make our grail.

Muhammad Hasanayn Haykal commented sarcastically, "If I had taken literature as a profession, I wouldn't have earned the price of a loaf of bread, and you're asking me about the Nobel Prize? Ask the educators in the schools and universities: primary responsibility for the economic straits in which the craft of literature finds itself in this country lies with them."

Anton al-Gumayyil wrote that a writer or poet who could win the Nobel Prize might exist but that the basic condition for winning was that the writer or poet be unique among the ancients and moderns, and a humanist in his approach. He traces the underlying reason for the failure of any of his generation to win the Nobel to the circumstances, environment, and only relatively recent appearance of creativity and innovation, and believed that the winning of the Nobel by an Egyptian was a possibility that lay hidden in the mists of the future.

Al-Mazini likewise deployed sarcasm: "And what is the literary value of the Nobel Prize? I don't see it as a ticket that will guarantee the writer's or the poet's entry into the annals of the immortals, or open him a tomb in the pantheon of long-awaited glory." He added, "The true assessment of a writer or poet cannot be made until fifty years have passed since his death, at which time all rancor will have died and the work of art will remain, in the presence of disinterested critics. Rarely do contemporaries do a good job of evaluating one another. The Nobel Prize should be given to the writer's heirs, after his death."

Under the heading "Egypt Twenty Years from Now," *al-Hilal* published an opinion poll, picking Khalil Mutran, "Poet of the Two Lands" (of Egypt and Lebanon), to write about the future of Arabic literature. The editor asked him, "Why has no Egyptian writer carried off the Nobel Prize?" Mutran responded, "In half a century, we will have what we long for now—world writers, writers whose reputation is known everywhere, and whose brilliant productions are translated into every language. This is not wishful thinking. I draw this conclusion with all due caution and expecting no more than the minimum. There can be no doubt that the writer's art will draw closer to the required perfection, for I believe that affluence and ease are requirements if the fine arts are to advance."

Mutran added: "The play and the story—whether the short story or the more expansive novel—will flourish in a new form. In 1982, the writer will be living a life of ease, and a single book or novel will bring its author thousands of pounds. In that time, publishers and printers will multiply, press standards will rise, and newspapers will sell by the million. I think it not unlikely that there will be schools teaching literature and criticism. Practitioners of the two crafts—prose and poetry—should have no fear: the future will give them their due in full."

In August 1939, *al-Majalla al-jadida* magazine, issued by Salama Musa, pondered the reasons why no Egyptian had been awarded the Nobel Prize in any of the branches of the sciences or in literature or in peace, while India had won it twice and small countries such as Denmark, Holland, Switzerland, Austria, and Belgium had also won it, as had a number of women; and "as for the reasons that have prevented us from receiving this honor, we leave those to the perspicacity of the Egyptian reader to decide, while we continue to hope that, one day, an Egyptian will be nominated."

In March 1958, *al-Risala al-jadida* polled a number of Egyptian writers to speak on their hopes for the third conference of the General Union of Arab Writers, which was to be held in Cairo. Naguib Mahfouz contributed a short piece in which he called on the Union to establish a prize for Arab writers along the lines of the Nobel Prize.

In a lecture on "Our Need for a New Style" delivered in 1959 at the University of Damascus, Yahya Hakki stated that Arabic literature was unsuited for translation and transfer to international culture by reason of two blameworthy characteristics that it possessed—"blandness and superficiality"—and called for a style that would be simple, even extremely simple. In his view, the skillful lute player was the one who did not let you hear the plucking of the strings; in the same way, the master writer should not let the reader hear the scratching of the pen.

'Abbas al-'Aqqad, for his part, was so preoccupied with the prize and its history that he wrote a whole book with the title *Jawa'iz al-adab al-'alamiya* (World Literary Prizes) and in his books justified his interest in the prize by claiming that he was above it, as he had refused more than once to be nominated ('Abbas Mahmud al-'Aqqad, *Jawa'iz al-adab al-'alamiya*, 81).

According to the Nobel Prize's archives, which are sealed for fifty years after the prize is awarded, the dean of Arabic letters, Taha Hussein, was the first Arab writer to be put forward officially for the prize. Hussein was nominated for the first time in 1949, his nominator being Ahmad Lutfi al-Sayyid, then head of the Arabic Language Academy and a member of the upper house of parliament. His nomination was supported by the French Nobel Prize winner André Gide and the orientalist Louis Massignon. At the time, *al-Musawwar* magazine published the citation for the nomination, which declared that "his writings, whether novels, works on social issues, or meticulous scholarship, make him worthy, when taken together, to receive this prize." However, the prize went in fact to the celebrated American novelist William Faulkner who, in an unusual departure from tradition, received it the following year.

According to those archives that are now open to the public, Taha Hussein remained on the lists of nominees for several years. In 1950, he was nominated by the board of Fuad I (now Cairo) University and in 1951 and 1952 by a number of foreign institutions. His name disappeared from the nominations after the July 1952 revolution, to appear again in 1961 with support from three parties, among them Muhammad Ahmad Khalafallah (then a member of the Arabic Language Academy and a vice-president of the University of Ain Shams). The "dean" continued to be a nominee up to 1964, when his name was put forward by DeWitt Wallace, owner–publisher of *Reader's Digest* magazine and therefore well known at the time.

In 1966, under pressure from numerous Zionist institutions in the West, the prize was divided between the Israeli writer Shmuel Yosef Agnon and the Swedish writer Nelly Sachs, who also had Israeli nationality and was author of *The Jews and Jewish History*. The prize committee had wanted to divide the prize that year between an Israeli and an Arab writer. However, according to statements published by *Rose al-Yusuf* magazine's then correspondent in Geneva, the foundation failed to find an Arab nominee for the prize, as no Arab institution had submitted Taha Hussein's name, even though it had, in the past, reached the list of finalists (Ibrahim 'Izzat, *Rose al-Yusuf*, 26 June 1966). The Higher Council for Literature and the Arts in Egypt had submitted the names of Tawfiq al-Hakim and Naguib Mahfouz but neither was well known to, or supported in, the West, and they therefore failed to reach the list; in addition, nominations by official bodies were not recognized. As a result, when the Nobel committee failed to find an Arab nominee, the prize was divided between two Israeli writers.

This was at a time when Gamal Abd al-Nasser was dreaming of an Arab winner of the Nobel and supporting most strongly Tawfiq al-Hakim, on the grounds that he was "the founder of modern Egyptian theater." Abd al-Nasser had sent al-Hakim to Paris in 1959 as an Egyptian delegate to UNESCO, so that he would be close to the nominating circles, given that Paris was not only the city of art, but also, in al-Hakim's words, "the greatest showcase in the world" (Tawfiq al-Hakim, *Zahrat al-'umr*, 85). According to contemporary reports, however, al-Hakim's parsimoniousness prevented him from communicating with any institution or individual, and he preferred to spend an entire year living in his ivory tower (Gamal al-Ghitani, *Akhbar al-adab*, 2 December 2001). Tawfiq al-Hakim returned after a year without having realized Abd al-Nasser's dream. The establishment had bet on al-Hakim but, when it despaired of him, added Naguib Mahfouz, leaving him as the primary candidate from 1966 onward. The late director Ahmad Badrakhan has recounted, in a special edition of *al-Hilal* devoted to Naguib Mahfouz (February 1971), that he was taking part in the Berlin International Film Festival when a number of young Germans called on him and asked him, "Do you know Naguib Mahfouz?" He replied, "I do. He's my boss." One of them then said, "You know Naguib Mahfouz; that is a fact. But you do not know the writings of Naguib Mahfouz and their depth; that is also a fact. If you did, you would spend millions of pounds on him, so that he could win the Nobel Prize."

Shortly before the announcement that Mahfouz had won the prize, there were, in literary circles in Europe and especially in Sweden, indications that he was close to doing so—expectations or prognostications or simply hopes. In 1988, France's well-known *Magazine Littéraire* ran an interview with French Arabist André Miquel in which he avers that "he has always asked himself why no Arab writer has won the Nobel Prize. He believes that Naguib Mahfouz is the Arab writer who may be expected to do so" (Sabri Hafiz, "Hikayat ja'izat Nubil wa Naguib Mahfouz wa-l-adab al-'arabi," *al-Naqid*, December 1988). In the same year, the Swedish magazine *Artes* dedicated an issue to Arabic literature; the magazine's principal editor was Östen Sjöstrand, a member of the Nobel Academy and the one most sympathetic, according to Sabri Hafiz, to the Arabs, and one who had called for the prize to be awarded to an Arab writer. In April of the same year, the Swedish magazine *Folket* issued a special supplement on Mahfouz that included a translation of his story *Taht al-mizalla* (Under the Sunshade) and a lengthy piece by Per Gahrton, who concludes his article with the words, "The experts agree that Naguib Mahfouz is one of the most prominent storytellers of the Arab world, and he must be given serious consideration as a nominee for the Nobel Prize" (Sabri Hafiz, "Hikayat ja'izat Nubil wa Naguib Mahfouz wa-l-adab al-'arabi," *al-Naqid*, December 1988). A few days before the announcement of the prize, a delegation from German television had been in Cairo to finish a film on the life of Mahfouz, and a number of newspapers around the world had included his name among those with caps in the ring.

Following the announcement of the prize, Naguib Mahfouz's life was turned upside down. Nothing was the same as before: now he had to become "an employee of Nobel's," as he once put it sarcastically, and busy himself facing a campaign organized against him by Arab organizations, certain writers of his own generation, and various groups within political Islam.

A deluge of charges brought by his enemies now rained down on Naguib Mahfouz. His support for the Camp David Accords (1978) was the first among these. Mahfouz's position on the accords was not an exception: most members of the liberal generation that had grown up and been formed following the 1919 revolution and who derived their ideas from the Wafd Party had no problem with negotiating with the enemy; indeed, the very idea from which the Wafd derived its name was the formation of a delegation *(wafd)* to negotiate with the British occupier, as a way to persuade him to leave the country and grant Egypt her freedom. To this one might add Mahfouz's skeptical, philosophical education, which took a non-racist, humanistic search for certainty as its point of departure. This is one explanation for Naguib Mahfouz's support for Camp David, and from it follows the conclusion that his position was not the product of any toadying to the authorities or taken with an international prize in mind; and this position of his had been pronounced openly, in one form or another, since the end of the 1960s.

In July 1968, Naguib Mahfouz wrote an article in *al-Katib* magazine under the title "The Modern State." In it, he speaks briefly of the elements essential to the existence of any modern state. At the political level, Mahfouz believes that "a basic political prerequisite, which may be summed up as the servicing of human rights, must be present. These rights begin with freedom—freedom of the individual to choose the ruler and the system of governance, freedom of expression and belief, and freedom to own property." At the social level, Mahfouz believes that the modern state "must be free of any partiality on the grounds of religion or creed." Thirdly, "The spirit of science, and not science alone, must prevail in every activity connected to the life of the individual, the family, or society. One, and only one, guarantee can bring this about—a constitution put in place by the people through its own power." At a conference convened by Sarwat 'Ukasha for leading officials of the Ministry of Culture under the title "An Open Dialogue on Escaping the Effects of the Naksa," Mahfouz declared, "The only way to get out of the crisis is to return to democracy and dialogue and to restore the freedom of a multiparty, multi-opinion system, while accepting the party that comes to power via free and honest elections, even if it negotiates with Israel."

These were daring, even at the time shocking, words, but the shock of defeat went beyond any sense of personal fear. The regime therefore allowed space for venting to a degree it never had before. Naguib Mahfouz repeated his words after Abd al-Nasser died, in 1971, at a meeting with Muammar al-Gaddafi that brought together a group of cultural leading lights at the invitation of Muhammad Hasanayn Haykal in *al-Ahram*. On that occasion, Mahfouz asked, "Is it in our capacity to fight Israel?" Ahmad 'Abbas Salih responded, "We cannot go to war." Mahfouz then commented, "If we cannot go to war, then we have no choice but to take the other path, the path of negotiation" (Raga' al-Naqqash, *Naguib Mahfouz: safahat min mudhakkaratihi*, 218).

This stand on Camp David made Mahfouz a pariah in most Arab countries. The Egyptian editions of his books were banned but the Beirut editions were allowed to pass without interference. His films were, likewise, semi-banned: movie producers would ask him to write screenplays for them on condition that he not put his name on them, so that they could be shown outside Egypt. They were hard years, during which Mahfouz completed his famous novel *Malhamat al-Harafish (The Harafish)* and was subjected to attack from almost all sides. His attackers would always claim that he had taken his stand in support of the accords in order to get the Nobel Prize. In fact, before winning the prize, he had attacked it in several press interviews, at times on the grounds that it was an expression of Western values and therefore extremely unlikely to be awarded to an Arab writer, and at other times because he considered that it was not a yardstick of good literature.

Similarly, in response to journalist al-Sayyid al-Shurbagi's question (*al-Idha'a wa-l-tilfizyun* [Radio and Television] magazine, 31 January 1976), asked in the course of an interview with Naguib Mahfouz before he won the Nobel Prize and reprinted after he won it, "If you were awarded the Nobel Prize, would you refuse it, like Sartre?," Mahfouz replied,

> Some people think that I call for peace and accept Camp David so that I can win the Nobel Prize, which is controlled by World Zionism . . . . In their view, I call for world peace so as to gain the approval of those organizations that supposedly can ensure that the prize is given to people they want. For this reason, if I were

> actually awarded the Nobel Prize, I would refuse it because I have no need, in fact, of the Zionists' approval . . . . This prize, like all prizes, rests on two bases. The first is a body of work, which has to be in some way outstanding, and the second is the embodiment of a certain kind of content, which is not devoid of adherence to a political line, in the general sense. (*al-Sharq al-Awsat*, 24 December 1987; reprinted in *al-Kuwayt* (Kuwait) magazine, January 1989)

Four years before the announcement of the award, the critic Sabri Hafiz led a harsh attack against Mahfouz in a number of articles in the magazines *al-Aqlam* (The Pens) and *al-'Iraqiya* (The Iraqi), as well as Libya's *al-Mawqif al-'arabi* (The Arab Stand), in which he described Mahfouz as having "deteriorated, in terms of his grasp of novelistic structure, the backwardness of his thinking, his declining artistry, and the superficiality of his vision" (Sabri Hafiz, "Tazyif al-wa'i wa-tashwih al-tarikh," *al-Aqlam*, July 1984).

A week after Mahfouz won the prize, Yusuf Idris attacked him in *al-Wafd* newspaper, writing,

> I was nominated for the prize five times before Naguib Mahfouz, and they always excluded me at the last moment because of my political stands. Mahfouz has got it because he has made peace with the Jews and does not criticize them. As to the idea that Mahfouz has "opened the door for other Arab writers," the opposite is true: it will be thirty years, at least, before they give it to another Arab writer. I would stress that Naguib Mahfouz has won the prize before any of his novels have been translated, and specifically that *Midaq Alley* is the only novel of his to have been translated into Swedish. (20 October 1988)

Needless to say, no one knows whether Yusuf Idris was nominated or not; it is, however, a fact that his name appears nowhere in the lists of nominees published in the press.

Idris kept up his attack on Mahfouz. At the Mirbad festival in Iraq, after receiving the Saddam Hussein Prize, he said, "Mahfouz's novels are of purely provincial interest, not just in terms of the people and the events, but of their thinking too." He states also that a member of the Swedish Academy suggested that he split the prize with an Israeli writer, a claim later denied by the Swedish writer Kjell Espmark, a member of the academy, who corrected this account of the incident by explaining that "it was a piece of foolishness on the part of a Swedish politician (the former head of a Swedish political party) who was visiting Egypt at the time and spoke with Yusuf Idris and made that suggestion to him" (France 24 interview with Espmark, 3 May 2014). Idris was furious when this correction by the Swedish writer was published, screaming in people's faces, "The suggestion was from a member of the Nobel Prize academy!"

Idris was not the only one to go on the attack. He was joined by the novelist Edwar Kharrat, who considered that neither Mahfouz nor Idris deserved the prize, writing, "They are both writers of middling stature by the standards by which the great, immortal works of literature are measured, even when we take note, as of course we must, of their pioneering role and how far they have had to travel in terms of the short story and the novel."

Mahfouz kept silent in the face of these attacks. As was his wont, he did not attempt to respond to the accusations, although he was obliged to clarify his point of view following the publication by Moshe Sassoon, Israel's former ambassador to Cairo, of his memoirs, in which the latter stated that Naguib Mahfouz had told him that "the opponents of peace are a bunch of mercenaries." Mahfouz commented, "I could never have said such a thing. Such words are not to be found in my dictionary and it is not my way of thinking to accuse those whose opinions differ from mine as being 'mercenaries' or adopting a position for money" (*Akhbar al-adab*, 30 November 1998). Mahfouz also revealed to *Akhbar al-adab* details he had not mentioned before:

> When I was at *al-Ahram*, at the beginning of the 1980s and before I had been awarded the Nobel Prize, somebody from the Israeli embassy in Cairo whose name I don't remember came to see me and offered me a nomination for a great world prize that had been won by the British writer Graham Greene. He said that they were thinking of giving me the prize and had come to ask my permission to do so. I told him, "I am very appreciative, but I cannot accept the prize being linked to my defense of peace, since that is a position of principle and was not adopted as a way to get prizes."

The prize referred to by Mahfouz was the Jerusalem Prize for the Freedom of the Individual in Society, worth ten thousand dollars, which had been won by Greene in 1981, and previously awarded to a number of writers, including Arthur Miller, Octavio Paz, Eugène Ionesco, Simone de Beauvoir, J.M. Coetzee, Mario Vargas Llosa, Jorge Luis Borges, Bertrand Russell, Susan Sontag, Max Frisch, Milan Kundera, and others. The prize was offered to Mahfouz in 1982 but he refused it. In the same interview, Mahfouz said, "After I got the Nobel, Shimon Peres wrote me a tactful letter in which he suggested that I nominate an Israeli novelist named Amos Oz, several of whose novels had been translated into Arabic, for the Nobel. I excused myself and said that Amos Oz would surely find someone to nominate him for the Nobel Prize and that if I were to nominate anyone, I would rather it be an Arab writer."

The attacks on Mahfouz's Nobel were not limited to the accusations by Yusuf Idris and some Arab newspapers that he received Zionist support, or of Edwar al-Kharrat that he was a conventional writer. Extremist religious groups also joined in, groups that believed that Mahfouz had won the prize because of his novel *Children of the Alley*. It was after all, an "atheistic" novel. Two weeks after the announcement of Mahfouz's winning the award, Interior Ministry forces attacked a terrorist organization in 'Ayn Shams, on the grounds that some of its members had harshly criticized Mahfouz in a mosque, referring to him as "the apostate writer." This may have been the day on which planning for his assassination began.

But was Yusuf Idris ever in fact nominated for the prize? And was he ever informed that he had been?

In 1981, most British newspapers, including *The Times*, published their predictions for who would get the Nobel Prize that year. Mahfouz's name appeared among the nominees, the papers depending, as usual, for their lists of nominees on leaks, often from influential personages within the Swedish Academy. Some of these predictions turned out to be true, others not. Mahfouz's name was bandied about based on a large quantity of data, the most important of which was that published by 'Atiya 'Amir, professor of Arabic literature and head of the Institute for Arabic Studies at the University of Stockholm, who has lived in Sweden since 1959 and has written in detail about the Nobel nominations in the book *Qissat Nubil Mahfuz* (The Story of the Mahfouz Nobel), edited by Wahid Muwafi. 'Amir's words may be summarized as follows:

- In 1978, the Swedish Academy asked me to nominate an Arab writer for the Nobel Prize. I nominated Naguib Mahfouz straightaway.

His works represent the true Egypt and contain a clear philosophy that links past and present and looks to the future. I replied to the Academy with the following letter: *I thank the committee for the Nobel Prize in Literature for its invitation to nominate an Arab writer for the Nobel Prize for the year 1979. I understand this to mean that the committee wishes me to nominate a writer who writes in Arabic, and it is my pleasure to recommend Naguib Mahfouz, as he is, in my opinion, the greatest representative of modern Arabic literature and one of the world's great novelists in this era.*

- I asked the Egyptian embassy in Stockholm to provide copies of all of Mahfouz's books along with their translations into the various languages. Al-Sadat knew about the nomination and telephoned the embassy, asking that I be told to nominate Tawfiq al-Hakim instead of Mahfouz, justifying this by saying that "Tawfiq al-Hakim is my friend and has been with the regime from the start. Gamal loved him and so do I. Please ask 'Atiya to change his nomination." So the Egyptian embassy began to support Tawfiq al-Hakim, which had a strong negative impact, given that the committee forbids government interference in its work.
- I was of the opinion that Tawfiq al-Hakim's writings did not represent the true, profound soul of Egypt. The French bent to his thinking was only too clear and none of his novels rose to the level of Naguib Mahfouz's.
- After Mubarak came to power, in 1981, the Egyptian ambassador phoned me and informed me that there was an important letter for me from President Mubarak. The gist of the letter was that they knew I had nominated Naguib Mahfouz for the prize and would I nominate 'Abd al-Rahman al-Sharqawi in his stead? I knew that his nomination could never be accepted, because of the prize's criteria, which stipulated that the bulk of the nominee's work should be literary, while most of al-Sharqawi's was on Islamic thought.
- In 1986, while on a visit to Cairo, I met my friend the minister of culture Ahmad Haykal and informed him that I would be nominating Naguib Mahfouz for the third time. I asked him that the government not intervene in the choice of nominee, so that there should be no repeat of what had happened with earlier nominees. Ahmad Haykal's undertaking not to allow the state to interfere in the nomination process was crucial to Naguib Mahfouz's winning.

- The Nobel committee contacted me to ask that another writer be nominated alongside Mahfouz and I did indeed choose Yusuf Idris, whom I had met in Stockholm, where he asked me, "Has the government written to you?" I replied, "No. The only one who has written is Saddam Hussein." Idris was wearing a wristwatch with Saddam's face on it. He had previously given a number of lectures to the students at the university, who had criticized him harshly for bragging of his relationship with the dictator. I told Yusuf Idris about his being nominated alongside Naguib Mahfouz. He was delighted to be nominated and told me, "Forget about Naguib Mahfouz. This prize will raise me to the skies. Why don't you want that for me?" I told him, "It should be enough that I nominated you as his competitor, but he couldn't not be nominated."

I asked Gabir 'Asfur for further details, especially as he had spent a year as a professor of Arabic literature at Stockholm University. He confirmed that it was true. "'Amir 'Atiya nominated Idris for the prize, and I personally wrote out, in Arabic, at that time, the detailed data relating to his nomination, which 'Atiya translated into Swedish."

At a gathering at Shepheard's Hotel in Cairo, Mahfouz commented on Idris's accusations for the first, and perhaps last, time. Mahfouz was asked, "What will remain of Yusuf Idris?" He answered, "His stories." He was asked, "Does he deserve to get the Nobel Prize for them?" He answered, "He isn't innovative enough to qualify for it." One of those present commented, "He was awarded the Saddam Hussein Prize and regarded it as the equal of the Nobel." Mahfouz responded, "If he got it, it must be bigger than the Nobel!" (Ibrahim 'Abd al-'Aziz, *Layali Naguib Mahfouz fi Shibard*, 87).

There can be no doubting 'Atiya 'Amir's account, especially as he backs it up with many documents, including his official correspondence with the Swedish Academy. Nevertheless, there is more to the truth than he provides. He was not the only one to nominate Mahfouz. Many other institutions did so, including the Department of Arabic Studies at the University of Stockholm, headed by 'Atiya 'Amir himself, and the Palestinian critic Salma Khadra Jayyusi, who has stated that in 1985 the Swedish Academy asked her to provide a report on Arab writers deserving of the Nobel Prize and that she had supported Mahfouz and Idris. There was also the American Arabist Roger Allen, who indicated his support for Mahfouz in an interview, and the universities of Georgetown and the Sorbonne and certain other European and Russian universities, which submitted reports to the effect that the author of *The Harafish* deserved the prize. In addition, Denys Johnson-Davies tells in his *Memories in Translation* of how in the 1980s he received a telephone call from a friend informing him that the wife of the French ambassador in Tunis, who was Swedish, was in Cairo and wanted to meet him. When he met her, she informed him that the Nobel committee was investigating the possibility of awarding the prize to an Arab author. With her she had a list of nominees, which also included Adonis, Yusuf Idris, and Tayeb Salih. During the discussion, Johnson-Davies explained to her that the poetry of Adonis was way over the heads of most readers and that Yusuf Idris had no works translated into English or French, the foreign languages known to members of the Swedish Academy. As for Tayeb Salih, and even though Johnson-Davies was his translator and friend, his limited output excluded him from the list. Thus it emerged from this meeting that Naguib Mahfouz was the best nominee for the prize.

In 1988, Mahfouz received a letter from the Orientalist Avihai Shivtiel informing him that he had nominated him.

> Dear Mr. Mahfouz,
> Greetings! It is my honor to send you these few lines by way of introduction, and to inform you that the Swedish Academy committee for the Nobel Prize has recently sent me a letter requesting that I provide them with the name of a writer as a nominee for the abovementioned prize for the current year. I was overjoyed to have this golden opportunity to draw the attention of the Academy to your much-admired works since I do not find anyone worthier or more deserving of this prize than your good self. I have therefore hastened to send them my humble recommendation, stressing that in giving you the Nobel Prize they would be crowning with laurels the head that best deserves them, given your oeuvre, which may be considered contemporary Arabic literature's strongest pillar and most solid cornerstone. Please forgive me for not giving your good self advance notice of submission of my recommendation, in view of the limited time available. I hope that you will win this lofty award and the riches of your literary output thereby win the international recognition they deserve. In closing, please accept our heartfelt good wishes, as we beseech the Almighty to grant you the strength, energy, and good health to continue to provide the

boon of your literary gifts to all the "people of the *ḍād*."
Sincerely,
Dr. A. Shivtiel
Head
Department of Modern Arabic Studies
University of Leeds
United Kingdom
(Masri Hannura, *Naguib Mahfouz wa-fann sina'at al-'abqariya*, 299)

Mahfouz responded with the following letter of thanks.

> I have received with pleasure, thanks, and appreciation your generous letter advising me of your kind recommendation of me to the prize committee. Whatever the outcome of your laudable effort, it is enough for me to have gained the appreciation of a great and learned scholar such as yourself. To me, as a writer, such appreciation is in no way less than the prize itself. I repeat my thanks, my dear sir, and send you my best wishes.

The Swedish writer Kjell Espmark, member of the Swedish Academy, head of the Nobel committee from 1988 to 2004, and one of the five members responsible for choosing the final winner of the prize in literature, explained in 2014 to the television channel France 24 the working method of the prize committee:

> We have a number of specialists and experts in Arabic and its literature to consult on the language used, the writing techniques applied, and the literary and structural make-up of the work. Thus translating the language is only one part of the translation as a whole. The second, which I believe to be the more important, is translating the basis, the techniques, the literary make-up, the phonic blending, the references used, and the means by which the book has been carried through and brought to completion.

Celebration over the Nobel Prize extended to the Arab nation as a whole. The official, "public" break with Egypt was breathing its last gasps. The previous ten years (1978–88) had done damage: first, through the assassination of al-Sadat; second, through the Iran–Iraq War; third, through the exit of the

Palestinian resistance from Lebanon; and fourth, through the failure to stand up to Israel. All these had, by the time of the announcement that Mahfouz had won the Nobel, made Egyptian–Arab relations more or less normal and friendly. Consequently, Mahfouz received congratulatory telegrams from leaders of all the Arab countries, Libya excepted. It was all the more of a surprise, therefore, when a Palestine Liberation Organization official visited Mahfouz at his home in the company of critic Raga' al-Naqqash (who recounts the incident without mentioning the official's nationality) (Raga' al-Naqqash, *Fi hubb Naguib Mahfouz*, 260). The official had with him a black case containing US$400,000, three times the value of the Nobel Prize. He asked Mahfouz to turn down the prize and to direct a certain amount of reproach and criticism (with a few insults as well, to be on the safe side) at the West, "which is hostile to us," in return for the sum in the black case. As usual, Mahfouz received the offer very calmly and apologized to the guest, stating that the prize was not for him but for Arabic literature as a whole and that refusing it would have an impact on every other Arab writer after him.

Every Arab magazine and newspaper celebrated the award and its winner, and Nizar Qabbani sent Mahfouz a letter, which *al-Ahram* published, defending him against his attackers.

> Naguib Mahfouz is one of "the children of the alley," one who makes friends on a daily basis with the newspaper vendor, the milkman, and the ironing man's boy, and stands on line in front of the bean sandwich seller. He owns two "safari" suits, one for sleeping and one for taking a bath in. Naguib Mahfouz is the good, hard-working schoolboy who copies out his homework neatly; the pious boy who says his prayers at the proper times; the young student at al-Azhar who sits at the foot of one of its pillars; the saint who wears a white gallabiya and wanders in the backstreets recording in a little notebook the sighs of the suffering, the groans of the downtrodden, and the tears of the tormented . . . and, in my view, Naguib Mahfouz's morals, his spiritual purity, and his inner and outer cleanliness are what won him the Nobel Prize, before even his literary works. Naguib Mahfouz, my friend: congratulations on the Nobel Prize that you have won with the sweat of your brow, by punishing your nerves, and the neighing on paper, for fifty years, of your courageous warhorse, not at the roulette table or from dealing in arms! (*al-Ahram*, 7 November 1988)

People expected that Naguib Mahfouz would quickly announce his departure for Sweden to receive the prize. However, he had taken the decision early on—two days after the announcement—not to go. At a gathering of the Hoodlums, he told his friends, "The problem is not being able to hear. Here it's a small matter. I say, 'Shout, Ali,' or 'Shout, Muhammad!' but there I'm supposed to tell the king or queen of Sweden, 'Speak up a bit!'?" (*al-Akhbar*, 16 October 1988). Also, his private doctor had advised him against traveling because of his diabetes and high blood pressure. On a visit by the permanent secretary of the Swedish Academy, Sture Allén, to make the arrangements for the ceremony, Mahfouz informed him of the impossibility of his traveling and nominated Egypt's ambassador to Sweden to take his place. However, the permanent secretary informed him that the prize was not something official and no official could therefore receive it; he must, therefore, choose a family member or other personal representative to receive the prize. Mahfouz chose the writer Mohamed Salmawy to receive the prize on his behalf, which in turn caused a media outcry, with some newspapers writing that the presidency of the republic should select Louis Awad, Sarwat Abaza, or Sarwat 'Ukasha to receive the prize on Mahfouz's behalf. This caused Salmawy to write to Mahfouz excusing himself, to relieve himself of the embarrassment. However, Mahfouz informed him that "the position of the presidency is noted, and the president has the right to choose whomever he pleases. I, however, have chosen my representative." Mahfouz told *al-Musawwar* magazine that he had chosen Salmawy because he wanted to "reach out, prize in hand, to the younger generation" (*al-Musawwar*, 25 November 1988). At the same time, Mahfouz's nephew, Muhammad al-Kurdi, went to the Swedish embassy in Cairo and asked to go to Sweden to receive the prize. This angered the family, and it was finally decided that Salmawy should go and deliver the speech while Umm Kulthum and Fatima, Mahfouz's daughters, should go and receive the prize.

Some hours after winning the Nobel Prize, Naguib Mahfouz was able to flee the lenses of the photographers who surrounded his house and the polite words he had to utter to his well-wishers among state officials and journalists, for his friends, the Hoodlums, whom he was accustomed to meet with every Thursday, where he could relax and speak naturally. When one of them asked him how he had felt when the prize was announced, he said, "I was happy because I'd broken the rule." "What rule?" they asked him. He replied, "The rule that requires that to win anything—never mind something like the Nobel Prize—these days needs special channels based on opportunism, public relations, and constant contacts between here and there. I can't say that I've established a new rule. I can just say that I've broken the prevailing one and offered a lesson to all serious, honest strivers—that devoting oneself to one's work and applying oneself to it wholeheartedly can lead even to the Nobel Prize" (Faruq 'Abd al-Qadir, *Fi al-riwaya al-'arabiya al-mu'asira* [On the Contemporary Arabic Novel], 45).

At the ceremony held by former president Hosni Mubarak ten days after the announcement of the award, to bestow on Mahfouz the Order of the Nile, Egypt's highest honor, a number of cultural figures brought up the case of *Children of the Alley*, to which Mubarak responded, "There is nothing to prevent its publication." This is what the minister of culture, Farouk Hosny, had been hoping to hear, and he gave instructions to the General Book Organization to begin publishing the book immediately, since there was no legal ruling preventing it from doing so. *Al-Gumhuriya* newspaper published this news on its front page. Surprisingly, a meeting of the cabinet on 30 November 1988 discussed the subject of the printing of the novel, and the cabinet was divided into two groups: the first was led by Farouk Hosny, who was enthusiastic about its publication, while on the other side was Safwat al-Sharif, minister of information, who rejected publication and asked that the matter be put to President Mubarak again. Finally, a consensus was reached that the novel should not be published until al-Sharif could speak to Mubarak on the telephone.

In a telephone conversation between myself and Farouk Hosny, Hosny failed to recall this incident, and stressed that he had given orders to Samir Sarhan, head of the General Book Organization, to print the novel without further intervention from Mubarak; Gabir 'Asfur and Yusuf al-Qa'id, who witnessed Mahfouz's investiture, confirm that Mubarak did indeed make the statement attributed to him. It is also clear that the Abd al-Nasser regime, throughout its various phases, consisted of more than one wing, and the victorious wing was always that of the security apparatus, as, only one day after the cabinet meeting, the Islamic Research Academy issued a statement renewing its opposition to the novel's publication, despite the fact that no one had asked its permission in the first place or presented it with a request for its opinion. Was Safwat al-Sharif behind this second ban and, consequently, the statement? To this day, no one knows the answer.

Mahfouz continued to defend the novel after he was awarded the Nobel Prize, putting forward in its defense, in these years during which religious terrorism was on the rise, a political interpretation. At the celebration in his honor put on for him by the Department of Philosophy of the Faculty of Humanities, Cairo University, most of the questions from the members of the department (of which Mahfouz was himself a graduate) bore on *Children of the Alley*. In response, Mahfouz explained that the vision that had guided him while writing the novel was "connected with political authority and how to confront it—the neighborhood bullyboys who represent the political authorities and use it against the alley. And that there are values that are necessary to support science, so the goal of the children of Gabalawi was to revive those values in support of science." Expressing himself more clearly, he explained, "There is no campaign against religion, or mockery of or contempt for the prophets." He added:

> It's true, the novel was supposed to raise political questions and did so to some extent, but when I discovered that there was something even more powerful, something that might destroy it, I stopped talking about *Children of the Alley*'s political implications. At the same time, it addresses, at some level, humankind in general, so, indubitably, it addresses those in government. At that time, 1959, there was ecstasy over certain triumphs, and along comes someone and says, "It's the same old estate, the same old alley, the same old bullyboys." I don't think the message escaped the authorities. This was hinted at to me, but was anyone going to come and ask me, "Whom do you mean by 'the bullyboys?'" The bullyboys are the bullyboys. The question here is the inner meaning. However, when those in power found that the novel had raised another issue, completely different from the one they were asking about, they shut up. (https://www.youtube.com/watch?v=DAhvXvR843o)

The whole crisis, from Mahfouz's perspective, was "a crisis of reading . . . no more, no less." This "crisis of reading," or "confusion of interpretation," was explained by Mahfouz in a letter he sent to Dr. Muhammad Hasan 'Abdallah on the occasion of the appearance of the latter's book *al-Islamiya wa-l-ruhiya fi adab Naguib Mahfouz* (Islamic Thought and Spirituality in the Works of Naguib Mahfouz; see the appendix for the full text). 'Abdallah considered *Children of the Alley* an Islamic novel, whose source was the

Noble Qur'an and whose interpretation of the outward manifestations of the universe and the sequence of apostleships was Islamic. He believed that Mahfouz had done the same in the novel *al-Tariq (The Search)*, which expresses the same Islamic position with regard to the bewildering choice between the paths of coercion and election, and that science is not an heir or successor to religion but one of life's tools, to be used for good or for evil, to build or to demolish, in keeping with one's motivations and moral and spiritual commitment. Mahfouz wrote:

> It may be that the confusion that sometimes arises from reading my works owes its origin to the way my heart combines a yearning for God, a faith in science, and a predilection for socialism. Any attempt to combine God and socialism is likely to give rise to suspicions of atheism among some and conservatism among others. I have always found it surprising that the communist philosophy should be taken as a religion, since I, as a student of philosophy, know that philosophy is a series of constructs that are renewed over time and is totally unsuited for worship. What I admire in communism is its absolute social justice (yet to be applied in Russia itself): from each according to his ability and to each according to his need! This is a perfect basis for interaction among humans and turns humankind into one divine family. But why is it that, in order to believe in this, I must first believe in materialism, or deny God? (Muhammad Hasan 'Abdallah, "Risala min Naguib Mahfouz" [A Letter from Naguib Mahfouz] in *al-Bayan al-kuwaytiya* [The Kuwait Report], May 1972)

Driven by the desire to repel the fierce attack on him, which continued for more than two months and came from a number of quarters, including jealous rivals, Islamic groups who impugned his religious belief, political organizations that believed he owed the Nobel Prize to "Zionism," and even the international press, which asked, "Who is this newcomer from the Middle East?," Naguib Mahfouz sat down to write his Nobel speech, to be delivered for him at the award ceremony. He did not address the techniques of writing or its esthetics. He wanted to tell the world, "I, of whom you ask, 'Who is this man?' am a son of the Third World." He wanted to show that he was the child of two great civilizations that had left their mark on humanity, and, seemingly, he wanted to affirm his position on religion.

He spoke not with his own voice but with the voice of the millions of Arabs who awaited his address. He spoke of their concerns, at the heart of which lay Palestine and its cause. Mahfouz wrote of personal concerns, of national concerns, and of human concerns. He wrote, "Good triumphs every day . . . but, in the end, evil is something loutish and noisy, with a loud voice." If we look through the handwritten draft of the speech, we find that he changed only one word: when speaking of Islamic civilization, he first wrote, "It aspires to freedom, equality, and tolerance." Then he amended it, by striking out "equality" and writing "justice" in its place. Did Mahfouz believe that "justice," as a value, was more expressive of Islamic civilization than "equality"? Was he truly convinced that equality was, always, marginal to Islamic civilization?

In June 1991, Sheikh Muhammad al-Ghazali was a guest at the Opera House's Ihsan Abdel Kouddous Cultural Hall. There he confessed, publicly and for the first time, that he had written a report that he had submitted to President Gamal Abd al-Nasser in which he had objected to the publication of *Children of the Alley* and that he had participated, along with Sheikh Muhammad Abu Zahra and Sheikh Ahmad al-Sharabasi, in the writing of other reports. He proclaimed his opinion with complete frankness: "The novel was saturated with the idea that civilization had wiped religion out entirely." Al-Ghazali called on Mahfouz to disavow *Children of the Alley*, while acknowledging that he was "a rich writer with works of lofty value to his credit" (*al-Akhbar*, 5 June 1991). Mahfouz commented briefly on al-Ghazali's demand: "A person cannot go back on what he has written" (*al-Akhbar*, 12 June 1991). He also announced that he was prepared to discuss the contents of the novel with the sheikhs of al-Azhar. For the second time, however, none of the sheikhs was prepared to have such a discussion.

The debate came back to life in February 1989, after Ayatollah Khomeini issued a fatwa declaring the blood of novelist Salman Rushdie forfeit for his novel *The Satanic Verses*. About the same time too, Omar Abdel-Rahman, spiritual leader of the Gama'a Islamiya, was asked by the Kuwaiti newspaper *al-Anba'* (The News) for his opinion of Rushdie's novel. He answered, "If the sentence of death had been carried out against Naguib Mahfouz when he wrote *Children of the Alley*, it would have been an eloquent lesson for Salman Rushdie." He repeated this response in a number of newspapers and in his Friday sermon, with different wording: "If we had killed Mahfouz thirty years ago, there would have been no Salman

Rushdie." Strangely, although Egyptian security forces contacted Mahfouz to offer him a personal security detail, he refused, saying, "Omar Abdel-Rahman's statement is not a fatwa calling for murder but a conditional sentence. He says '*If* we had killed Mahfouz thirty years ago.'" And what 'Abd al-Rahman said was not, indeed, a fatwa: it was a message, or a signal, that Mahfouz should be killed.

14 OCTOBER 1994

Stifling dust in the air, like that described by Naguib Mahfouz at the outset of *The Thief and the Dogs*. Sandstorms strike Cairo, causing accidents and the collapse of buildings. Thundery rains, with floods inundating a number of the southern provinces.

At 5:30 p.m., Naguib Mahfouz usually left his house to head for his weekly discussion group at the Casino Qasr al-Nil. Waiting for him in front of the house was the physician Fathi Hashim, who was supposed to take him in his car to join his friends and the Hoodlums. Fathi Hashim was not the only one waiting. There was another young man, carrying a flick knife, who approached Mahfouz after the latter had settled into the car's front seat and stabbed him with his knife. Mahfouz said he had seen a terrifying monster leap at him and slash at his neck with its claws. A fountain of blood erupted, and the perpetrator fled. When the news was broadcast, the exclamation on most Egyptians' lips was "God protect us!" (see appendix: Minutes of the Questioning of Naguib Mahfouz Following His Attempted Assassination).

A few days later, the police announced the name of the perpetrator: Muhammad Nagi. The incident was the climax of a violent struggle between the state on one side and those who espoused religious terrorism on the other. Terrorists' bombs had targeted tourists and Copts, and political assassinations had targeted intellectuals and politicians. This context led many to believe that "the locomotive of the religious state was coming down the track and there was nothing to be done about it, so some decided to book a seat," in the words of Nasr Abu Zayd (*al-Qawl al-mufid fi qadiyat Abu Zayd* (What May Be Usefully Said on the Case of Abu Zayd) and created an atmosphere hostile to all the liberties. However, events preceding the incident make it clear that there were many contributing factors.

A year before the incident, the Ministry of Education had stopped teaching Mahfouz's novel *Kifah Tiba (Thebes at War)*, which had been a set text for middle-school students. The committee in charge of text selection attributed this decision to an argument with the novel's publisher over 8 piasters, with the publisher requesting 104 piasters per copy while the ministry insisted on paying 96. Oddly, the committee then chose the novel *al-Saqr al-jari'* (The Bold Hawk) by 'Abd al-Salam Zaydan to replace the canceled novel, with a price for the former of 124 piasters, or 20 piasters more than that turned down by the ministry for *Thebes at War*. A few days previously, the committee had taken it on itself to lighten the curricular load on high-school students by removing Naguib Mahfouz's Nobel Prize speech from the Arabic language curriculum, a move *Akhbar al-adab* newspaper considered part of a plot within the Ministry of Education against the "dean of the novel" ("Mu'amara did Naguib Mahfouz fi Wazarat al-Ta'lim," *Akhbar al-adab*, 29 August 1993).

Around the same time, Dr. Nasr Hamid Abu Zayd was roaming the hallways of the courts in connection with the case against him that had begun a few months previously. In March 1993, he had presented three studies on Imam al-Shafi'i in support of his request for promotion at Cairo University and new critical discourses for the analysis of religious texts, only to find himself under wide attack. Certain faculty members at the university, chief among them 'Abd al-Sabur Shahin, felt that the expulsion of Abu Zayd from the university would be a way to "expose secularism at the university." With this in mind, Shahin was quick to write a damning report rejecting the promotion and accusing Abu Zayd of abandoning Islam. He also began attacking him in Friday sermons and the terrifying sequence of events came full circle with a call for his forced separation from his wife and colleague, Ibtihal Yunus, a professor of French literature at Cairo University, on the grounds that she was a Muslim while he was an apostate.

On 10 February 1994, the General Assembly of the Council of State, chaired by Tariq al-Bishri, issued a fatwa (*Akhbar al-adab*, 30 March 1994) asserting that the opinion of al-Azhar, and al-Azhar alone, was binding on the Ministry of Culture for the evaluation of Islamic matters when it came to the licensing or non-licensing of works of art and of audio and video productions that dealt with Islamic issues or conflicted with Islam, and that it had the right to prevent their printing, recording, publication, distribution, and circulation ("Muthaqqafun fi warshat ʻamal al-Warsha al-Misriya li-Huquq al-Insan: al-fatwa laysat mulzima wa-in kanat mukhifa," *Akhbar al-adab*, 30 March 1994). By the same token, the Islamic Research Academy with its constituent committees and departments, which included the Department of Research, Writing, Translation, and Publication, had the authority to check printed editions of the Noble Qur'an and undertake investigations of writings, both nonfiction and fiction, that ventured to deal with Islam or expressed an opinion on it, making this institution the arbiter of everything connected to Islamic affairs. It followed that the opinion of al-Azhar, as expressed via its various organs, was binding on the parties charged with issuing any decision. Civil society considered the fatwa "participation by the Council of State in the demolition of the foundations of the civil state and an attempt to resurrect the religious state." Gabir ʻAsfur, secretary general of the Supreme Council for Culture, criticized it and noted, "This does not mean that a religious institution can be transformed into a judge and censor of people's consciences or an obstacle to creative freedom ("Muthaqqafun fi warshat ʻamal al-Warsha al-Misriya li-Huquq al-Insan: al-fatwa laysat mulzima wa-in kanat mukhifa," *Akhbar al-adab*, 30 March 1994).

Strangely, the censor's office was in no need of legal fatwas, as it had been practicing its rule with brutal self-confidence ever since a member of the Egyptian parliament, Galal Gharib, had tabled an interpellation for the minister of culture protesting the publication by *Ibdaʻ* (Creativity) magazine of a painting by Austrian artist Gustav Klimt titled *Adam and Eve*, and likewise the holding of an experimental theater festival and the existence of an orchestra at the Cairo Opera, on the grounds that there was no need for such things in the land of al-Azhar. Within hours of the interpellation, a committee from the Administrative Control Authority had set off with a list in hand of works of fiction such as Yusuf Abu Rayya's novel *Wishsh al-fajr* (Daybreak), Hasan Talab's long poem "Ayat Jiim" (The Miraculous Sign of Jiim), Farid Abu Siʻda's poem "Wardat al-Qayz" (Highsummer Rose), Ibrahim ʻIsa's novel *al-ʻUrah* (The Naked), Muhammad Adam's poem "Ana baha' al-jasad" (I Am the Pride of the Body), Edwar al-Kharrat's novel *Makhluqat al-ashwaq al-taʻira* (Creatures of Fleeting Appetites), Muhammad ʻAbd al-Salam al-ʻUmri's short story *Bustan al-Azbakiya* (The Azbakiya Garden), Gamal al-Ghitani's novels *Khitat al-Ghitani* (al-Ghitani's "Topography") and *Waqa'i' harat al-Za'farani (The Zafarani Files)*, and Mukhtar al-Suwayfi's short-story collection *Qissa li-l-atfal* (A Children's Story). The committee questioned the officials of the General Book Organization regarding the circumstances surrounding the printing of these works and how they had come to be selected. It then took specimens of the confiscated books and issued directions forbidding the handling of any copies present in the Organization's bookstores and warehouses and referred the seized copies to al-Azhar for its opinion. At about the same time, the Organization's workers' own censorship system had come into being, with the workers at its presses refusing to print Ni'mat al-Buhayri's story *Saff* (Line), which had been slated for publication in *Ibda'*, as it was, in their opinion, "sexual." One of them told the magazine's editor-in-chief, Ahmad 'Abd al-Mu'ti Higazi, "I have orders from the head of the Organization [Samir Sirhan]: If there's a story you don't like, let me know!" (*Akhbar al-adab*, 17 July 1994).

It was in this atmosphere that a number of cultural figures signed a statement titled "In Defense of Culture." It read,

> We, the undersigned cultural figures, writers, artists, and thinkers, have followed with increasing surprise and anger the brutal interference with cultural magazines and artistic and cultural creativity embodied in the uncivilized and unseemly confrontation between a member of the People's Assembly and the minister of culture. This campaign is an inseparable part of the terrorist activity that confronts the Egyptian people. We condemn this feverish campaign, proclaim our opposition to it, and affirm our unity in confronting it. (*Akhbar al-adab*, 2 January 1994)

Naguib Mahfouz was among the signatories to the statement, a rare and unusual act of participation on his part, not seen since he signed the 1972 statement supporting student demands for democracy and an end to the state of no-war no-peace that prevailed at that time.

The campaign of attacks on the United Nations Conference on Population and Development, hosted in Cairo a few days previously, continued likewise, with al-Azhar's Fatwa Committee and the Islamic Research Academy issuing a joint statement before the opening of the conference protesting at the conference's agenda, which "conflicted with Islamic law." Some stigmatized the conference as promoting homosexuality, spreading fornication, and calling for uncontrolled abortion and the moral and physical corruption of children.

The ruling National Party held its own conference, at which Yusuf Wali, the party's secretary-general, affirmed that Egypt should be subject to the control of its Islamic identity, while the Mufti of the Republic, Muhammad Sayyid Tantawi, declared that 90 percent of the issues to be discussed at the conference facilitated mortal sins. The minister of housing, Mahir Mahran, said that he felt deeply concerned to defend the teachings of his religion and the traditions of his society and that the discussion of certain views at the conference did not mean that we had to apply them; they were the business of other countries and cultures.

During the same time period, *al-Ahram* had begun publishing Mahfouz's *Asda' al-sira al-dhatiya (Echoes of an Autobiography)*, which Mahfouz described as "the ramblings of an old man" ("Ta'ammulat Naguib Mahfouz bayn al-taraddud wa-l-ihmal," *al-Hayat*, 7 March 1994) or "meditations difficult to fit into the short-story genre." Mahfouz was anxious about the experiment, which he had refused to publish in book form, especially given that *al-Ahram* had failed to give the work appropriate publicity: it had neither announced it nor tried to promote it beforehand and it was printed in the midst of other articles in a manner inappropriate for a work by Mahfouz, considering his importance and status.

A month before the attempted assassination, Ibrahim Kamil asked Naguib Mahfouz about Egypt's confrontation with terrorism. Naguib Mahfouz replied,

> The police have won the present battle but I fear that society as a whole has lost the war. The appeal to the authority of religion has spread to an unprecedented degree. Take any educated person and see how much he talks about religion and how he makes it a cornerstone of daily conduct—and this despite the current terrorism, which has no relationship to Islam beyond the fact that we have all taken the slippery slope into their territory and do battle on their terms, not ours, which is the biggest danger of all. (*al-Musawwar*, 21 October 1994)

In this atmosphere, the stabbing seemed to take the educated classes by surprise despite the dozens of pointers that preceded it and, particularly, Mahfouz's refusal some years previously to have a personal guard assigned to protect him following Omar Abdel-Rahman's fatwa. At the time, Mahfouz had said, sarcastically, "If a guard has to walk behind me then he'll be the one who kills me because I'll torment him with my love of walking and he'll have to walk with me every day, and after a while he'll get fed up and kill me himself!" (Raga' al-Naqqash, *Naguib Mahfouz: safahat min mudhakkaratihi*, 145).

Mahfouz was taken to the Police Hospital, close to his house, and it became clear that the stabbing had injured his neck muscles and torn the arteries. A delicate operation was performed and when he came around, he turned to those surrounding him and said, according to Gamal al-Ghitani's account, "They're trying to scare you. Don't lower your voices" (Gamal al-Ghitani, "Dhikr ma jara," *Akhbar al-adab*, 21 October 1994).

Two days later, the police succeeded in arresting the group tasked with carrying out the crime. It became clear that they belonged to the military wing of the banned Gama'a Islamiya (Islamic Group) organization. The chief witness, Fathi Hashim, recognized the prime suspect, Muhammad Nagi, from his photo, and investigations revealed that their original plan had been not to kill Naguib Mahfouz but to force him into a taxi and hold him hostage at their hideout in al-Khanka, to be exchanged for a number of their leaders who were in prison. The suspects, however, were late in bringing the car, preventing implementation of the kidnap plan, and this panicked the perpetrator into stabbing Mahfouz. The investigation also revealed that the group had planned to bomb the Cairo International Book Fair, due to be held in January 1995, and to assassinate Nasr Hamid Abu Zayd: "There is a writer called Nasr Abu Zayd who lives in al-Haram, at Tir'a; he will be killed by someone going up to his apartment and stabbing him with a knife," as it says in the minutes of the interrogations. There was also a plan to blow up Cinema Heliopolis (Mahmud Salah, *Awlad shari'ina: Naguib Mahfouz, muhawalat ightiyal* [The Children on Our Street: Naguib Mahfouz, the Attempted Assassination], 91–95).

The suspect said that he committed the crime because of Mahfouz's defiance of Islam in the novel *Children of the Alley*. He said, "We haven't read the novel but we were given the assignment to kill its author after the Gama'a killed Farag Foda," adding that he did not regret what he had done and would try again if he ever got out of prison (*al-Ahram*, 27 October 1994). Mahfouz replied to these statements the following day, saying,

> No one can be judged an infidel in their absence and without a discussion being held with them. Likewise, sentences cannot be issued

> by persons who are not qualified to make religiously informed determinations and do not understand their religion correctly. I repeat, *Children of the Alley* is simply a work of literature and must be looked at from that perspective. It is a novel that ends with the affirmation of the importance of faith in the divine essence. (*al-Ahram*, 27 October 1994)

When the public prosecutor questioned the victim, Mahfouz once more repeated his aim in writing the novel.

> *Children of the Alley* is like *Kalila wa Dimna*: it creates an imaginary world for the purpose of revealing another world beyond it. We find ourselves among animals living in a forest, but you know, and the ordinary reader knows, that we mean a critique of the human world with its forms of government, individual relationships, the wisdom of the wise, the stupidity of the stupid. However, so long as we maintain that we are in a forest, our heroes have to be animals and we are not to be held to account for dealing with them as we would with animals because we are dealing with something that is represented symbolically by animals. I used the same principle in *Children of the Alley*. I present Egyptians living in an alley, with their way of life and its injustices in all their detail.

Mahfouz added:

> These people (meaning his would-be assassins) do not read works of fiction with a literary or humanistic eye that seeks to understand truth and the struggle between good and evil. The only thing that matters in their eyes is that the work be in literal accordance with the teachings of religion, and they go too far even in that, because religion itself is an exposition of the story of good and evil and of Satan's disobedience to the divine essence. All my novels revolve around clear ideas. Never, under any circumstances, could they be intended to defy or mock any of the divinely revealed religions, and anyone who says that I am an infidel is a liar.

Once Mahfouz had made his statement, the public prosecutor asked him to sign his deposition, but Mahfouz's injured hand was unable to hold the pen and the prosecutor was obliged to take Mahfouz's thumbprint.

According to Ashraf El-Ashmawi, one of the prosecutors charged with investigation of the incident, Mahfouz asked him during the investigation, "Why did they stab me, Mr. Prosecutor?" El-Ashmawi said,

> I answered in a way that I thought would comfort him and said that the one who'd tried to kill him had done so to make society better. Then he asked me, with the same concern, "How did he arrive at that view?" and I answered warily, "Because they think society can only be made better by killing 'the infidels.'" After giving him this answer, I apologized, telling him that that was the term that occurred in the statements of the suspect whom I had questioned, and he smiled at me affectionately and told me not to apologize. Then he surprised me with another question: "I know they haven't read the novel, but I'd like to know if they've read any of my other novels." ("Fi al-dhikra al-tasi'a li-rahil adib Nubil Naguib Mahfouz wa-li-awwal marra mundhu 20 'aman . . . asrar jadida fi muhawalat ightiyal al-adib al-'alami . . . shahda bi-qalam Ashraf El-Ashmawi wakil al-niyaba al-ladhi haqqaqa fi al-qadiya," *al-Yawm al-sabi'*, 30 August 2015)

Naguib Mahfouz then asked the members of the prosecutor's team to allow him to make a gift to the suspects of some of his books and asked his wife to fetch three novels from his house, which was next door to the hospital. In the dedication he wrote, "To those who disagree with my views I dedicate lines I have written for a society that can only be made better through culture" (*al-Yawm al-sabi'*, 30 August 2015).

The first thing Naguib Mahfouz wrote following the incident—on the morning of Friday 28 October 1994, according to the novelist Yusuf al-Qa'id—was to grant *al-Ahram* exclusive rights for the publication of the novel. The aim of the grant was to give *al-Ahram* the right to have urgent recourse to the courts to prevent publication of the novel by several newspapers that had declared their intention to do so. This feverish race had begun with two newspapers—*al-Masa'* and *al-Ahali* (The Native Sons), the first of which had already begun publishing it, starting Saturday 29 October 1994; the newspaper had announced that publication was at the express wish of Naguib Mahfouz, which Mahfouz denied. It published six installments of the novel before publication ceased in accordance with Mahfouz's request; this would be the second time that *al-Masa'* had announced its publication of the novel; it had also published one chapter following Mahfouz's winning of the Nobel Prize. On that occasion, Sarwat Abaza, in his capacity as head of the Writers Union, had intervened to stop publication. Similarly, *al-Ahali*, the organ of the Tagammu' Party, had announced that it would be publishing the novel "so that *Children of the Alley* should appear in full, for the first time, within days of the incident in a special issue" (Sunday, 30 October 1994). The issue was sold out, according to the newspaper's announcement at the time. The first page of the issue bore the headline "For the First Time in Egypt, the Complete Text of Naguib Mahfouz's Masterpiece *Children of the Alley*—Available to the Egyptian People for the First Time after 35 Years." The newspaper paved the way for the text with articles by the prominent critics and journalists Mahmud Amin al-'Alim, Shukri 'Iyad, Farida al-Naqqash, Gabir 'Asfur, and Salama Ahmad Salama, as well as the actor 'Adil Imam, plus drawings by 'Abd al-Ghani Abu al-'Aynayn and Gouda Khalifa.

Following its publication in *al-Ahali*, a number of writers and artists issued a statement asking that the novel not be published in Egypt against the wishes of Naguib Mahfouz himself. The signatories argued that publication of the novel in this fashion constituted a clear infringement of the author's literary, legal, and material rights and that defense of freedom of expression was no excuse for such an act of aggression. Fifteen cultural figures, including Ahmad 'Abd al-Mu'ti Higazi, Ghali Shukri, Gamal al-Ghitani, Yusuf al-Qa'id, Mohamed Salmawy, al-Sayyid Yasin, Sa'd Ardash, Tahiya Halim, Sami Khashaba, 'Abd al-Wahhab Mutawi', and Fathi al-'Ashri, signed the statement.

At the same time, a number of cultural and literary figures and writers collected donations toward the publication of a popular edition, in response to Mahmud Amin al-'Alim's call, at the meeting of cultural figures convened in solidarity with Naguib Mahfouz at the Balloon Theater; it was to be published immediately as a riposte to the extremists. This writers' initiative for the printing of the novel constituted, in effect, a rejection of the concept of the confiscation or banning of any literary work, although some of those involved made it a condition that Naguib Mahfouz's written consent be obtained before the collection of donations was begun.

The official mood in Egypt was in favor of publishing the novel, especially after minister of information Safwat al-Sharif, who had objected previously to its publication, visited Mahfouz in the Police Hospital where he was being treated and was asked by the writer's wife to stop publication of *Children of the Alley*. He told her and the journalists present, "No idea can be banned in Egypt today." This was taken to be a new official position on *Children of the Alley*. Indeed, *al-Ahali* even presented to Egyptian Television an announcement of *Children of the Alley*'s publication and this was broadcast without objection. Likewise, Nabil Abaza, editor-in-chief of Kitab al-Yawm (Book of the Day), a monthly book series issued by the Akhbar al-Yawm publishing house, contacted a number of critics, asking them to write introductions to the novel and telling them that he had the word of Dr. Muhammad Sayyid Tantawi, Mufti of Egypt, that he too would write an introduction, and that the novel and the studies would appear in the famous series in December 1994. A book bearing the title *Hikayat Awlad haratina* (The Tale of *Children of the Alley*) and including articles by Mahmud Amin al-'Alim, Samir Sirhan, and Sheikh 'Abd al-Galil Shalabi, former secretary-general of the Islamic Research Academy, did indeed appear. Shalabi had attacked *Children of the Alley* in the wake of Mahfouz's receipt of the Nobel Prize, going so far as to claim that it was "the proven father of Salman Rushdie's *Satanic Verses*" (Muhammad Wahdan, "Awlad haratina marratan ukhra . . . lajnat al-fatwa bi-l-Azhar tatlub muhakamatiha," *al-Masa'*, 28 June 1991), an assertion he justified by saying that "the novel had been printed in numerous living languages, including English, French, and Hebrew, and it would not have been difficult for Salman Rushdie to read it and weave his novel on the same loom." In his article included in the book, however, no such claim is made. In fact, he reads the novel as "alluding to the repression, stress, and property theft to which people were subject at that time as a result of the wave of nationalization and against which they were unable to raise their voices in complaint to God. The novel tells them that the prophets also suffered in their day and met with the fates that met them, so they should take them as a model, as night would inevitably end and day would come." Despite the clever allusions in his reading, he does criticize

> the novel's excessive concern with drinking, drunkenness, and drugs. Even the righteous prophets whom he has chosen do not hold aloof from hashish dens and are not above drinking and smoking hashish. This, though, is Mahfouz's trademark, and most of his novels contain similar scenes. It seems that his immersion in the life of the common people has led him to take note of such phenomena, which continue to be widespread in Egyptian life,

despite the rigorousness of the measures and the harshness of the penalties against them.

The sheikh also reveals that he had met with Mahfouz and discussed the novel with him and that it was the secret police who had presented the novel to al-Azhar, requesting that the latter issue a ban on it because, in Mahfouz's words, "Azharis did not read that kind of fictional literature."

The introductions written for the novel were published, but the novel itself was not, and the mufti never wrote a word about it.

Mahfouz was not keen on publishing the novel at that time. While he was still recovering from the attempt on his life and learned of the attempts to publish the novel, he told Gamal al-Ghitani and Yusuf al-Qa'id, "Don't I have enough to deal with? Is it such a small thing?" (*al-Wasat*, 7 November 1994). In statements to *al-Ahram*, Mahfouz said that he was afraid now that the novel would be misinterpreted and that "the reader will not be able to read it objectively. He will read it in order to find in it that interpretation and, given that the novel is symbolic, it won't be hard for the reader to give it the interpretation he is looking for" (*al-Ahram* 27 October 1994).

He justified his insistence by saying that the issue now was the attempted assassination of a writer and that publishing the novel would make it a party to the case, and maybe the whole thing would end up being about the novel and its position on religion. Mahfouz also added, according to Yusuf al-Qa'id, "In this context, the novel can only be given a religious reading, while it's supposed to be read simply as literature. And if that happens, the door will be opened to a renewed review of all fictional writing exclusively through the eyes of religion. What is needed now is effort, explanation, and analysis to remove the charge of blasphemy from the novel and of apostasy from its author. It can be published once that is done" (*al-Wasat* magazine, 7 November 1994).

Following the incident, Muhammad al-Ghazali visited Mahfouz. Al-Ghazali had written the first report calling for the novel to be banned, and the visit was a declaration on his part that he refused to associate himself with the attempted murder. Yusuf al-Qa'id has related details of the meeting. Al-Ghazali commented on the possibility of the novel being made available in Egypt by saying, "Poison also spreads unseen, and people accept it." He emphasized that he was against the novel but condemned the attempted assassination, which "was acceptable neither to the law nor to religion." In response to the charge that certain provocative books, including Sheikh Kishk's *Kalimatuna fi al-radd 'ala Awlad haratina* (Our Contribution to the Refutation of *Children of the Alley*), had prepared the way for the attempt, al-Ghazali declared that the man was "an ignoramus." Mahfouz brought the exchange to an end by affirming that he respected al-Ghazali's position on the novel: "All opinions are welcome, but the problem doesn't lie in the opinions. It lies in the ones who kill" (Yusuf al-Qa'id in *al-Musawwar*, 2 December 1994).

Mahfouz could see no harm in an opinion, however extreme. He was not angry at the critics of *Children of the Alley* so much as at the fatwa permitting the killing issued by Omar Abdel-Rahman, one of the most distinguished disciples of the spiritual father of the violent religious groups, Sayyid Qutb, whose book *Ma'alim fi al-tariq* was the primary authority for all the jihadist tendencies that took violence as their basis and for whose operations the book provided legal justification. The stab wound in Mahfouz's neck came, as it were, from an old friend. But how did Qutb and Mahfouz meet, and how did their paths diverge? It may be that Mahfouz, on his sickbed, went over in his mind his long relationship with Qutb.

CONFRONTING SAYYID QUTB

In keeping with his liberal upbringing and education, Naguib Mahfouz felt a profound aversion toward any group that believed it held a monopoly on the truth. Following the spread of the Muslim Brotherhood's ideas and the rise of Hasan al-Banna's star, many of his friends tried to convince him to "get to know" the group. One such was 'Abd al-Hamid Guda al-Sahhar, who pressed Mahfouz to do so and even set up an appointment for him with Hasan al-Banna. The dean of the novel, however, refused the meeting, on the grounds that the Brothers and Misr al-Fatah were simply organizations that were "simultaneously fascist and opportunist." Al-Sahhar told him, "Come and meet al-Banna and then make up your mind" but Mahfouz "could not abide the whole business" (Ibrahim 'Abd al-'Aziz, *Ana Naguib Mahfouz*, 160) and proclaimed his unwavering hatred of the group. He told Ghali Shukri, "The ones I've hated from the very beginning are the Muslim Brothers. At the start, the Brothers were a religious society that included Wafd Party members and non-Wafdists, but when we found they were beginning to compete with the Wafd, we treated them as enemies. We saw any competition with the Wafd as undermining its clout" (Ghali Shukri, *Min al-Jamaliya ila Nubil*, 74).

In his novel *Cairo Modern*, Mahfouz had attempted to present a panorama of Cairo society in the mid-1940s, in which he deals with the intellectual and ideological struggles of that period. Mahfouz selected the novel's main characters in such a way as to make each an expression of a different intellectual tendency. Ma'mun Radwan represents what might be called the Islamist tendency and the Muslim Brothers specifically, making this the Brothers' first appearance in an Arabic novel.

Ma'mun is a young man from the country wary of and angry at unbelievers and their modern innovations. He dreams of restoring the Islamic caliphate to its past glory. At university, they used to call him "the Unexpected Savior" or "Islam's imam for Our Age" (*Cairo Modern*, 4). The narrator mocks his way of thinking, saying, "Mr. Ma'mun Radwan is Islam's imam for our age. In ancient times, Amr ibn al-'As introduced Islam to Egypt, through his brilliance. Tomorrow, Ma'mun Radwan will extinguish Islam in Egypt thanks to his insensitivity." Mahfouz ends the novel with a prediction of the coming struggle between Ma'mun, representing the Brotherhood, and the leftist 'Ali Taha, which is perhaps the same struggle as that between the two brothers Ahmad and 'Abd al-Mun'im Shawkat with which Mahfouz's *Trilogy* also ends.

When it was published, the critics paid no attention to Mahfouz's *Cairo Modern*, an omission that caught the attention of Sayyid Qutb, who launched a violent attack on them, declaring that the novel was no less important than Tawfiq al-Hakim's plays *Ahl al-kahf* (The People of the Cave) and *Shahrazad* (Scheherazade) (Sayyid Qutb, "'Ala hamish al-naqd: *al-Qahira al-jadida*," *al-Risala*, issue no. 704, 30 December 1946).

Mahfouz's attitude to the Brotherhood, to which his friend, 'Abd al-Hamid Guda al-Sahhar, was attracted, never changed, even when Sayyid Qutb joined it and became its foremost thinker. They had first met as members of the Publishing Committee for Academics, which later became the publishing house Maktabat Misr and which had been created by 'Abd al-Hamid Guda al-Sahhar in partnership with his brother, Sa'id Guda al-Sahhar. Mahfouz says of the enterprise, "The Publishing Committee for Academics was founded at a time when a whole generation of writers, and I'm talking here of the generation that came after the pioneers, suffered from the publishing issue. We all had books stowed away, and when the committee was set up, we began publishing them in an orderly fashion" (Ibrahim 'Abd al-'Aziz, *Ana Naguib Mahfouz*, 105). Sayyid Qutb had arrived in the literary world earlier than these young people and used to encourage them by writing about their works. Mahfouz often stated that Qutb had been the first critic to pay attention to and write about his work. In fact, while Sayyid Qutb was not the first to write about Naguib Mahfouz, he was undoubtedly the first to attract major attention to him (Raga' al-Naqqash, *Fi hubb Naguib Mahfouz*, 181), particularly in view of the fact that most of the articles written on Naguib Mahfouz before Sayyid Qutb were either reportage or written out of friendship.

The first time Sayyid Qutb wrote about Mahfouz was following the publication of the novel *Thebes at War*, of which he wrote in *al-Risala* magazine (2 October 1944) that "If I had anything to do with it, I would put this story into the hands of every boy and every girl. I would print it and distribute it to every household for free and I would hold an award ceremony—of which Egypt has so many, both deserved and undeserved—for its author (whom I do not know personally)." Subsequently, Sayyid Qutb wrote a further three articles praising Mahfouz for his novels *Khan al-Khalili*, *Cairo Modern*, and, finally, *Midaq Alley*, which were published in *al-Fikr al-jadid*. Qutb also wrote of Mahfouz in a letter he sent to Tawfiq al-Hakim from America (also published by *al-Risala* on 9 May 1949) in which he praised Yahya Hakki, "who has found inspiration in the depths of the Egyptian character by picturing faith through the miracles of Our Lady Umm Hashim and the beliefs and legends associated with her." He also wrote of Mahfouz that "he depicts in his works the mockery of Fate, as well as people's hopes and dreams." Qutb ends his letter as follows: "I am certain that we shall have an immortal literature and intellectual and humanistic life of note the day we feel that we have something to give, the day we draw our inspiration from our original nature, the day we find the path within ourselves to that deep wellspring."

Although Mahfouz was happy with Qutb's writings and regarded them as the first to point to his rising talent, these writings were celebratory, evangelistic, and propagandistic rather than truly critical. Qutb was always talking in them of "identity" and of the search for a literature that was "strong, with clearly defined characteristics and distinctive markings and with an Egyptian soul, one purified of the impact of, while benefiting from, foreign intrusions, one that we can serve up, in all its national particularity, on the banquet table of the world" (*al-Risala* no. 650, 17 December 1945). Similarly, Qutb considered *Cairo Modern* to be "the story of the struggle between spirit and matter, between religious, moral, social, and scientific beliefs, between virtue and vice, riches and poverty, between love and money in the arena of life" (*al-Risala* no. 704, 30 December 1946). In all his critical writings, Qutb was looking for dualities within the work in question, dualities that led him, in the end, to divide the world into two camps—"Muslims" and "infidels." Qutb could not grasp, as a true critic would have, that a writer is not a political leader or propagandist but rather someone who plays, who has fun while he writes, and who bestows on others, too, the pleasure of playing and observing along with him.

The relationship between Mahfouz and Qutb was not that of a disciple to his guru, for the dean of the novel made no secret of the fact that his mentors were two—Sheikh Mustafa 'Abd al-Raziq and Salama Musa. From the first he took, according to Raga' al-Naqqash, "his enlightened view of the Islamic and Arabic heritage" (Raga' al-Naqqash, *Fi hubb Naguib Mahfouz*, 21); from the second, "hopes of civilizational renewal, a call for social justice, and increased attention to the ancient roots of the Egyptian personality." His relationship with Qutb may, therefore, be seen more as one of respect than of friendship or discipleship, a relationship that was "more literary than personal," to use Mahfouz's own words (Raga' al-Naqqash, *Naguib Mahfouz: safahat min mudhakkaratihi*, 328), since Qutb used to attend the discussion group organized by Mahfouz at the Casino Opera every Friday.

Just as Qutb wrote three articles about Mahfouz, so Mahfouz wrote three about Qutb. The first was when Qutb's book *al-Taswir al-fanni fi al-Qur'an* (Artistic Depiction in the Qur'an) appeared, the second when his novel *Ashwak* (Thorns) was issued (by Dar Sa'd in 1947) and Mahfouz wrote a review of it that Qutb himself published in *al-Sawadi* weekly newspaper, where he was employed as a culture editor. The latter piece disproves the statements by some to the effect that not one critic wrote about the novel and that as a result Qutb was afflicted with a hatred for the literary and cultural milieu. Mahfouz's article also demonstrates that Qutb's novel is an autobiographical account of his falling in love, citing the dedication with which Qutb opens the work: "To her who plunged with me into the midst of the thorns, so that I bled and she bled, I suffered and she suffered, and who then went one way while I went another, both wounded after the battle, she unwilling to make a decision, I unwilling to wait for one." In his review, Mahfouz does not evaluate the novel, seeing it rather as "a personal experience and as such . . . excused the requirements of creativity with regard to both content and characters, although we must point out that a novelist only truly merits the name when he leaves the boundaries of his own self and writes about others."

The third time Mahfouz wrote about Qutb was in his novel *al-Maraya (Mirrors)*. Here Qutb has been transformed into an imaginary character existing only on paper, and Mahfouz, as was his custom, has turned his experiences with people he knew into a source for his creativity, not, however, narrating those persons' lives as they really were but rather using them as symbols and charging them with meaning. In *Mirrors*, he gives Sayyid Qutb the name "'Abd al-Wahhab Isma'il" and observes of his transformations, "Today he is a legend, and as a legend, interpretations vary. Although he always showed me generous fraternity, I was never comfortable with his face or the look in his bulging, serious eyes" (*Mirrors*, 131). Mahfouz adds:

> Although Abd al-Wahab Isma'il never spoke about religion, pretended modernity in his ideas and dress, and adopted European habits in food and going to the cinema, yet the effect religion had on him, his belief, even fanaticism, were not a secret to me.
>
> A young Coptic writer had offered him his book of articles on criticism and sociology. He talked about him one day at Fishawi's.
>
> "He's intelligent, well-informed, sensitive, original in style and ideas."
>
> "When will you write about him?" I asked innocently, as I was fond of the writer.
>
> He smiled mysteriously. "Wait, and it'll be a long wait!" he said.
>
> "What do you mean?"
>
> "I will not help build a pen that tomorrow will slander our Islamic heritage in every twisted way," he replied decisively.
>
> He added, "I don't trust people of other religions." (*Mirrors*, 132)

Sayyid Qutb began his literary career by writing satirical pieces for the humorous magazine *Ishmi'na?* (How Come?), published by the Egyptian cartoonist Rakha. Three issues appeared at the end of 1929 and the beginning of 1930. Rakha, according to his biography published by *Akhbar al-yawm* (Sa'id Abu al-'Aynayn, *Rakha: faris al-karikatur* [Rakha: The King of Caricature], had become acquainted with Qutb in 1928 at the office of the owner of *al-Balagh* (The Report) newspaper, 'Abd al-Qadir Hamza, who had noted Qutb's intelligence and talent and put him in charge of the poetry page of *al-Balagh al-usbu'i* (The Weekly Report), where his job was to receive the letters of poetry-writing readers, select the best, and publish them. If he found nothing worth publishing, he would choose examples of the best poetry and print those. A number of Qutb's articles were written for the same humorous magazine. The first was titled "My Mother-in-Law" and gives evidence of a writer of grotesque satire of the first order. The second was titled "Our Friend the Poet" (Sa'id Abu al-'Aynayn, *Rakha: faris al-karikatur*). Later, this satirist would write an article for *al-Ahram* (17 October 1937) in which he called for total nudity, asserting that

> Pictures of naked people and descriptions of what goes on on beaches are more arousing than actual naked bodies, the pictures and descriptions leaving plenty of room for the imagination while the naked body leaves it little room and the appetite soon tires of looking at it. All you reformers who are so worried about morals, let the beaches be nude and playful! It will be the best way to ensure that rampant lust is stilled and morality observed.

In the same article he also says,

> There is nothing alluring about a naked body on the *plage* for those who behold it and can feast their eyes upon it all the time. The charms of the body there are the ones that are hidden beneath the burnoose or the dress. Those in a swimsuit neither attract nor arouse. If they arouse anything it is an artistic pleasure that is far—as far as can be—from that terrible, frightening gaze. (*al-Ahram*, 17 October 1937)

The distance between where Qutb began and where he ended up is vast, especially if we compare these liberal positions of his and those that he held following his fascinating transformations. Following the July 1952 revolution, Qutb worked as an adviser on labor issues for 'Abd al-Mun'im Amin, a Free Officer who was a member of the Muslim Brotherhood. During this period, Qutb wrote an article calling for the execution of labor leaders Mustafa Khamis and Muhammad al-Baqari and demanded that no workers' union, such as that whose formation had been announced in September 1952, be allowed. Sayyid Qutb's closeness to many members of the revolutionary leadership also allowed him to advise them to ban songs from the radio and demand the silencing of "dirty voices," such as those of Muhammad 'Abd al-Wahhab, Umm Kulthum, Farid al-Atrash, Muhammad Fawzi, Layla Murad, Sayyid Darwish, and 'Abd al-'Aziz Mahmud. In his words, "the radio has fallen over itself for the last quarter of a century trying to make the king happy and what is needed now is a new acculturation process for the masses that will give expression to their manliness. The masses loved the singers who sang the king's praises the way they loved drugs. It is the revolution's duty to safeguard thoughts and morals from softness and morbid appetites" (Sayyid Qutb, "Adab al-inhilal," *al-Risala*, 25 August 1952). It was then made a requirement that only religious songs written in classical Arabic be broadcast, and listeners woke up to find nothing on the radio but songs such as "Wulida al-huda" (Guidance Is Born) and "Salu qalbi" (Ask My Heart!). Bored, Egyptians deserted their own broadcasting service for the Near East Broadcasting Station, especially given that a new voice was beginning to be heard at that time, the voice of "Fairouz of Lebanon," that had the power to attract listeners. The Near East Broadcasting Station had a colonialist orientation and was linked to the forces of British imperialism, but Egyptians listened to the news on it and failed to return to the newscasts of the Egyptian Broadcasting Service. Abd al-Nasser was furious at the decision and called a meeting of the Revolutionary Leadership Council to discuss the matter. Then he canceled the previous decrees, which had been in force for eighteen days. Egyptians, however, no longer paid attention to Egyptian broadcasting stations and the Near East Broadcasting Station remained a source of information for them, so Abd al-Nasser gave instructions that a new radio drama series should begin broadcasting at the same time as the Near East Broadcasting Station's news bulletin.

When Qutb took another path, one that would lead him to accuse the whole society of unbelief, he lost his ability to smile, as Naguib Mahfouz indicates when describing his last meeting with him, which took place at Qutb's house in Helwan following his release from prison and one year before his execution.

> On that visit, we talked about literature and its issues. Then the conversation turned to religion, women, and life. It was the first time I sensed the depth of the change that had come over Sayyid Qutb's personality and ideas. I found a different person in front of me. Aggressive in his thinking, extreme in his opinions, he believed that society was returning to "the first Age of Barbarism" and was now a society of infidels that could only be set to rights by the application of God's law, starting with the idea of "divine rule"—that only God could rule. I heard him out without getting into any debate or discussion. What use could there be in debating a man

> who had become so fanatical in his beliefs?" (Raga' al-Naqqash, *Naguib Mahfouz: safahat min mudhakkaratihi*, 328)

Mahfouz adds that "On that visit, there were a number of bearded types. Qutb looked nothing like my old friend, and I wanted to break the tension of the heavy silence, so I made some trifling joke, thinking they would cheer up and laugh, but they looked at me askance and no one, not even Sayed, laughed. As I left the house in silence, I felt the extent of the change that had overcome him" (Gamal al-Ghitani, *al-Majalis al-mahfuziya*, 49).

Mahfouz and Qutb represent two different models. Each was searching for some truth. Qutb had a career full of sudden upsets and sharp turns; every time he discovered a path, he found it blocked, in an itinerary that began within the embrace of the political authority (whether that of the Wafd or of the July 1952 revolution, for which he worked during its early stages as an adviser) and which may not in fact have ended even when he claimed to own the absolute truth, a truth that permitted him to find the entire society guilty of unbelief. Naguib Mahfouz, on the other hand, resisted on some occasions the authorities and on many more the report writers, the tyrant makers, and the extremists' knives, as well as all the other difficulties that threatened to come between him and writing.

PUBLICATION BY *FORCE MAJEURE*

The attempt to assassinate Naguib Mahfouz failed, and he survived. A few weeks after he left the hospital and while still recovering, he met with a surprise: he found himself a suspect in, and summoned for, Case No. 1787, 1995, at Mansura Criminal Court. A lawyer named al-Sayyid 'Abd al-Rahman from Mansura had brought a case against Mahfouz accusing him of contempt of religion and of adding a new name to the list of God's Most Beautiful Names, namely, "Gabalawi." The charges carried a sentence of imprisonment and a fine, not to mention, by analogy with what happened to Nasr Abu Zayd, separation from his wife. This was the first time *Children of the Alley* had been taken to court, for, despite all the debate it had stirred up, the latter had remained at the written level, in the form of articles and official statements put out by the Islamic Research Academy, or oral agreements not to publish the book in Egypt.

The lawyer based his case on the fact that *al-Akhbar* had reported that when Mahfouz woke from the anesthetic, he had asked his wife when the operation was to be. She told him, "The operation's over," and Mahfouz had laughed and said, "So Gabalawi's happy with me!" According to the investigating magistrate, the lawyer (like Mahfouz's would-be assassin) had not read *Children of the Alley*; in fact he declared, "God forbid I should read it, with all the deviance it contains!" (Ahmad al-Sayyid 'Awadayn, *Muhakamat Awlad haratina* [*Children of the Alley* on Trial], 264).

Mahfouz was defended throughout the trial by Ahmad al-Sayyid ʻAwadayn, who later published the details of the trial and his arguments in his book *Muhakamat Awlad haratina* (p. 271). After five sessions over the period from 23 May to 30 November 1995, the court ruled that the case could not be heard, due to its failure to meet two requirements: interest and capacity. It also required the plaintiff to pay legal costs. Mahfouz's lawyer explains his failure to be acquitted by the fact that

> the law requires that the court not proceed to judgment on the substance of any case before it has reached a ruling on the formal arguments or, to put it differently, the judgment will only review the substance of a case that is accepted formally. If any infirmity renders the form defective, that makes the case unacceptable, the case concludes, and a judgment is passed that the case is unacceptable in view of the establishment of the said formal defect in the requirements for its acceptance, chief among which is the failure to meet the requirement of interest on the part of the plaintiff.

During the same period, Islamic thinker Khalid Muhammad Khalid asked to be allowed to write an introduction to the novel and did in fact meet with Mahfouz and ask him a number of questions about it. Mahfouz responded to his questions by telling him about the circumstances in which the novel was published and how it had been understood by al-Azhar, stating, "Al-Azhar read it as history, not as literature." For further clarification, he added:

> When I now ask myself how and why I wrote *Children of the Alley*, the answer that comes to me is that in 1959 I had begun to feel a certain disappointment in the 1952 revolution. It had come and done tremendous things but we'd begun to hear "Today so-and-so was arrested. Today they tortured so-and-so." And there were people who were benefiting enormously, till they'd become better off than the feudalists. Things of that sort. So after the first joy one had begun to have a bad feeling about where things were heading. So I imagined a thoroughly Egyptian neighborhood, with a band of bullyboys who wanted to plunder it and another group who were good and wanted to preserve its inheritance (the estate). These were all specifically Egyptian things and given the political

> perspective of the times I was thinking of something I could take from human history as a cover, so I thought about our larger heritage and about the people who had tried to make it a reality for humankind. It was as though in the end I was trying to tell the leaders of the revolution, "Whose side are you on? The bullyboys' or the prophets'?" That's what was in my mind when I wrote it. Did it come out exactly like that or did other things come out at the same time? That's what it all comes down to, but the one thing I am certain about is that I have never in my entire life doubted the existence of God and though I may have begun to understand Islam in a special way when I was an adolescent, I came to understand it properly later.

Mahfouz added,

> When you write a work of literature, you may have one idea about it, the reader another, and the critic a third, and only God knows which is correct. But that's the nature of art: it radiates meanings, and readers never cease to discover new ones in it as long as the work is read. Ideological books, on the other hand, have a single, delimited idea. Some viewed *Children of the Alley* as an ideological work, with the result that its meaning was lost, because it wasn't read as a novel and was understood as having only one, delimited meaning. (Naguib Mahfouz, *Asatidhati*, 143)

At one of the gatherings of the Hoodlums, talk turned to *Children of the Alley*. Mahfouz said, "Circumstances denied *Children of the Alley* its critical due," explaining that "it is above all a political work, a work that offers a political vision, and the people I had in mind understood its meaning. They knew whom I meant by 'the bullyboys,' so I think that they were probably behind the religious turn things took, so that I'd be hoist with my own petard" (*Akhbar al-adab*, 3 December 2001) (that is, when the critics saw that the book could be read in a religious sense, they encouraged this interpretation in order to get Mahfouz into trouble with the religious authorities).

And so Mahfouz's numerous interpretations, some brief, some expansive, follow one another, changing with the times. After the assassination attempt, Mahfouz interpreted the novel purely politically, unlike before, when he had alternated between "religious" interpretations (throughout the 1960s) and a combination of the religious and the political (in the 1970s and 1980s). This shift was not limited to Mahfouz alone: it also extended to a number of critics whose interpretations of the novel changed, among them Mahmud Amin al-'Alim, who said of the novel on its first appearance:

> It is not, as some claim, a history of mankind and it is not a history of Egypt alone. It is quite simply—in my belief—an affirmation that the essence of religion is justice. It is security, it is dignity, it is freedom, it is love, it is the good, it is the progress of humanity. The work is also an affirmation that this human essence of religion's makes science an extension and continuation of the mission of the various religions. Indeed, it is the means to the realization of their noblest goals. (*al-Hilal*, 1 July 1965)

In the aftermath of the assassination attempt, al-'Alim offered a different interpretation, stating that the essence of the novel was

> a symbolic, ideological, values-based critique of the Nasserite regime from the perspective of the contradiction between its slogans and principles and some of its practices, especially when it came to those related to political democracy. At the same time, the novel attempted to offer an evangelistic vision that eliminates the opposition between the ideal and the actual, between authority and society, between the political and the moral, between the theoretical and the practical, and between the objective and the subjective in Egypt generally speaking. (Mahmud Amin al-'Alim, in Nabil Abaza, ed., *Hikayat Awlad haratina*, 105)

It took thirty years for Muhammad Amin al-'Alim to offer two opposing points of view on one novel. The same occurred in the positions of certain government figures who agreed to its publication after the attempted assassination but who had rejected the idea after the Nobel award, and the same happened with the positions of the various tendencies of political Islam.

In December 2005, in the wake of the elections that resulted in eighty-eight successful Muslim Brotherhood candidates entering parliament, a member of the Guidance Office of the Muslim Brotherhood, 'Abd al-Mun'im Abu al-Futuh, went to congratulate Naguib Mahfouz on his birthday. The visit was, according to Abu al-Futuh, a "personal initiative" on his part because he felt a special gratitude to Mahfouz for writing against oppression at a time when members of the Brotherhood were suffering in the torture chambers in the 1950s and 1960s. At the same time, he wanted with this visit to send the message that Egypt's writers were regarded with appreciation and respect and that the tactics certain writers were using to create fear among cultural figures and authors, of the Muslim Brothers following their arrival in such large numbers in the Egyptian parliament, were unnecessary. *Children of the Alley* was present at the meeting: Abu al-Futuh said that he had no objection to the publication of the novel and in fact blamed Mahfouz for having made it conditional on al-Azhar's consent. Mahfouz listened. Then he said that he was "against requiring the permission of religious authorities for the publication of creative works but that *Children of the Alley* was a special case . . . a very special case indeed" (*Akhbar al-adab*, 18 December 2005). In the context of the struggle within the Brotherhood's leadership, Abu al-Futuh's visit laid him open to attack. A crisis erupted between him and the Brotherhood, which announced that it disagreed with his statement. This fierce attack on Abu al-Futuh was the expression of a strong current of opinion that still saw *Children of the Alley* as an unbelieving and atheistic novel and thought that its author deserved to be killed, and Abu al-Futuh was obliged to publish a retraction in which he said that he "did not agree with or agree to some of what was to be found in the novel" (published on the website of the Society of the Muslim Brothers, ikhwanonline.com, 2 January 2006).

A few days after this visit, in mid-January 2006, Dar al-Hilal announced that it was preparing "a major surprise and the most important literary event of the new year" for readers of its *Riwayat al-Hilal* (al-Hilal Novels) series.

Despite the publishing house's concern to keep the matter secret from everyone, including Mahfouz himself, Magdi al-Daqqaq, then editor-in-chief of *al-Hilal* magazine, appeared on television to announce that the surprise was *Children of the Alley* and to affirm that he had sent it to the printer's, prepared the cover, and was using the same illustrations that *al-Ahram* had when the novel was first published at the end of the 1950s. Al-Daqqaq stated that he had not received permission from any security service and that "I am simply benefiting from the democratic atmosphere that prevails in Egypt. I refuse to get any light, green or red, from any security, religious, or party apparatus. I have no personal religious or political point of reference that I consult when publishing creative works, and no one has the right to monopolize the right to be creative or to publish." He also expressed the opinion that "*Children of the Alley* is no longer the personal property of Naguib Mahfouz. It follows that it is unacceptable that the novel should be banned in Egypt under any pretext or for any reason. Naguib Mahfouz's gifts, like those of Umm Kulthum, do not belong to him alone but to everyone" (*Akhbar al-adab*, 15 January 2006).

Mahfouz, for his part, requested respect for his rights and sent a warning to Dar al-Hilal demanding that it halt the printing of the novel. It was one of the rare occasions on which he resorted to the law; in keeping with his personality and quiet demeanor, he usually chose to face controversies in his own particular way. This was especially true given that the timing of the announcement gave the impression of being more a political ploy, or an attempt to play the hero at Naguib Mahfouz's expense, than a defense of creative freedom, all the more so given that in January 2005 al-Daqqaq had published the novel *Kharif al-jiniral* (The Autumn of the General) by Hamdi al-Batran and omitted passages in which the author violently insults the Egyptian regime. Al-Daqqaq's position on *Children of the Alley* was simply a journalistic squib, a trial balloon to test the attitude toward the arts of the Muslim Brotherhood, now that it had reached parliament. It was aimed at either provoking them into moving against publication of the novel and so revealing their true face before the international community or at embarrassing them before Egypt's cultured classes, especially in the light of the visit to Mahfouz by 'Abd al-Mun'im Abu al-Futuh, a member of the Guidance Office, and his affirmation that he had no objection to publication of the novel.

The novel was not in fact published at this time. The attempt to do so did, however, highlight fraught questions concerning freedom of expression and publication on the one hand and the writer's financial and literary rights on the other. Should publication against the author's will of a novel that had become a part of human history be regarded as yet another assault on the author and his original publisher?

Everyone respected Mahfouz's desire to prevent publication of the novel, whose printing he opposed until the last moment of his life, fearing reactions against his family, whom he had always kept out of the spotlight. This was why he had sought the consent of al-Azhar. It was a position he clarified in an interview following the attempted assassination:

> *Children of the Alley* is a faith-based Islamic novel that has been unjustly treated. This is why I did not agree to its being published

> in Egypt without al-Azhar's consent, meaning until al-Azhar accepted my understanding of it. Why did I impose this condition? Because I am not against religion or al-Azhar, and if I and the novel had been against al-Azhar, I would have challenged al-Azhar and made every effort to publish the novel to spite it. But I am not like that, because I am neither against al-Azhar nor against religion. I am an Azhari by birth and upbringing. I'm a civilian Azhari! (*Rose al-Yusuf*, 13 February 2006)

In spite of Mahfouz's having made al-Azhar's consent a condition for the novel's publication in Egypt, he refused an offer made him by Sheikh 'Abd al-Zahir 'Abd al-Raziq, director of research, writing, and publication at the Islamic Research Academy, according to which Mahfouz would himself present a request to the Academy to reexamine the novel without reference to the Academy's earlier decisions calling for its proscription. 'Ali Abu al-Hasan, the Sheikh of al-Azhar's counselor on fatwa-related matters, declared that he had no objection to the novel's publication on condition that "Mahfouz delete the sentences and expressions that insult the wives of the Prophet, his Companions, and other Islamic symbols" (*al-Misri al-yawm*, 19 January 2006). Mahfouz rejected this offer vehemently, regarding it as "a dangerous precedent for creativity and its freedom" (telephone conversation with Mohamed Salmawy, July 2016).

The Islamic Research Academy's hardline position against the novel was countered by a more understanding position on creative work on the part of the Dar al-Ifta', the country's leading source of fatwas, whose head, the Mufti of the Republic, stated in an interview at the Cairo International Book Fair that "al-Azhar has never issued a decree for the confiscation of *Children of the Alley*, which we have to treat as a work of literature to which we cannot apply the same rules as we would to an ideological work" (*Akhbar al-adab*, 5 February 2006).

Despite this statement, Mahfouz insisted on sticking to the two conditions that he had set for publication of the work in Egypt, affirming, once again, to his new publisher, Dar El Shorouk, that al-Azhar's consent must precede publication and that Kamal Abu al-Magd must write an introduction. Mahfouz wanted to obtain a "driver's license" for the novel, stamped and signed by an intellectual who had credibility with the ordinary followers of the Islamist groups but who was not regarded as wedded to an extremist perspective on the position of religion in modern societies. And this is what in fact occurred, with Kamal Abu al-Magd writing an introduction to the novel when it was published in Egypt, legally, for the first time. While the introduction may have seemed "Islamist," it acted as a verdict of innocence for the novel on the charge of demeaning the divine essence or the prophets, which so many intellectuals had found unacceptable.

30 AUGUST 2006

"A good ending and a calm death"—that was what Naguib Mahfouz hoped for, and when Mohamed Salmawy asked him, "What do you mean by 'a good ending'?" he responded, "I had two brothers. The older died of cancer and suffered torments during his final days. My other brother drank some tea, rested his head on my shoulder, and died in less than a second. I hope that my death will be that calm" (Mohamed Salmawy, *Naguib Mahfouz, watani misri: hiwarat ma'a Mohamed Salmawy*, 100).

However, Mahfouz suffered from illness during his last days. After he tripped and fell in the parlor of his home, he went into a coma, and on waking from it he declared, "I want to go home." The doctors were unable to gain control over his condition, which continued to deteriorate for almost a month and a half.

Naguib Mahfouz departed this life on the evening of 29 August 2006 and the news of his demise was delayed until the presidency of the republic could be informed. By the time of the official announcement, security personnel from the presidency had proceeded to the hospital and Mahfouz's body had been placed under "total surveillance" by presidential explosive experts, who became, from that moment on, responsible for all the details of the funeral, as they were for the thorough frisking of members and friends of the family, to ensure the security of the president, who would take part in the obsequies of Egypt's great writer. Despite all these precautions, it was thought necessary to pass the body through explosives detectors and then guard it so as to prevent anyone from approaching it before the funeral. Mahfouz had never dreamed of a public occasion. It came as a shock to his family and impelled his wife to inform close friends that she would rather the body leave from Sayyidna al-Husayn Mosque, in the quarter in which Mahfouz had been born and where he had grown up and to which he was attached. However, this dream too was not to be realized: the bier that was borne to the al-Husayn mosque contained no body; the body itself was taken directly to al-Rashdan Mosque, where the president and generals were waiting. The president managed to walk in the procession for just three minutes, for the sake of the cameras, before withdrawing, along with his companions and guards, leaving the body unattended.

Public funeral processions may perhaps be considered a barometer of the relationship between the authorities and the masses. Saad Zaghloul's funeral procession was, by Mahfouz's own account, the biggest and most impressive. The masses carried the bier on their shoulders from Opera Square to the Imam al-Shafi'i cemetery and people of all social groups, classes, and parties were overwhelmed with grief. Zaghloul was, after all, "the spiritual father of the entire nation" (Raga' al-Naqqash, *Naguib Mahfouz: safahat min mudhakkaratihi*, 209). The same happened with Prime Minister Mustafa al-Nahhas Basha, who had been forbidden to appear in any media and all news of whom was banned from 1954 until his death in 1965. Despite the Nasserist regime's warnings against "assembly" and its threats against anyone who might attend, on the excuse that the common people were obsessed with such processions, vast numbers of mourners were present and the occasion was regarded at the time as a popular rehabilitation of the Wafd and its leader. Nor was the funeral procession of Field Marshal 'Abd al-Mu'im Riyad normal and traditional. We had before us a military leader killed by the enemy's bullet while on the frontline inspecting his forces. So many Egyptians came out spontaneously to participate that Abd al-Nasser's security detail completely disappeared amid the throngs of mourners, who themselves surrounded the president and joined hands to form a new security detail around him. The same happened with Abd al-Nasser himself, in whose funeral procession four million Egyptians marched in Cairo alone, while informal popular processions were held for him in all the provinces and even in a number of Arab countries. At the funeral processions of 'Abd al-Halim Hafiz and Umm Kulthum, millions marched, everyone coming out to bid them farewell in a celebration of the power of human creativity and innovation. In contrast, Muhammad 'Abd al-Wahhab, Su'ad Husni, and Mahfouz all had the bad luck to die during the Mubarak era, and their funeral processions were models of the cold official cortege, presided over by the authorities, while the masses were forbidden to participate. That mass participation in Mahfouz's procession would send a message against violence and extremism never occurred to the authorities; anything of that sort was forbidden throughout Mubarak's reign out of fear of the public, which was permitted to express its joys and sorrows only under the patronage of the authorities themselves.

Nor was *Children of the Alley* absent from the final farewell—an impressive scene, crafted with the skill of a novelist, at which those in authority, and their sheikhs, dressed themselves in line to pray for his soul. Would Mahfouz's funeral be the occasion for the announcement of a reconciliation between the religious establishment and Mahfouz? This question was addressed by a journalist to the Sheikh of al-Azhar, Sayyid Tantawi, the Mufti of the Republic, 'Ali Gum'a, and the minister of religious endowments, Hamdi Zaqzuq, following the first funeral prayers, which took place at the mosque of al-Husayn. The question angered Mahfouz's Hoodlums, who said that it was inappropriate to raise it at that time. The Sheikh of al-Azhar preferred to say nothing, while the mufti responded briefly that "it's all fabricated" and stated that "this is a sad day because we are bidding farewell to a literary giant who loved Egypt and humankind" (*Akhbar al-adab*, 3 September 2006). The minister delivered a short address in which he described Mahfouz as "a fourth pyramid, who placed Arabic literature among the ranks of world literature" (*Rose al-Yusuf*, 1 September 2006).

At this precise moment, according to Gamal al-Ghitani, "a young man pushed himself forward and voiced his objection to the prayers on the grounds that Mahfouz was an unbeliever" (Gamal al-Ghitani, *al-Akhbar*, 30 August 2015).

Mahfouz's funeral was something larger than a happenstance encounter of all the opposing parties to bid farewell to a man who had been forbearing to all and yet in opposition to all. Everyone in authority attended Mahfouz's funeral, along with the official religious establishment and representatives of the Muslim Brotherhood, despite the latter's hesitation over taking a positive stand toward publication of *Children of the Alley*. The Gama'a Islamiya was quick to issue a statement noting Mahfouz's death and claiming that his attempted assassination had not been part of the Gama'a's general line of thinking. However, while enumerating in its statement Mahfouz's virtues, the Gama'a praised him for "refusing to publish or print *Children of the Alley* without the agreement of al-Azhar. This is something that we consider—by God!—to be a way on his part of backing away from the novel, of disassociating himself from it, and of repenting unto God for the sin he committed in writing it" (*al-Riyadh*, 2 September 2006). Thus, while on the face of it the Gama'a was apologizing for its earlier crime against Mahfouz, its apology was incomplete since it supposed that Mahfouz had repented of his novel.

Mahfouz had not announced his repentance, as the Gama'a Islamiya imagined, nor was his bier booby-trapped with explosives, as the authorities feared. He mocked them all, in his creative life as in his farewell scene, one that was not without its comic side too, vis-à-vis the novel, some people picturing Mahfouz handing out copies of *Children of the Alley* to its protagonists in the heavens while giving each a smile and saying, "Look what I wrote about you!" (Wa'il 'Abd al-Fattah, *al-Akhbar* (Lebanon), 15 September 2006).

Funeral rites over, the attack turned to the sheikhs who had performed the prayers over the dead man. The Partisans of Consultation and Peace group in Kuwait issued a statement titled "Fear God!" in which it attacked both the Sheikh of al-Azhar and the Mufti for praying over Mahfouz and asking for mercy on his soul: "How could they ban his novel yesterday, then pray over him and ask for mercy and forgiveness for him today?" (Gabir 'Asfur, *Naguib Mahfouz: al-ramz wa-l-qima*, 412).

THE WASTE LAND

The identity of the unknown thief who had robbed the villa of Ahmad Shawqi, "the Prince of Poets," on the day in 1959 when Naguib Mahfouz began publishing *Children of the Alley* in *al-Ahram* was now known. A few days later, he had robbed Umm Kulthum's villa and the police had managed to catch him. During questioning, he stated that he had committed fifty-eight similar crimes. Unfortunately, he managed to escape before he could be brought to trial.

Mahfouz did not concern himself for long with the tumult and outcry caused by *Children of the Alley*. He was more interested in the mysterious thief, who had become the talk of the whole country. Indeed, he was so preoccupied with the case that when Yahya Hakki asked him, "What are you reading these days and what's on your mind?" Mahfouz replied, "The only thing on my mind and in my thoughts is Mahmud Amin Sulayman." Hakki describes the scene:

> At that period, whenever I went into his office (we had offices next door to one another at the Arts Authority and would leave together), I'd find him pacing up and down. It would be as though I'd woken him from a coma or brought him back from some unknown world to this. If a cannon had gone off next to him, he wouldn't have noticed. His hands were clasped behind his back, his head raised and tilted a little backward, and I could tell from

his voice that his throat was dry. If I'd rapped with my knuckles on his body, it would have rung like a mattress-fluffer's bow. From time to time, he'd raise his hand to his forehead and wipe it, as though removing sweat or trying to bring its temperature down. At first glance, one might have thought that his face was implacable, frowning, in a state of crisis, but in reality it was the face of a man sunk in deep thought, totally absorbed by his emotions. (Yahya Hakki, *'Itr al-ahbab*, 113)

Mahfouz published *The Thief and the Dogs* one year and eight months after the publication of *Children of the Alley*, on 11 August 1961.

Now, Egypt is building the High Dam, the Egyptian revolution is entering a new era with the announcement of the so-called "socialist decrees," and nothing that has yet been made public muddies the clear waters of Egyptian–Syrian unity (which will collapse one month from that day). A German mission is visiting Egypt to study the construction of a nuclear power station in Wadi al-Hawf and the authorities are bringing the country's citizens the glad news that three million pounds have been set aside to convert the city of al-Qanatir al-Khayriya into an integrated tourist city that will include the Orient's first floating amusement park. Umm Kulthum's song "Thuwwar" (Revolutionaries), 'Abd al-Halim Hafiz's "Bi-l-ahdan" (In Each Other's Arms), and 'Abd al-Wahhab's "al-Gil al-sa'id" (The Rising Generation), after being performed at the ninth-anniversary celebrations of the revolution, will be made into short movies, while film director Youssef Chahine begins preparations for his movie *al-Ard* (The Land), based on 'Abd al-Rahman al-Sharqawi's novel. The most notable international event and the focus of attention of most Egyptian newspapers is "Russia's Ascent into Space," which raises fears of a Third World War. The United States president Kennedy declares, "We expect further Soviet achievements but will never let our enemies gain control over space" (*al-Ahram*, 11 August 1961), while, at the UN General Assembly, America demands guarantees that space be used only for peaceful purposes. In the midst of all this, *al-Ahram* announces on its first page the start of publication of *The Thief and the Dogs*—"a new long story in serial form"—that will appear weekly in its literary supplement with illustrations by 'Abd al-Mun'im al-Qassas.

In the supplement (*al-Ahram*, 11 August 1961), Muhammad Hasanayn Haykal writes his weekly article for his column *Bi-saraha* (Frankly Speaking), under the title "Six Questions and Their Answers." The piece appears to be a continuation of six articles by Haykal known as "The Crisis of the Intellectuals" that were published during June and July 1961. In the article, Haykal poses the question: "Have the revolutionary measures, with all the fundamental changes that were announced at the time of the celebrations for the ninth anniversary of the revolution, come to an end?" Answering his own question, he says, "In my view, the main lines of revolutionary change have been clearly drawn. In his speech in Alexandria on 26 July 1961, Gamal Abd al-Nasser said the following: 'The necessary revolutionary measures are complete and in process of implementation.'" Haykal published his six articles on the crisis of the intellectuals in an effort to rally the latter to the side of the revolution following "their inability—given their class affiliations and social aspirations—to stand shoulder to shoulder with the masses before the army took action, or to respond to the new regime brought into being by that action—a new regime that realized what the intellectuals had been incapable of realizing, filled the vacuum they had left, adopted the demands of the masses, and led the popular struggle" (*al-Ahram*, 2 June 1961). The articles were the start of discussion and debate around the issue, on which Lutfi al-Kholi had begun writing following his release and in which others, some representing the regime, others the few intellectuals who remained out of prison, took part.

During the *Children of the Alley* crisis, a journalist asked Naguib Mahfouz, "When are you going to write your next story?"

"When I retire, God willing!" Mahfouz replied (*al-Kawakib*, 24 January 1961).

His answer was heavily ironic, given that he had lost his job as director of the office for the censorship of literary works and been transferred to work in the Arts Sectors' Cinema Authority as director of censorship for film. The new job may have been a relief to him, taking off his shoulders many burdens, including the contradictions between his vision of art as "resolute" and aimed at bringing about change, on the one hand, and his work at the censor's office on the other. At the same time, and feeling that he was under surveillance by the authorities following *Children of the Alley*, Mahfouz never stopped thinking about "the solution" or "salvation."

It was during this period that the critic Ahmad Rushdi Salih wrote on "The Short Story and the Novel under Socialism" (*al-Idha'a*, 11 November 1961). "Story writers and novelists are entering a new era, the era of socialism. They are living through wonderful events that must have an impact on a writer's heart, as they must on his taste and his orientation, while opportunities to publish are also multiplying." "How," he wondered, "should the story and the novel address this new era and how should they give expression to it?"

Salih continued:

> What if a talented writer such as Naguib Mahfouz were to directly experience the construction of the High Dam and return to Cairo to write a trilogy, or a quartet, on this wonderful experience, in which age-old mountains are turned into fragile dunes and level expanses covered in water; an experience through which the River Nile appears first as a wonderful, untamed monster and then, following the building of the dam, as a docile, friendly being; an experience through which the emotions of thousands upon thousands of peasants, workers, engineers, contractors, women, children, and so on are intertwined, as though weaving the threads of the future, so that we can visualize this as something that has really happened and see what the result may be? Presumably, the novels of Naguib Mahfouz or al-Sharqawi would live up to the standards of world socialist literature.

Salih cites as an example of what he has in mind the works of the American Howard Fast, author of *Freedom Road* and *Citizen Tom Paine*.

In the same issue, *al-Idha'a* asked Naguib Mahfouz how he chose the ideas for his novels. Mahfouz responded:

> I live the novel before I write it. It begins with some idea or other or with a situation or a character or a time or a certain place. I can't pin down how the idea begins. I'm always thinking. Thinking is a part of life. When I feel that I'm totally immersed in an idea, to the point at which I've become a part of it and it has become a part of me . . . when I feel this, I find myself in a state of dazzling radiance and luminescence, a state of incandescence that moves me to the core. Then, my attention becomes focused on this radiance and incandescence and I feel joy, and deep inside me I am transformed into a small child full of vitality and energy and I know I've stumbled upon the starting point of a new work. The days pass and I

remain engrossed in thinking about this new exciting thing that has saved me from haphazard thinking, and various aspects of this now orderly thinking become clearer—situations emerge, characters coalesce, and little by little the idea takes shape. The dialogue flows, the work begins to grow, and these spontaneous, slow processes take place with the help of day-to-day life, of past life, of memories that have lain dormant in the silence of forgetfulness. After a while, I find that I've arrived at a rich and fertile idea even if it is still shapeless or indeed just scraps scattered here and there, confused thoughts that just need structure, meaning writing. Here the regular work begins, the work that is to a considerable degree conscious. I make a general plan that collects these scraps into a meaningful picture. The general plan doesn't pay attention to every detail, it traces the broad lines that the work will follow. Finally the writing process, with its regular time allotment, begins. During writing the entire plan may change, and the novel be born as a creation almost foreign to the general plan that was drawn up for it originally.

Mahfouz never wrote a new trilogy on the High Dam, as Ahmad Rushdi Salih had demanded. He was preoccupied with the story of "the killer" or "the mysterious thief" who specialized in robbing the villas of the rich, was caught while trying to rob Umm Kulthum's villa at the end of January 1959, and confessed during questioning that he was having a love affair with one of Umm Kulthum's maids; the man stated that he had entered the villa to see the girl, nothing more. In March 1960, *al-Akhbar* published, over a prominent frontpage picture, a sensational story headlined "Umm Kulthum Villa Intruder Suddenly Turns Killer!" This was the start of a much more sensational story whose chapters were reported one after the other in the months that followed and which became the Egyptian press's favorite topic. The papers followed the steps of the thief, whose name—Mahmud Amin Sulayman—was now known and who himself wanted every detail of his life to be familiar to all. The papers sent people to rummage through his relationships, his history, his family, his failed marriage. "The Killer," the nickname by which he had become famous, was easier and had a better ring to it than his long real name, not to mention that he was no longer simply a burglar who robbed the houses of the famous but was now also a murderer, and one "seeking justice," or so he claimed. The press treated the Killer's case as a public opinion issue. For approximately three months, the papers followed the life of this person who had turned, in the words of Bakr Darwish in *al-Masa'*, into "a folk hero in some people's imagination—a sort of Abu Zayd al-Hilali or 'Antar ibn Shaddad" (Bakr Darwish, *al-Saffah: qadiyyat Amin Sulayman*, 5). However, this did not imply admiration for "the substance of his crimes, only for their outward form," meaning "his quick intelligence, his astonishing daring, and his amazing ability to cope with the most ticklish and difficult situations."

Who, though, was this "killer" who fired bullets right and left "as naturally as one might light a cigarette," to use the words of Bakr Darwish, author of the book *al-Saffah: qadiyyat Amin Sulayman* (The Killer: The Case of Amin Sulayman, 5)?

Mahmud Amin Sulayman had read the Arsène Lupin novels and wanted to be like him. He was a thief of a rare kind, the most brilliant of the breed who enter houses through their windows or balconies without being seen, who are skilled at opening shutters and leaping into homes like a cat, and he had a thousand and one tricks for escaping the police. When caught, he would resort to an infallible method: he would swallow pins and razorblades, be taken to the hospital, and from there escape unnoticed. Once he had escaped, he did not bother to hide or disappear: he went on with his life as normal, living in everyone's midst. On one occasion, he opened a publishing house, on another he owned a store for selling and mending watches, on a third he ran a grocery. Once, following an escape, he even used in his labors the help of a policeman working at the prison! He wanted to be like Robin Hood or Arsène Lupin, stealing only from the rich, although he differed from them in that "he kept what he stole for himself, not for the poor," in the words of Bakr Darwish, crime editor at *al-Masa'* in the1960s (Bakr Darwish, *al-Saffah*, 7).

The poet Ahmad Fu'ad Nigm devotes a chapter of his memoirs *al-Fagumi: al-sira al-dhatiya al-kamila* (al-Fagumi: The Unabridged Autobiography, 161–69) to Sulayman, whom he met in prison, concentrating mostly on the police chase that followed his escape:

> We followed the news of him with enthusiastic admiration, like fans at a soccer game. Even the wardens, when the officers weren't around, couldn't hide their admiration and sympathy for Mahmud. Once I asked Sergeant 'Abd al-Ghaffar (the cruelest warden I came across in the prison system), "Is it true what they say, Uncle

> 'Abd al-Ghaffar, that you were praying for the Killer at afternoon prayers yesterday?" He answered, "Are you threatening me, boy? Yes, I was praying for him and I'll go on praying for him. There's nothing wrong with Mahmud. He's a kindhearted boy and a good lad too. Please, dear Prophet, let the Lord protect him from those unjust sons of bitches and send him victorious over them!" Ahmad Fawzi, the guy who stole "cats," meaning women's bags, laughed and told 'Abd al-Ghaffar, "So if Our Lord grants Mahmud victory over them, the thieves get to rule Egypt, Uncle 'Abd al-Ghaffar?" For the first time ever I saw 'Abd al-Ghaffar smile as he replied, "They already do, smartass!"

Sulayman's sufferings began in childhood, when his father took him from their village of Abu Tisht in the governorate of Qena in southern Egypt and went to work in Lebanon. The young child was always in trouble with his family and at school, stealing his father's money to spend it on his own pleasures, then stealing from the neighbors, until he was arrested and sent to prison in Lebanon for five years, while the submissive, conciliatory father was forced to leave Lebanon for Alexandria in 1953. The son managed not simply to escape from prison and disappear but also to marry, four times in succession and, like some modern-day Shahriyar, was forced, after each of these adventures, to leave Lebanon and go back to Alexandria, announcing to his family that he was sorry, and would not do it again. In Alexandria, he opened a publishing house called Dar al-Fikr. Then he married Hamida Ahmad Ibrahim, aka "Bella," only to divorce her soon after and resume his former career, the number of his crimes in Alexandria keeping pace with the number of his arrests and escapes. Every time, he was defended by his friend, the lawyer Badr al-Din Ayyub. Months passed and then suddenly he met the love of his life, Nawal 'Abd al-Ra'uf, aka "the Belle of Alexandria," and married her and they had a daughter, Iman, and moved to Cairo and opened Iman's Grocery. Mahmud had never been so happy. He had a beautiful wife who loved him and whom he loved, a daughter, and a lawyer friend who could get him out of all his scrapes. And he had money too. But, just as the happiness had arrived all of a sudden, so, all of a sudden, it left, turned into a boundless misery that could only be described as hell when he discovered that his wife was cheating on him! And with whom? With his friend! And that wasn't all. She confessed everything, revealing that she had not only cheated on him with his friend but with many others too, and she stoked his already blazing inferno by informing him that his sister was having an affair with yet another friend of his. From then on, his eyes saw nothing before them but revenge, revenge on everyone. Except that he could not get to his treacherous wife as she was very good at escaping whenever he managed to get close to her, and then the police provided her with a security detail to protect her and trap him.

Even though all the newspapers were interested in Sulayman, *al-Akhbar* was the one that followed most closely the reports of his doings and the details of his life, even going so far as to come to an arrangement with his wife to publish her memoirs, after a journalist called Sabri Ghunaym convinced her he would marry her once the Killer had been caught and had divorced her. The memoirs were duly published (Sabri Ghunaym, *al-Misri al-yawm*, 24 September 2009).

Almost every day, the newspapers published sensational stories about the Killer, some true, many simply rumors or inventions made up to enhance their authors' media profiles: detectives believed the Killer was hiding in the house of a woman who wanted him all to herself, was afraid for him, loved him, wanted to help him, and was feeding him information; the actresses Maryam Fakhr al-Din and Tahiya Carioca were receiving threatening letters from the Killer. The strangest rumor was that Sulayman had offered Gamal Abd al-Nasser in a telephone call to bring him the head of Iraqi president 'Abd al-Karim Qasim, who at the time was engaged in a furious quarrel with him.

On 6 April 1960, *al-Akhbar* published on its front page a statement by Cairo's chief of police threatening anyone who assisted or sheltered the Killer and offering a reward of one thousand pounds to anyone who helped get him arrested. Sulayman then started on his flight from Cairo to Upper Egypt. He dodged the checkpoints set up to catch him and got as far as Badrashin, where he flagged down a truck and tried to convince the driver to take him to al-Wasiti. The driver grew suspicious and at the next traffic checkpoint pretended that he was going to give the police officer his driving license and informed the officer that the Killer was in the truck. Sulayman, however, quickly escaped with the truck, after shooting and killing the officer. A few hours later, police found the truck with his clothes in it and, on sniffing these, trained police dogs led them to a cave in the hills surrounding Helwan where he was hiding. Now began a short, but very exciting, moving, and dramatic stage. According to *al-Ahram*, an extended conversation took place between the thief and the police chief, as follows:

> Police Chief: Give yourself up, Mahmud!
>
> Thief: If you want to kill me, I am ready to take my own life. One shot and it will all be over.

The thief did not, however, commit suicide but resorted to cunning. At first, he agreed to hand himself over but only on condition that the police bring him his wife, the cause of his tragic situation. Then he asked that they bring him the journalist and editor-in-chief of *al-Ahram*, Muhammad Hasanayn Haykal, along with some white paper, as he wished to write his memoirs. More than an hour and a half passed in conversation with the police, who were well aware of his prevarications, and then the storming of the cave in which he was hiding commenced. *Al-Ahram* wrote that Sulayman took seventeen bullets, dying instantaneously; *al-Masa'* wrote that Sulayman shot himself in his head with his revolver and died a suicide. "The night Sulayman died of police bullets, the entire prison mourned—the warders, the sergeants, the soldiers on night duty. B Wing was sunk in sadness, silence, and depression," as Nigm recounts (*al-Fagumi*, 196).

Following his killing, the police inspected the last apartment the thief had occupied, on Muhammad 'Ali Street, and there they found a letter addressed to Muhammad Hasanayn Haykal, who published the text on the front page of *al-Ahram*. In it, Sulayman asks Haykal to have *al-Ahram* print his life story, in installments, providing even the title ("Muhammad Amin Speaks at Last! Picks *al-Ahram* to Publish This Letter!"). In three school copybooks and using a novelistic style full of grammatical mistakes, he explains to Haykal the driving forces behind his thefts, details of his wife's betrayal, and his anger at an unjust society. He also denies being a killer and states that he is, rather, a simple human being, the victim of a wife's infidelity and the circumstances surrounding his marriage to her. He also attempts to analyze his personality and explains his miserable situation. His victims were killed by mistake. His defense is that he is a victim of society: "I must write. Maybe it will help this sick society that fights against me so hard. I don't know where to begin but the best thing for me and for society is for it to understand that particular incident [of his wife's infidelity] because it's the one that changed the course of my life." He then devotes some pages to talking about his wife Nawal, whom he "snatched from an impure past" and who he imagined, when he thought of marrying her after he divorced Bella, would be his servant, and therefore loved . . . though betrayal was his destiny.

The copybooks are full of expressions that Sulayman believed would appear to be those of a sage, one who had lived and learned. He writes, "If the world turns dark before your eyes, take your anger out on society because it is society that is responsible, and have no mercy," and "Mercy is above justice and strength is above justice," and so on.

The day following Sulayman's death, Gamal Abd al-Nasser was on a visit to Pakistan. *Al-Akhbar* led with a full-page heading "Death of the Killer" and beneath it another, "Abd al-Nasser in Pakistan," with no clear division between the two so that it looked as though they formed a single headline: "Death of the Killer Abd al-Nasser in Pakistan" (*al-Akhbar*, 10 April 1960). Some claim the authorities used this headline as one excuse, among others, for the nationalization of the press on 24 May 1960. What is certain is that the authorities were greatly annoyed by how much space the press was devoting to the crime, believing that enemies of the regime might exploit the story to embarrass it and that it presented an embarrassing picture of the new, renascent society. The authorities' desire for hegemony and social control did not, however, prevent the leaking of news of the arrest of 1,055 prostitutes in Cairo alone, some of whom were earning as much as 206 Egyptian pounds a month (*al-Bigha' fi al-Qahira* [Prostitution in Cairo], a report by the National Center for Social and Criminal Studies).

Following his demise, more than one cinema producer proposed to turn the Killer's life story into a film. Farid Shawqi did so, and so did Madiha Yusri. However, the censor, Muhammad 'Ali Nasif, refused to issue a license, as it was his opinion that the Killer was "a perverse example of society, a nonchalant criminal whose life does not deserve to be glorified or put on show" (*al-Kawakib*, 14 November 1961).

The story of the Killer came to an end, journalistically speaking. The press, occupied with its own nationalization, failed to concern itself with other stories. From a distance, however, one mind was following developments, linking events and motives. It kept its eyes on the signals, and worried over them. Naguib Mahfouz had set to work immediately on writing the story of "the dogs" and "the thief," for, as Said Mahran tells Nur in Mahfouz's novel (which realized the Killer's dream of seeing his life story serialized in *al-Ahram*), "Most Egyptians neither fear nor dislike thieves . . . but they do have an instinctive dislike for dogs" (*The Thief and the Dogs*, 69).

Naguib Mahfouz's passion for detective stories, of which many were available in Arabic translation, began when he was ten. During his childhood and boyhood he was preoccupied with questions about the world around us. What went on there? What role might he play in it? And he found the answer.

> The only thing I instinctively took to in those days was detective stories. Isn't it odd, the way we tend to laugh at this period in our lives? When one imagines himself in one of two situations—either challenging the law or defending it, and with no middle way between the two. The hero is a child's dream. No one feels the terror and holiness of being a hero like a child. When I was small, I wanted to be a hero. Now, my wish is to write a hero on paper. That is my modest measure of heroism. (*Sabah al-khayr*, 11 August 1966)

His passion for detective stories led Mahfouz to enter cinema as a writer, with that same goal in mind. His first film was *al-Muntaqim* (The Avenger, 1947), based on the tale of the Upper Egyptian desperado known as "Khutt," his second *Rayya wa Sikina* (Rayya and Sikina, 1953) based on the story of the two celebrated Alexandrian murderesses whose crimes held the whole of Egypt in thrall. Then it was *Ja'aluni mujriman* (They Made Me a Criminal, 1954), followed by *al-Wahsh* (The Beast, 1954), and other early films of his that show his love of crime stories. There was, therefore, nothing strange in Mahfouz's preoccupation with Mahmud Amin Sulayman. In his character he found an embodiment of all the questions whose answers he was seeking during that period. Mahfouz says:

> I remember that one of the regulars at the Casino Opera literary circle told me, "You're going to write about that man, Naguib." I had developed an obsession with him, and the maelstrom inside me made me feel that this man was my chance to put into living form all the reactions and thoughts I'd been keeping to myself and which I hadn't been able to work out how to express—the relation between the individual and authority, his Creator, and his society. I had taken an interest in Mahmud Amin Sulayman's story and that interest had compelled me to thinking of writing about him, and the first thing I felt I needed to think about was *how* to write about him. I found something intimate in him. He was like a part of me. And when I did in fact write about him, it wasn't the story of Mahmud Amin Sulayman but an existential, philosophical tale that gave expression to many things within me that had been crying out for expression.

> From the moment I began writing the story, Mahmud Sulayman ceased to exist. What was there was Said Mahran, a man who leaves prison as one might leave one's mother's womb, looking for something to believe in and to belong to, facing everything that the world contains, good and evil, and dying in the waste land. This was a new character, not Mahmud Sulayman. Said Mahran and Mahmud Sulayman provide an example of the difference between artistic reality and true reality. (Naguib Mahfouz, *Atahaddath ilaykum*, 112)

With Naguib Mahfouz, Said Mahran becomes a "fictional" character far removed from the original. The novel is no longer a mere story of murder and betrayal, but one of philosophical issues. As Mahfouz says, he felt that "this man was my chance to put into living form all the reactions and thoughts I'd been keeping to myself and which I hadn't been able to work out how to express—the relationship between the individual and authority, his Creator, and his society" (Gamal al-Ghitani, *Naguib Mahfouz yatadhakkar*, 70). He found that these preoccupations of his could be expressed in the character of Said Mahran, making *The Thief and the Dogs* both the detective story through which Mahfouz gives expression to the idea of heroism and at the same time an exemplar expressive of his own self. Mahfouz confessed in his interview with Charlotte El Shabrawy, a writer for the *Paris Review*, that he saw himself as Said Mahran, adding:

> At the time I was suffering from a persistent and peculiar sense that I was being pursued, and also the conviction that under the political order of the time our lives had no meaning. So when I wrote the criminal's story, I wrote my own story along with it. A simple crime tale became a philosophical meditation on the times! I subjected the main character, Sayyid Mahran, to all my confusion, my perplexities. I put him through the experience of looking for answers in the sheikh, in the "fallen woman," in the idealist who has betrayed his ideas for money and fame. The writer, you see, is not simply a journalist. He interweaves a story with his own doubts, questions, and values. That is art. (Charlotte El Shabrawy, "Naguib Mahfouz, The Art of Fiction No. 129," *Paris Review*)

The Thief and the Dogs was the first of Naguib Mahfouz's novels to criticize the regime severely and in depth. It was his bullet fired at the errors of the July 1952 revolution and he wrote it straightforwardly, without the symbols or hidden meanings he had used in *Children of the Alley*. In the latter, he had wanted to send a message to the July officers: before you lie two paths; either you choose to be "bullyboys" or you choose to be "prophets." It was clear that they had chosen to be bullyboys. In *The Thief and the Dogs*, Mahfouz was playing a sad tune, a lament for the death, after nine years, of the dreams of the revolution. Despite the talk of "major triumphs" and "the sacred advance of socialism" that adorned the pages of the newspapers, the children of the alley remained downtrodden, without dignity, without justice, without freedom, torn apart by the dogs.

In the novel, Mahfouz broadens the characters' horizons to express the human longing for and need of justice. Said Mahran is no longer the thief, or "the Killer." He has been transformed into a revolutionary with a case to bring against the conditions of an unjust society. His mother is thrown into the street after a famous doctor at Qasr al-'Ayni Hospital refuses to treat her, his wife betrays him and denies him access to his daughter, and his mentor, Rauf Ilwan, whom he wants to kill just as Rauf has killed his past, has turned his back on him. In the end, though, the bullets with which he had hoped to "rip out the betrayal by its roots" miss him, and he dies "meaninglessly" amid the graves.

On publication, the novel gave rise to a major critical debate, and the critics found it hard to classify. Louis Awad regarded it as "classical in form, romantic in content" (Louis Awad, "al-Liss wa-l-kilab," *al-Ahram*, 16 March 1962), while others regarded it as belonging to the existential movement, in that Said Mahran's crisis was (in the eyes of Anwar al-Mi'dawi and Ghali Shukri) an existential crisis (Anwar al-Mi'dawi, "Fi al-riwaya al-misriya al-qasira," *al-Majalla*, August 1962; Ghali Shukri, *al-Muntami: dirasa fi adab Naguib Mahfouz*, 354).

Many critics, however, believed that the novel could not be viewed separately from *Children of the Alley*. Among these were Ghali Shukri, who pointed out that

> we can catch glimpses of most of the ideas found in *Children of the Alley*—the ideas of "the estate," the big house, Gabalawi, the overseers of the estate, the neighborhood bullyboys, and finally Arafa and the serpent—in Mahfouz's remaining works, starting with *The Thief and the Dogs* and ending with *Miramar*. However, in so doing, we will also observe that the change they have undergone is too

great to allow any acknowledgment of the distant original. (Ghali Shukri, *al-Muntami: dirasa fi adab Naguib Mahfouz*, 354)

The Thief and the Dogs was simply a rewriting of the banned novel. Said Mahran was simply one of the "children of the alley," seeking, like his peers, for justice through the use of his own personal prophetic powers, and, like them, failing.

Naguib Mahfouz had learned from his mentor, Salama Musa, that censorship of ideas could never be allowed. In the 1930s, Musa had published his book *al-Ishtirakiya* (Socialism) and it had been confiscated and banned. Mahfouz was unable to read the book even at the National Library, since it was forbidden to issue it to a reader. Later, after Mahfouz and his mentor had met and become friends, he did not ask Musa for a copy, explaining in a personal interview by this author with him that this was because "Salama Musa had expressed the ideas in the book in *al-Majalla al-jadida*, but in different form" (*Akhbar al-adab*, 26 August 2007).

Because for Naguib Mahfouz a novel is a journey of exploration, an open question, he sought to test out the forbidden questions of *Children of the Alley* in his other novels, rewriting it again and again in different forms—in *The Thief and the Dogs*, in *The Search*, in *The Beggar*, in *The Harafish*, and in his short story *Za'balawi*. Ironically, *Children of the Alley* has also been considered a rewriting of the *Trilogy*, the two even being referred to as "one novel" (*Akhbar al-adab*, 3 December 2000). Perhaps this is why he did not insist on its being published when so many, following his winning of the Nobel Prize and again following the attempt on his life, demanded that he do so. His position seemed to mock everyone, as though he were saying, "Seek the same ideas in different shapes in all my works!"

Thus the debate around the novel never ceased. It was a leading topic in all Mahfouz's meetings with visitors, Arabs and non-Arabs, while in his interviews with the press the question was always raised of the "forbidden" novel—would it or would it not be published?—along with other questions about its "real meaning" and what Mahfouz had hoped to achieve with it.

In 2003, the thinker Nasr Abu Zayd returned to Egypt from his exile in the Netherlands to sort out his paperwork with the university prior to his retirement on reaching sixty. On an earlier visit to one of his friends, he had asked the latter to arrange a meeting for him with Naguib Mahfouz. Abu

Zayd had from time to time attended Mahfouz's literary circle at the Café Riche, but they had never spoken privately. At the meeting, on 3 December 2003, Abu Zayd was concerned with *Children of the Alley*. All his questions about this "problematic" novel poured out. First of all, he asked Mahfouz about *The Harafish*. Was it another version of *Children of the Alley*? Mahfouz denied this, saying, "They are two separate novels." Abu Zayd asked, "Why was there an outcry following the publication of *Children of the Alley* when there was no such outcry when Tawfiq al-Hakim wrote *Ahl al-kahf*?" Mahfouz answered, "The reason may lie in the difference of period, or maybe al-Hakim was more successful at explaining his ideas than I was." Mahfouz expressed his sorrow at the passing of the liberal atmosphere of the 1920s and 1930s, which was the opposite of that currently prevailing. Abu Zayd's questions appeared to stem from his desire to understand the secret behind the *Children of the Alley* crisis. Was he engaged in writing something about book-banning at the time, or about Naguib Mahfouz? More to the point, Mahfouz spoke about the novel in detail that day. He spoke, in his mocking way, of a meeting between him and a sheikh from al-Azhar. "He came to meet with me at the Ali Baba café, before the Nobel award, and we discussed *Children of the Alley* at length. Once the sheikh was convinced of my interpretation of the novel, he pulled a copybook out of his pocket and said, 'I've written a play and I'd like you to read it and tell me what you think!'" Abu Zayd then spoke at length about his crisis with the university, Mahfouz listening with interest, sometimes interrupting the conversation with one of his celebrated ironic quips (*Akhbar al-adab*, 28 December 2003).

After his short visit, Abu Zayd returned to his place of exile, for his life too, as a victim of the lack of freedom of research and thought in a still immature society, was threatened, and when Mahfouz died, Abu Zayd wrote a number of articles of farewell. In these, he revisited *Children of the Alley*, which he regarded as the literary expression of a long-established current in modern Egyptian thought in Arabic, a current that went back to Muhammad 'Abduh, the pioneer of modern religious reform, who considered that "religious narrative consists of 'representations' of greater truths that lie behind them." Abu Zayd clarified this by saying

> The novel treats religious narrative as though it were literature, distilling its human and social significations in such a way that the prophets become the defenders of the oppressed and the exploited in the hospice of existence, in the universal sense. The writer

employs the concept of the "bullyboy" to represent power, which may stand with the truth and by so doing even the scales of existence, or with tyranny, and by so doing upset the scales and spread ruin. ("Literature Is Intellectual Resistance," *al-Misri al-yawm*, 12 December 2006)

THE NEGLECTED COMMANDMENTS

Naguib Mahfouz was given two pieces of advice at the start of his literary career. The first came when he was being questioned following the publication of his novel *Cairo Modern*. The interrogator asked him, "Why do you make problems for yourself writing about the scandals of the rich and powerful? Write about love. It would be better for you, and safer."

The second came from Ibrahim 'Abd al-Qadir al-Mazini, at their only meeting. Al-Mazini told him, "What you're writing is realist literature, and that kind of literature causes its writers all sorts of problems because the common idea about literature is that it's about personal confessions. If you're going to go on being a writer of realist literature, you'll bring hardship and headaches upon yourself without even realizing it" (Raga' al-Naqqash, *Naguib Mahfouz: safahat min mudhakkaratihi*, 75). Mahfouz paid no attention to either recommendation. He didn't write about love, and hardship and headaches pursued him from the day he began writing.

When he received copies of his first novel, *Khufu's Wisdom*, from his publisher, he took one to the home of Sheikh Mustafa 'Abd al-Raziq, his teacher at Fu'ad I University's department of philosophy. On arrival, Mahfouz found a number of sheikhs from al-Azhar visiting 'Abd al-Raziq. When these looked at the book, they were incensed at its title. Mahfouz was taken aback by the attack, but the sheikh saved the situation by defending his student.

When he finished his second novel, *Radubis (Rhadopis of Nubia)*, published in 1943, the censor refused to allow it to be published, on the grounds that it was "an inflammatory work" because the people in the book rise up against a king who has abandoned himself to the indulgence of his personal pleasures, and he asked that the ending be changed. Mahfouz explained that it was just a story from history and that it would be difficult to change the ending because to do so would be to distort history. The censor then gave him permission to publish it, the main reason perhaps being that the stories about the king's (Faruq I's) womanizing were not yet widely known.

Following the appearance of his novel *Cairo Modern*, he was called in for questioning because he criticizes the government in it and the work was read as though it consisted simply of essays criticizing its members. During questioning, the interrogator, Ahmad Hussein (brother of Dr. Taha Hussein), asked him, "What are you getting at?" He replied, "They are imaginary scenes. I don't have particular persons in mind. This is a novel like the ones your brother Taha Hussein taught us to appreciate." A few years later, Mahfouz agreed to change the title of the novel to *Fadiha fi al-Qahira* (A Scandal in Cairo) in response to a request from Ihsan Abdel Kouddous, who wanted to publish it in his series al-Kitab al-Dhahabi (The Golden Book) and was afraid that people would understand from the original title that the novel criticized the society of the 1952 revolution.

When he submitted his novel *The Mirage*, published in 1948, for the Arabic Language Academy's award, the academy rejected it for "moral" reasons, one member telling him that "I understand very well what you wrote, but our social environment here will never accept such things. We are an official institution and if we encouraged such literature, it would mean that we officially acknowledged it, which is a responsibility we cannot assume" (Raga' al-Naqqash, *Naguib Mahfouz: safahat min mudhakkaratihi*, 150). This was not the only problem the novel caused him. A certain habitué of a café Mahfouz regularly patronized, who knew Mahfouz, believed that he was the person on whom the novel's main character, Kamil Ru'ba Laz, who was impotent, was based. The man loaded a revolver and determined on killing Mahfouz, but Mahfouz went for a whole year without going near the café and, to put an end to the matter, phoned the angry bearer of the revolver to point out to him the vast differences between him and the character in the novel and asked him to assure himself of that by reading the book.

The publication of *The Beginning and the End* in 1949 passed quietly but, after the revolution, Anwar al-Sadat met with Mahfouz in Ihsan Abdel Kouddous's office and told him, "I'm upset with you." "Why, God forbid?" Mahfouz asked. Al-Sadat answered reproachfully, "How could you make the officer in *The Beginning and the End* kill himself? Don't you know that the officer is us?" (Ahmad Hashim al-Sharif, *Naguib Mahfouz: muhawarat ma qabl Nubil*, 60).

Publication of the *Trilogy* (1956–57) also passed without incident, with the exception of a few reviews that labeled him as "bourgeois." In the late 1950s and through the 1960s, Mahfouz would return to form and write one of his most critical works, *Children of the Alley*, a novel that exposed the dictatorship and criticized the nationalization of the public sphere, and in which Mahfouz would go so far as to write, "Overpowered by fear, the overseer and his men sent their spies everywhere to search homes and shops and impose the cruelest punishments for the slightest offenses. They beat people with sticks for a look, a joke, a laugh, until the alley endured a nightmarish atmosphere of fear, hatred and terrorism" (*Children of the Alley*, trans. Theroux, 416).

Influential members of the Nasserist regime were so infuriated by *Adrift on the Nile* (1966), *Miramar* (1967), and some of Mahfouz's short stories that Field Marshal 'Abd al-Hakim 'Amir would have had Mahfouz arrested were it not for Abd al-Nasser's personal last-minute intervention.

At the start of the 1970s, *al-Hubb taht al-matar (Love in the Rain)*, published in 1973, and *al-Karnak (Karnak Café)*, published in 1974, were subjected to the censor's savage scissors, the deletions seriously disfiguring both novels.

With each new novel, a storm and a crisis. In the midst of those storms, however, Mahfouz protected himself. His storytelling remained neutral, giving the impression of not accusing or seeking to direct, a narrative that placed on its heroes', and not its writer's, shoulders the responsibility for what they said or did. The writer was merely a witness, an uninvolved sage, a god observing and mocking. This may explain why the storms passed. *Children of the Alley*, however, was different.

As a novel, it is central to Mahfouz's world. What came before was pure realism, what came after was always experimental and distanced from classical realism. The novel bore the burden of what one might describe as the transition from the society of the oral to that of the written, with the narrator responding to the recommendation of Arafa, one of the righteous children of the alley: "You are one of the few who know how to write, so why don't you write the story of our alley? Right now it is subject to the preferences and partisanship of those who tell it, so it would be good if it could be noted down honestly, in a single, complete, form, so that good use can be made of it."

Mahfouz, as narrator, wrote down the spoken stories that are passed from generation to generation as a way of speaking of his dream—his dream of justice and of the rule of knowledge, his dream, and all humankind's, that life might be passed in the garden, with flute and song, and that the alley might witness the demise of the tyrants and the dawn of the light. The novel was a parable of our relationship to the authority that chokes humankind until it can no longer breathe, be that authority political, religious, or societal. It follows that all the latter were disturbed by the novel's ability to strip them naked and expose them for what they are, making the novel Mahfouz's great "sin" in the eyes of them all.

Children of the Alley was a special case. According to Mahfouz's own description, it became no longer a novel in which he raised his usual questions about justice and freedom; it had instead become an enactment of the story of our relationship with authority and censorship, the story of society itself and its yearning to think outside the red lines. It became both a book and the symbol of a political, social, and cultural battle that is not yet over but which takes, with each era, a new and fascinating form. It is as though Mahfouz, in writing it, brought to life—without realizing or intending to do so—the old dream of Kamal 'Abd al-Gawad (his spirit double, or portrait, in the *Trilogy*, in the eyes of most critics). Kamal used to

> dream of writing a book. What book? It would not be poetry. There was poetry in his diary, but it originated with Aïda, who changed prose into poetry, not with any poetic gift of his. Thus the book would be prose. It would be a large, bound volume about the size and shape of the Holy Qur'an, and, like the Qur'an, its pages would have margins filled with notes and commentaries. But what would he write about? The Qur'an embraced everything, did it not? There was no cause for him to despair. He would find his subject one day. It was enough for him to know the size, shape, and style of annotation for the book. Surely a book that would shake the world was better than a civil service position, even if the latter shook the world too. Every educated person knew about Socrates. Who remembered the judges who had presided at his trial? (Mahfouz, *Palace of Desire*, 65–66)

Mahfouz lived through the days of sultans, kings, and presidents. He was there during revolutions and coups, wars, plagues, and catastrophes. He lived through political upheavals and sharp twists in the road, through revolutions, regimes, and wars, from the Naksa to the War of Attrition and the October War, from the 1919 revolution to the July 1952 revolution and Camp David, and from the Nobel Prize to the villainous dagger that was plunged into his neck. He was able to endure in the face of the upheavals, storms, and changes that afflicted society and culture and he was able to endure in the face of fundamentalist hatred. And he was able, throughout the years of his life, which covered almost a century, as also after his death, to maintain his impact and effectiveness and become a symbol across time.

Fashions have changed and esthetic criteria have been upended. Names have changed and great writers have retired to the museum of "history." Yet he remains in place, provoking interest, admiration, and raucous debate. Mahfouz continued to resist every obstacle that might come between him and writing.

The accusations upset him, but he faced them with a whole-hearted laugh that would ring out from time to time. When a journalist asked him to imagine a rehearsal for the Final Reckoning and decide for himself whether his good or his bad deeds would weigh heavier in the scales, Mahfouz laughed for a long time before replying, "I haven't killed anyone in my whole life. I haven't stolen and I haven't committed any major sins. All my sins have been little ones and won't weigh heavily in the scale. If 'one good deed is worth ten bad,' then the scales will definitely be in my favor" ('Abd al-Hayy, *'Asir hayati*, 134).

As we have seen, *Children of the Alley* remained in the spotlight from the time it was first published as a serial in *al-Ahram* in the fall of 1959 and continued to be there even after Mahfouz's death, when it appeared for the first time in Egypt as a book, accompanied by an introduction that was like a theological writ granting absolution to a work of art and fiction.

APPENDIX: DOCUMENTS

"On Bernard Shaw's *Back to Methuselah*"

This essay by Naguib Mahfouz was published in al-Ma'rifa *(founder and editor-in-chief, 'Abd al-'Aziz al-Islambuli; April/May 1934). Reference is made to a second part to the essay to be published in the forthcoming issue; however, consensus has it that this was the last issue published. Despite this, the critic 'Abd al-Muhsin Taha Badr refers in his* al-Ru'ya wa-l-adah *(Vision and Instrument) to having seen the second part of the essay; he also refers to a third part.*

To start with, Methuselah is a patriarch. It is said that he lived so long that he passed the nine-hundred-year mark by half a century or so. To go back to him, therefore, is to take humanity back to the long lifespans of old, the point being to introduce the pivotal concept that underlies the plot and which will be revealed to the reader later. In a word, the writer aims to write a history of so-called Creative Evolution. He begins with the story of Adam and Eve and brings into the picture the eternal desire for the "philosopher's stone" that gives people the power to conquer death's sting. In addition, the story is a review of the defects of civilized life, especially its political side, as acted out through the plot.

We are somewhere in the Garden of Eden where Adam and Eve are sitting. Close to them lives a serpent, whose head is hidden, and there is a fawn with a broken neck. The fawn has attracted Adam and Eve's attention with its motionless and unnerving appearance, which has scared the man into wondering what if he, too, should trip and break his neck and his life be extinguished. Eve senses some of what he is going through and each commiserates with the other at the idea that one of them should leave their companion behind on that eternal migration, abandoning them to a lonely life without a companion. All the same, Eve is amazed at Adam's fear, because he is always going back and forth between anger at immortality and fear of death! Adam picks up the fawn and takes it away to throw it into the river. While he is absent, the serpent moves and speaks to Eve in her own language, which the long time she has spent listening to Eve's dialogue with Adam has allowed her to learn. The serpent speaks to Eve when she sees how afraid she is of death and tells her of its cure, which is birth and resurrection. She cites herself as an example: she gives birth to new serpents; Lilith did the same when the idea of death caused her pain and she gave birth to Adam and Eve! To create is not impossible: you just have to have the desire and the imagination; then you make a wish and create. And why not? Was not Eve unable to climb trees? Did she not desire, imagine, and make a wish, and then create the muscles and the willingness that enabled her to climb trees? In other words creation consists of practice and effort. Eve must not hesitate if she wishes to overcome death and the horror of death. When Adam returns, Eve rushes to him and tells him everything that has transpired between her and the serpent. The man is pleased, but conceives a fear that whatever may be born to the serpent will kill him. All the same, he feels a strange tranquillity and believes he hears a voice telling him that no harm will come to him from whatever may be born. He confesses to Eve that it is the same voice that has turned him against the idea of killing her. At this point, Eve tells him, "The Voice does not tell me not to kill you. Yet I do not want you to die before me. No voice is needed to make me feel that." Adam says, "Oh no: that is plain without any voice. There is something that holds us together, something that has no word . . . "

The Serpent: "Love. Love. Love."

Adam: "That is too short a word for so long a thing."

The Serpent: "Love may be too long a word for so short a thing soon. But when it is short it will be very sweet."

Adam: "You puzzle me. My old trouble was heavy; but it was simple and the marvels you promise may tangle up my being before they bring me the gift of death. I was troubled with the burden of eternal being, but I was not confused in my mind. If I did not know that I loved Eve, at least I did not know that she might cease to love me, and come to love some other Adam and desire my death. Can you find a name for that knowledge?"

The Serpent: "Jealousy. Jealousy. Jealousy."

Adam: "How can I help brooding when the future has become uncertain? Anything is better than uncertainty. Life has become uncertain. Love is uncertain. Have you a word for this new misery?"

The Serpent: "Fear. Fear. Fear." Then Adam says, "Have you a remedy for it?" and the serpent says, "Yes. Hope. Hope. Hope." He asks, "What is hope?" and she says, "As long as you do not know the future you do not know that it will not be happier than the past. That is hope."

Adam: "It does not console me. Fear is stronger in me than hope. I must have certainty. Give it to me; or I will kill you when next I catch you asleep." Eve says, "My beautiful snake. Oh no. How can you even think such a horror?" Then the serpent says to Adam: "Bind the future by your will. Make a vow."

Adam: "What is a vow?" The serpent replies, "Choose a day for your death; and resolve to die on that day. Then death is no longer uncertain but certain. Let Eve vow to love you until your death. Then love will be no longer uncertain." Eve protests, "But it will destroy hope." Adam says, angrily, "Be silent, woman. Hope is wicked. Happiness is wicked. Certainty is blessed."

The Serpent: "What is wicked?" Adam answers, "Whatever I fear to do is wicked. Listen to me, Eve; and you, snake, listen too, that your memory may hold my vow. I will live a thousand sets of the four seasons—"

The Serpent: "A thousand years? A thousand years?" Adam repeats: "Yes, I will live a thousand years; and then I will endure no more: I will die and take my rest. And I will love Eve all that time and no other woman," and Eve says: "And if Adam keeps his vow I will love no other man."

The serpent exclaims that they have invented marriage. Then she takes Eve aside so as to divulge to her the secret of this "marriage." She whispers in Eve's ear and her face brightens with joy, which is soon replaced with repugnance, and she buries her face in her hands.

Centuries pass. Adam has fallen from Eden and lives with Eve. Here he is digging and here she is spinning. They no longer retain the fresh garb of youth but have submitted to the rule of time, which has stripped them of its bloom and let old age have its way with them. For the first time, a new human appears alongside them. It is Cain, swathed in a warrior's cloak and full of the pride and conceit of a fighter. The misunderstanding and patent anger that stand between father and son are there for all to see, the son's sin being that he killed his brother Abel. He offers as an excuse that it was his brother who invented fire and killing and that he had put an end to his life in just the same way that Abel had put an end to the life of other things, and that in any case he was not grieved by what he had done and in fact was proud of it because his life, in his view, was more full of greatness than his father's. What did Adam's life consist of other than digging? To boast of being a digger is like boasting of having been created a man! He, for his part, could take pride in being the first murderer, and the life of a murderer was one of power and freedom!

Eve does not like her son's words and is afraid that Adam will be influenced by him. She heaps reproach upon her son for boasting of something that deserves neither boasting nor praise and rebukes him for claiming for himself a power and freedom that he does not in fact possess, for he is a captive to his wife, who drives him to do battle with wild animals through some silent power of suggestion, since he knows happiness only at the moment when he throws his prey at her feet, proud of his strength and brutality. When all is said and done, he is nothing but a destroyer. If he had known the torment and toil that she had to produce and build, his logical faculties would not have let him think so foolishly. However, the young man is not fazed by his mother's words and keeps insisting that he would rather be upbraided for his way of life than be like his father. When his father looks to the soil and declares that it is the source of life, he looks to the sky, and he says that the soil is the source of all diseases. His fury at the soil and everything about it that pertains to food and reproduction increases and he wonders, "If this is all that humans have, what's the difference between them and bears?" The father gets angrier and angrier and the son more and more arrogant until they are in danger of doing one another harm. This causes Eve to intervene to calm them down. When she sees that they are inclined to be quiet, she confesses that she is not content with either Adam's way of life or Cain's. The first bores her with its monotony and repetition, the second repels her with its cruelty and destruction. The only thing that consoles her and makes things easier to bear is hope for the future. She has begun to sense harbingers of good things that hold out a promise of happiness, meaning the things that some of her sons are starting to achieve. One gazes at the stars, gives them names, and takes note of their movements. Another has made for her this wonderful spinning wheel. A third wanders through the forest listening for the Voice, which will inspire in him ideas with which he can guide his brothers. These are her hope for the future, the ones who are building and creating new things without being enchanted by the knife or dazzled by the excitement of fighting. Cain appears not to understand what she has said and he takes his accoutrements and leaves. Adam goes back to his digging, and she sits and spins, saying, "Man need not always live by bread alone. There is something else. We do not yet know what it is; but some day we shall find out; and then we will live on that alone; and there shall be no more digging nor spinning, nor fighting nor killing."

We are now in the period after the Great War, in a room in the house of Franklyn Barnabas, a former clergyman, and his brother, Conrad Barnabas, a biologist. The brothers are men of talent who live for the betterment of humankind. They have agreed that human life is too short to allow the individual to achieve the wisdom and insight that he craves. Franklyn left the church when he saw that he still needed 150 years to achieve wisdom. Conrad wants to live to 960, like the patriarch Methuselah, so that he can attain true scientific knowledge.

As we listen pleasurably to their conversation, the rector, Haslam, enters, followed by his fiancée Savvy, who is Franklyn's daughter. They have hardly settled down before a third person, Mr. Burge, enters. He is a prominent political figure; suffice it to say that he was prime minister during the war and is now leader of the opposition. He has not come just for a visit but has a political objective in mind: he has heard that Mr. Franklyn intends to "make a move." Does the move have a political goal? If so, is the gentleman one of his supporters or an opponent? The situation is critical, and the people are unhappy with the present government, which represents none of them. Franklyn, however, has absolutely no desire to engage in political propaganda and has not given a thought to politics. Politics, in its current form, cannot attract him, and he gives Mr. Burge his frank opinion of the styles and elections of politicians, which he sees as worthless, comical farces.

During this conversation, the maid enters and announces the arrival of Mr. Lubin, Burge's old boss and prime minister before the war. Between the two men there is fierce competition, repressed antagonism, and mutual contempt. Everyone discusses politics and whether politicians think of anything other than politics, as though the world had been created to serve as a battleground for their elections and as though people only existed to support them and hand them the reins of government. In the end, Savvy grows bored with the talk and makes fun of it, suggesting that her father and uncle inform the two politicians of their new gospel.

The politicians are aghast, thinking that the brothers intend to set up a new party to crowd them out of the arena, but Conrad assures them that such an idea could never appeal to them. What then could this gospel be? At this point, Franklyn says, "Our program is only that the term of human life shall be extended to three hundred years." Savvy says, "Our election cry is 'Back to Methuselah.'" But what does all this have to do with politics? Here, Franklyn begins explaining his book, or gospel, saying, "Politicians die just as they reach the age of discernment. They die just as a flicker of light shines over their darkling souls. Their lives must, therefore, be extended until they can reach wisdom and benefit from the experience of the centuries." When Mr. Lubin hears this, he agrees but can see no point in going into it: we must hold on to the birds in our hands even if the heavens fall. The two men ask Conrad whether he has discovered the elixir of life. Will he offer it to them in the form of food or give it to them to drink? The scientist tells them that he is sorry but he is speaking to them about science; they must not come toward him with mouths open and eyes closed. Lubin, however, does not put a great deal of trust in science, pointing to the repeated mistakes made by scientists. His trust in poetry is, perhaps, greater, a point to which Franklyn agrees, citing as an example of the truth of poetry the legend of Eden. Then he says, "Well, you remember, don't you, that in the Garden of Eden Adam and Eve were not created mortal, and that natural death, as we call it, was not a part of life, but a later and quite separate invention?" When Lubin objects that unnatural death existed, Franklyn continues, saying, "Precisely. Adam and Eve were hung up between two frightful possibilities. One was the extinction of mankind by their accidental death. The other was the prospect of living forever. They could bear neither. They decided that they would just take a short turn of a thousand years, and meanwhile hand on their work to a new pair. Consequently, they had to invent natural birth and natural death, which are, after all, only modes of perpetuating life without putting on any single creature the terrible burden of immortality."

Life, then, is eternal, even if individuals get worn out, and we are its repeated representations. It proceeds toward unlimited omnipotence and omniscience, which have to remain unlimited if life is to have room for us. Lubin asks him about the origin of sin and Franklyn answers him by saying that in Eden, Adam lived safe from death. It was his eternal home so he took great care to preserve it and take care of it. When natural death was invented and he became a tenant in the house and not its owner, his concern for it waned. He even dared to beat Eve, when before, if anything harmed her, he had felt pity for her, so he ended up alone and companionless. When his sons came, they reached his age and more, and there was killing and there was conflict and there was suffering. This is the story of Eden, and you can call it "phylogenesis" if you are one of those people who love scientific names. Evolution is not a large phenomenon that generates power. We are an experiment it is conducting. If we welcome success, it will let us survive, and if we think we are a failed experiment, it will put an end to us and come up with something else. How many creatures have become extinct leaving nothing but their traces in ancient rocks!

This is all well and good, but what is the path to a lifespan of three hundred years? Is there an elixir or some such? The fact is there is no elixir or anything else. The most that can happen is, in Franklyn's words, that "we can put it into men's heads that there is nothing to prevent its happening but their own will to die before their work is done, and their own ignorance of the splendid work there is for them to do."

Lubin and Burge are disappointed. Their mindset is persuaded only by material things; will and psychological conviction are another matter! Do we not all want to live three hundred years, despite which it is not granted to us to pass our allotted span? Conrad, however, does not believe this and says, pettishly, "Everybody would like to have a million of money. Why haven't they? Because the men who would like to be millionaires won't save sixpence even with the chance of starvation staring them in the face. The men who want to live forever won't cut off a glass of beer or a pipe of tobacco, although they believe the teetotalers and non-smokers live longer. That sort of liking is not willing. See what they do when they know they must."

These ideas are beyond Lubin, and he despairs of lengthening his life. Burge believes he can turn the issue into the basis for an electoral battle, and Haslam does not believe any of it. Even his fiancée Savvy has strong doubts about it, finding it absurd that the parlor maid could live for centuries and get back to Methuselah. The two brothers, on the other hand, are unassailed by doubts. But will any of them live so long? That is something no one knows.

It is 2170, in England again and in the parlor of the president, who looks like both Mr. Burge and Mr. Lubin. We are aware of progress in terms of material culture: the president speaks to the health minister by telephone, from a distance of many miles, and can see him and the place where he is sitting as though they were just feet away. We are astounded to see that control over public services is in the hands of foreigners: the health minister is a negro from Africa, the chief secretary is named Confucius and is from China. The reason for this, as stated by Confucius, is that, following a devastating war, the English have become convinced that they are unfit to govern themselves and have handed things over to others. The machinery of government is now well ordered and the government is free to think about policy. An English civil servant, who looks very much like Conrad Barnabas, enters to see the president. He seems upset and makes violent motions. The president had earlier sent him in his place to meet an American inventor who has invented a machine for breathing under water and had seen it fit that the government should show the American a reel of film representing the great men who have died by drowning. Barnabas has beheld the following great men—Bishop Stickit, Minister Dickenson, and General Bullyboy. He has examined them minutely and to his extreme astonishment discovered that these persons and the current Archbishop of York are one and the same. True, there is no great resemblance between them but it is one essence. The president and chief secretary are amazed at what the civil servant has said, and even more so when the Archbishop of York joins them. He looks very much like the rector Haslam, Savvy's fiancé, whom we met two centuries ago. He has barely taken his place before Barnabas accuses him of being a thief because he is still collecting a salary from the state after passing the legal retirement age, which is around forty. The archbishop sees that it is necessary that he clear away the clouds enveloping the matter, so he tells them a story of which he claims to be the hero. They are nearly struck dumb, they are so astonished. He tells them that in 1924 he married the daughter of the Franklyn from whose family the current Barnabas is also descended. He had read a book by his wife's uncle announcing the good news that humans would live for three hundred years. The days passed, his wife died, and nothing whatsoever happened to him. So it occurred to him that he was indeed going to live for a very long time. At the end of each lifespan, and after having become known as one personality, he would rid himself of it and take on a new one. He did this by going to the seashore, leaving his clothes there, and traveling to some distant land, so that people thought that he had drowned. Using this method, he was sometimes a bishop, had assumed the post of president once, and had been head of the army once. Now he was getting on for two hundred and fifty years of age! When Haslam finishes his story, each person present is affected in a different way. Barnabas does not believe him, Burge-Lubin is very suspicious, and Confucius thinks and thinks in the hope that he may be guided to the light of certainty in the midst of this impenetrable darkness. While they are thus occupied with accusations and doubt, a lady minister enters to see the president on some matter of state. She is a woman of awe-inspiring presence, despite her youthfulness, but as soon as her eyes meet those of Bishop Haslam, she is taken aback, as is he, and he tells her that he remembers having seen her in some place and at some time that his memory refuses to help him identify. All that he remembers is that she was opening a door for him to let him through. The lady minister is also amazed, because it seems to her too that she was receiving him and letting him through a door, but where, and when? Confucius asks the bishop if he knows anyone who has lived as long as he has, but the other does not. He has hidden it from everyone because he knows that people, like animals, hurt those who are unlike them. The lady minister now remembers the bishop and confesses to him that she is his fiancée Savvy's parlor maid who received him at Barnabas's house in 1924! She tells him how she had read Barnabas's book and it had made the sort of impression on her that only an uneducated person could feel. She had married and lived a hard life of drudgery without tasting any of life's sweetness or leisure. Then her husband died and she was amazed to find that she retained, and continued to do so over all these years, her youth and the bloom of her childhood. Then she thought about the fact that she would live to a very great age, as she had read in Barnabas's book, and was overtaken by terror, as she had been unable to bear life when it was short, so how was she to put up with it for three hundred years? What consoled her and gave her resolve was the exponential progress that had accompanied political and social life, which had made her live for herself until she came to hold a place in the cabinet! Burge-Lubin casts doubtful glances at her. The truth has nonplussed him and he dares to ask a question: "Have you never married?" She answers that long ago she married an eighty-year-old painter and lived with him for a period. The man died just as he was starting to create truly great work. He died at the instant that the gates of Heaven opened to him! He asks her again why she didn't marry again at that age? Was it because she did not want to have to deal with the childishness of another eighty-year-old? And does she think he was happy, at his age, to marry a twelve-year-old girl? A wonderful conversation ensues between the bishop and the lady minister about the English way of life, which they subject to withering criticism. The English shrink away from important work and leave it to the negroes and the Chinese. It is not unlikely that the day will come when the English become servants in their own country! They note that it is the yellow, black, and brown minds that are creative now and come up with new inventions, just as in the old days it was the Scots, the Germans, the Jews, and the Italians. The English are now happy just to play golf and other such childish games. Naturally, the bishop and the lady minister are attracted to one another and they get up to leave, each having it in mind that they will marry the other. Barnabas guesses their intention and bars their way, but they leave in spite of him. Barnabas proposes that they be killed and, if need be, that a legal age limit be established for the very old. Might they not give birth to children like them and their offspring spread, making them children in comparison to them? Is it not probable that their stature should also increase in keeping with the age, making them dwarves beside them?

Confucius hears Barnabas out but is not persuaded and can see no good in them. Barnabas grows angry and leaves in a fury. Confucius approaches the president and says, "The English could achieve wisdom if they could only reach adulthood, but there is no possibility of that happening so long as they go on dying as children," and mocks their claim to exist to be masters and take over the leadership of other peoples. He compares it to the claims of a jealous child who will not let go of a wooden toy he is playing with. He asks the man, "I wonder if there are other people like the bishop and the lady minister. Who knows? Perhaps they are themselves destined to live extremely long lives."

While they are talking, the negro lady health minister invites the president to a picnic which involves his being parachuted into Fishguard Bay. He hesitates, which is unusual for him when this woman invites him anywhere. Life was once short and ephemeral, and he used to depend on that and never let anything make him forego an hour of pleasure. Now, though, that he might live on like others, for a long time, how can he risk such a precious treasure? Suppose he survives the parachute, might he not be smitten by rheumatism for three hundred years? No, no! It would be better to refuse the invitation than to risk all that. This time he takes it easy and suffers the indignity of the negro woman's anger. Confucius is happy with this outcome in which the spirit of wisdom has overcome the instinct for revelry and sport and that the man has become a wise, sensible coward! Burge-Lubin pays no attention to this characterization. Coward or not, only one thing concerns him and makes him worry and that is his safety, given that he may now live for three hundred years!

My New Direction and the Future of the Novel

Article by Naguib Mahfouz published in al-Katib *magazine in February 1964.*

At the writers' conference in Moscow, the French novelist Alain Robbe-Grillet stood up and announced that the novel had exhausted all topics and that nothing was left to the novelist but form. By so doing, Robbe-Grillet was offering a justification for the new form, or method, he has been following in his novels and which some critics have dubbed "the phenomenological school." Robbe-Grillet describes ordinary things at great length, as though he were a naturalist who has happened on some rare find and made a complete descriptive study of it. For example, he describes, over a number of pages, a doorknob or a window so accurately and at such length that it becomes boring—more than boring, in fact, or so boring that the abundance of superfluous detail leaves the reader confused as to the point the writer is making.

Through this prolixity of description and his amazed and curious interest in things, Robbe-Grillet seeks to revoke the individual's familiarity with the objects that he sees and uses in his daily life and create a kind of alienation between nature/the universe and the individual, and especially with those manifestations of the physical world that are closest to the individual, namely the tools he uses and the places he constantly inhabits. He wants to say that the individual is alone in the universe and that any real connection between him and what is outside of him has been severed. He goes so far in his denial of everything that he even accuses a writer such as Jean-Paul Sartre of having faith!

This exaggerated attention to form that has spread among writers of the modern novel is the result of a paucity of subject matter and of the charges directed by critics at the novel as an art, charges that allege that the novel is finished as a literary genre because it has touched on everything and has been left with nothing with which to engage.

It is true that the novel has touched on every conceivable field. It has dealt with the individual, society, and the family. It has dealt with streets, cities, and even continents. Dos Pasos, for example, has circumambulated more than one continent in his stories; they have, in fact, crossed the continents, the entire earth, and ascended to the stars. There is, likewise, no human emotion that has not been the repeated subject of the novel, and over long periods.

Those who view the novel from this perspective have decided that it has outlived its purpose, and this has thrown contemporary novelists into a crisis, as they have the sense that everything they think of doing has been thought of before and everything they want to say has been said before!

These novelists have, therefore, focused on form, and the novel, at their hands, has begun to take the same direction as the plastic arts. It has been transformed into something purely formal, to which content is extraneous.

However, if we take these opinions as an excuse to bury the novel, we shall have to bury all literature—nay, all other arts—along with it. Art has already touched, in general terms, upon every topic. When the arts are considered as a whole, every subject has been used more than once. However, the matter is not that simple. What has been used renews itself, just as life renews itself, and what is new is never the already-touched-upon subject, but the artist. The artist is an individual and an age and a civilization. Each generation gives its point of view on subjects that are constant throughout time.

If we speak of resemblance and difference, it is useful to bear in mind that when we look at people from an airplane at a certain height above the earth, everyone seems to look the same. When we get closer to them, however, we are surprised at all the ways in which they differ. The individual members of humankind, taken as an organic whole, do not differ. In every individual there is a certain fixed percentage of minerals and compounds that does not vary from one person to another, yet despite that each individual has their essence, or something that distinguishes them. In terms of the arts, the question is not that of whether something is old or new but of the function it performs in deepening and enriching life through experience, and the contribution that this richness of understanding and experience makes to the development of human life as a whole. I do not believe that art should be judged on how new it is but on the pleasure and benefit that it brings into being. This is the criterion by which the entire human heritage has been judged, and on its basis many literary and artistic works have seen their lifespans curtailed, while others have lasted the test of time.

If we take the emotion of love, for example, what is there in it that is new (setting aside here the question of its relationship to the novel or its occurrence as one of its subjects)? If we measure this emotion with the yardstick of newness, we will have to kill it off and have nothing more to do with it!

It is not the subject itself that is important, when we look at it from the esthetic, artistic, and critical perspectives. To follow the domestic incidents reported in any daily newspaper is to discover dozens of stories. In some lower-class neighborhood we will find a tale like the plot of *Othello* and others identical to those of *Hamlet* and *Lear*. But these tales do not rise to the level of art simply by virtue of having been recounted. Art is the way in which the subject is handled or treated.

This being so, there is no danger to the novel as an art form. On the contrary, it will remain well loved for as long as the desire and need for literature remain in people's hearts and reading matter remains available, easily accessed, and not surpassed. André Gide has said, "We write in the hope of finding a reader who hasn't read the works that were written before us."

The crisis of the novel is not, moreover, universal. In many other countries, such as the Soviet Union, India, and China, novelists do not voice the complaints that we hear in France, England, and Italy, whose conceptual paradigms are never, at the present time, free of the crisis. "Paucity of subject matter" translates into other words that lie behind that concept, namely, "We have no subjects and we hold no values." When an individual holds no values, all subjects worthy of treatment are nullified. When an individual holds no values, life becomes meaningless and trivial, unworthy of treatment. Europe's crisis is that it no longer believes in anything. It no longer believes in life, or in anything after or before life. Without faith in something, writing becomes a performance in a vacuum, and when an inclination toward literature appears in someone in such a nihilistic atmosphere, it immerses itself in form, seeing this as its sole remaining refuge. Thus the issue of art for art's sake returns in its true sense, a sense that has never been applied to European art in any age to the extent that it is now, and not only with regard to literature, but to music and the plastic arts too.

A further phenomenon worthy of attention in the art of the modern novel is the metaphysical tendency. While it is true that novels never fail to contain some philosophical concepts, the modern tendency in the novel grants metaphysical philosophy much space.

This is a further indicator of the European cultural crisis. During the periods of stability and industrial efflorescence that Europe experienced before being torn apart by modern contradictions, experimental science was its ruling principle. It flourished, ignoring spiritual values. Just as the human body may suffer a biological or psychological crisis, so may a culture, and just as the human rouses himself from his crisis to seek refuge in spiritual values, so does culture. When an individual, and likewise a culture, go bankrupt, they remember God. Europe believed in science, then lost its faith in it and, as a result, began to turn to metaphysics. If a writer may be permitted to speak of his own experience in a general matter such as the future of the novel, I will permit myself to use as an example my novel *Children of the Alley*, since it does, in fact, reflect my thoughts on the crisis of the modern age.

In this novel, Science (Arafa) thinks that it has no need of Gabalawi, so it kills him. This outcome leads Arafa to a sense of emptiness and of the bitterness of life. It is the same conclusion that Albert Camus reached when he decided that life has no meaning and only absurdity is meaningful.

From an objective standpoint, the refusal to acknowledge any higher meaning to life, though it may find evidence and proofs, has no stronger a basis than the possibility of the existence of such meaning, and this refusal, whose soundness cannot be categorically affirmed, is a moral error that drives the individual to the furthest reaches of despair. When people had faith in society, the realistic novel and the pastoral novel emerged. Then, when the era of doubts about society and the mind began, all the old questions that success had consigned to oblivion returned and began insisting on answers.

It may be said, concerning the future of the novel, that the distinguishing mark of this new age is the asking of questions and the attempt to answer them, and that intellectual debate is the main characteristic of contemporary thought. It would follow that the literary form most appropriate to the crisis of the age is the theater, given that the theater is the art form that depends most basically on debate, dialogue, and the clash of ideas. Based on this, those who speak of the end of the age of the novel believe that the prevailing metaphysical posture cannot find its best expression within that framework; it can find it only in the theater. This is, to some degree, true. The novel may have paled a little compared to the energy that has overtaken the theater. The current crisis will not be forever; progress continues on its way and what seems now to be the first signs of the crisis for the European societies may be the end of a culture rather than the end of humanity.

Despite this, the novel in general has not stood idly by, observing the new situation. It has changed its approach and discovered a new technique, which explains the new experiments in the contemporary novel. When novels concerned themselves with life in and of itself, the traditional narrative was the style most appropriate, with the human character appearing with all its details. But when life itself becomes a problem, the human being is no longer a specific person but rather a mere human. He is not a person in and of him- or herself, distinguished from other people by his or her peculiar and specific details. It follows that details disappear, narrative disappears, and discussion takes precedence over all other elements. *Children of the Alley*, for example, even though it chronicles the entire history of humanity, is shorter than any one part of a novel such as *The Cairo Trilogy*. When mankind finds itself face to face with its destiny, details lose their value. This is the difference between Arafa, hero of *Children of the Alley*, and Kamal Ahmad 'Abd al-Gawad, hero of the *Trilogy*. However, if the novel should try to renew itself after the fashion described by Robbe-Grillet, it certainly will cease to exist. The strange thing is that Robbe-Grillet does not believe in anything, even science.

The future of the novel in the light of the circumstances of the age may be a problem to writers whose values have collapsed, and the search for new techniques may be important for them. In my experiments with the novel, however, I have not been aware of any acute problem of technique. On the contrary, I have solved any such problems with the greatest of ease: the subject matter which I ponder, and my reactions to it, are what define the form for me, without any great effort and without fretting over whether it is old or new. Technique, as far as I am concerned, is either appropriate or inappropriate.

When I was preoccupied with life and its meaning, the most appropriate style for me was realism, and it was in this style that, for many long years, I presented my works. The details, whether of the social environment, the characters, or the events, were extremely important. It is a style that reflects life in all its aspects, one from which ideas may follow, albeit indirectly.

Now, though, that abstract ideas and a sensitivity to them have started to preoccupy me, neither settings nor persons nor events are called for per se. Characters have come to resemble something closer to exemplars or symbols, and settings no longer need to be presented in detail; in fact, they have become something closer to décor, and the choice of events depends on the need to crystallize the main ideas.

The danger here is that the idea may impose itself on the reality inharmoniously, or you may be obliged to create a special reality for it. However, when the idea springs from the reality and is a result of a fertile coexistence with it, there will be no contradiction between them when it attempts to incarnate itself in a particular form. One difficulty, however, does face the writer: the events, characters, and general atmosphere of a work of art must come naturally and without evoking the process of fashioning and planning that precedes it. It is this that distances this expressive procedure from that of the literature of ideas. The fundamental difference, in my opinion, between this method and that of the conventional literature of ideas, such as Kafka's, for example, is that Kafka created a world different from ours, with its own special dimensions—a different world, in which it is okay for a person to have a charge about which he knows nothing, and regarding something equally unknown, leveled against him, a world in which such events can unfold, and unfold in that way. Here, the ideas have created a world that is appropriate to them. The play *Shahrazad* by Tawfiq al-Hakim is another example of the creation of a special, unfamiliar reality to serve the idea. There is nothing with which we are familiar in ordinary life that would make King Shahriyar behave as he does in the play. These works have their own special realities and should not be compared with ordinary reality. In my latest efforts, my ideas spring from reality because it is that which inspires them. It follows that they can be traced back to it without forcing or contradiction. These efforts are not something new to literature. Many writers, through the various literary eras, have shifted from naturalism to expressionism, among them Strindberg, Thomas Mann, O'Neill, and Hemingway.

As an art form, the novel is very flexible and has proved itself capable of digesting all the forms that preceded it, such as theater, poetry, and epic. It may rely on expatiation, or it may equally rely on the dramatic form that lends itself best to concentration and on putting dialogue at the fore. It can discuss ideas just as it can give expression to life. Indeed, it can set forth long and complex discussions whose introduction into the theater would be seen as distinctly adventurous, such as those that take place in Thomas Mann's novel *The Magic Mountain* or those long discussions, and especially those concerned with philosophy and art, set forth by Proust in *Remembrance of Things Past*, which could easily be extracted from the novel and issued as a book on their own.

It follows that I do not believe that my new experiments with the novel are linked to that so specifically European crisis of which we have spoken. The novel, as a field, remains wide open before the novelists of the many nations of the world that possess a philosophy of life and humanistic creed.

Finally, the novel possesses one major distinguishing feature that separates it from all other literary forms. It addresses the human being as a thinking, conscious individual without relying on any legerdemain, while the collective forms require that the receptor be present in a totally passive state; this is the case with cinema, television, radio, and, to some extent, theater. The receptor at the cinema exerts no creative effort, while, in the case of the novel, he plays a creative role, participating with the author in the conversion of words into incidents, events, and reactions.

There is another issue that used constantly to force itself upon me, the issue of commitment, for commitment rescues art from committing suicide among the molds of form, something toward which the modern European novel is tending, hard though it is to envision the existence of a writer, or even a citizen, without commitment. Though "commitment," in its normally accepted sense, means commitment to a progressive position on life, I believe that the sole foundation of art is truthfulness. The socialist writer does not have to be committed to socialism to be so described. For him to be a socialist it is enough that the signs of socialism be manifest in what he does, provided he holds fast to the one and only basic commitment in art, which is truthfulness. This basic commitment excludes spurious art from the scope of true art. An honest reactionary writer may even be of greater benefit to literature and society than a spurious socialist writer, because the honest reactionary will stimulate the reader's and the critic's thinking and create an arena for conflict where ideas are clarified, while the spurious socialist implicates socialism in his own dishonesty and does it harm.

Sayyid Qutb's *Ashwak* (Thorns)

Review of Qutb's novel by Naguib Mahfouz published in al-Sawadi *weekly newspaper*, 25 August 1947.

This novel seems like an extended, lyrical, poem—lyrical in every sense of the word. From one perspective, it is a personal experience; from another, it describes deep feelings experienced during a much-heightened state of incandescence, sensitivity, and excitement, a state in which the body melts away through emotion, and the spirit is turned into a furnace of feelings, ideas, and illusions. It is the story of two hearts whom love brought together and led to the happy night of the engagement ceremony. But, on that night, when he took her hand to place on it the ring, he felt her tremble and her hand pull back, and looked and saw a tear escape her eye. The man, bewildered, then fearfully takes her aside and she confesses everything to him, confident in his gallantry and trusting to his tender feelings. She concludes her story as follows: "This tear that you saw had to be shed. With it, I bade farewell to a part of my life that was dear to me. The music around me was the music of the funeral at which I paid my last respects to his (she means her first love's) bier for the last time. And now it is over!" But no! It is not over! Rather, a new page of respect and love is followed by pages of jealousy and doubt, and then by more, of forgiveness and happiness, followed by others still, of misgivings and pains, the two of them in an unending and fearful struggle, trying to forget the past and be true to the present and the future, until it kills them. The past stretches out its black hand and interposes itself between them, cruelly and monstrously, and we find that our friend has gone back to his old self—a despairing heart in an arid world. Time passes and he strives unceasingly to pluck out his past dreams from his heart but finds himself unable to do so. A certain affection has taken root in his heart and a certain image in his soul; his feelings are all the former, his imaginings all the latter. More time passes, and one day he meets a young woman leading a child by the hand. Forgetting himself, he goes toward her, and she receives him with a smile of distant sadness, asks after his wellbeing, and presents her child to him—and how delighted he is to find that she has named it after him, albeit the name is all that remains of what his loved one had won!

The writer's success is dazzlingly impressive, success in such stories depending above all on the portrayal of the emotions. Such stories are unlike objective stories in which the field of expression burgeons because of the multiplicity of their elements—the topics, the characters, the various artistic values. Instead, it focuses on the basic emotion around which motive, topic, and story all coalesce.

The writer's success is dazzlingly impressive, as I have said. He has fulfilled his goal in terms of accuracy, sensitivity, depth, and the capturing of even those fine-grained emotions that are the most deeply buried within the labyrinth of the soul. He knows how to move hearts and involve them in his tragedy, to live inside it, to participate in its love and its repulsion, its pleasures and its pains, and all this in a radiant, beautiful, smoothly flowing rhetorical style that captures the reader's soul with its poeticism, dazzles it with its precision, and seduces it with its epical stamp.

The author has decided not to present a direct description of his two protagonists. Nevertheless, their characters crystallize and form their separate selves as the emotion that binds them is depicted and the events between them unfold. Through these, it transpires that his young man is one of those who migrate from the countryside in search of an education; then life keeps them in Cairo and they live on the margins of life there, clinging to the purity of their early upbringing and responsive to what the city offers only to the extent that it in no way offends against virtue. They adopt its dress, inhabit its lodgings, and mix with its people until the moment when some experience that it offers plays havoc with their emotions and strips away the acquired exterior to lay bare their authentic natures, and their true hearts take them back to their original traditions in a burst of unmitigated impetuosity and merciless rage. It follows that the emotion the protagonist feels cannot be without conflict and struggle, and, if we add to this his extreme innate sensitivity, it turns him into an easy prey to suspicion and doubt. His pride and sense of self-worth drive him to adopt toward the girl on more than one occasion the posture of a teacher and guide, to the point that he comes, without realizing it, to look down on her. When we add this all up, we can understand the forces that were ready to kill his love at any moment. He appears not to be aware of the strength of his doubts and of his pride, but the comments of his fiancée's family confirm this defect. Thus the girl's mother tells him, in exasperation, "If she were a slave girl tortured by her master, she wouldn't have to put up with so much. Every day reproaches, every day discussions, every day rebukes!" Her brother tells him, during a quarrel, that he was never really serious about their plans, and that he has become so full of doubts and fears that he is intolerable. The two descriptions point, without doubt, to his true nature, but our young man has simply been true to his own nature and logic and is therefore unaware that he has become intolerable and has buried his love alive while weeping copious tears.

The girl is a fully endowed female, sure of her allure, reveling in her charms. She has tried them out on two men with whom she was previously in love and many more whom she did not love. Her pride in her femininity is no less than his pride in himself and, as a result, the struggle that erupts is between two despotic forces which seem, in the end, to prefer the torment of separation and deprivation to the humiliation of the self and submission. She is not looking for just a husband but for a man who will worship her and take pride in her, affording her femininity at least as much respect as she affords it herself. When circumstances decree that she must show herself before him "exposed" (to use her expression) and that he become acquainted with things in her past that may destroy his dreams and illusions, she shies away from him and refuses to be his, trampling on her heart and her future. She consents to withdraw into her family's home, waiting for "any man" but him, a man who may not possess his manliness and other qualities but with whom she will never feel humiliated; for a proud and sensitive soul such as hers this will suffice. Listen to what he has to say about her during one episode of their struggle: "She was afraid to show him the affection he wanted, for he would see in that the depravity of a confession on her part and the shame of a self-revelation. She would measure her status in his eyes by the possibility of his indulging her." On another occasion, she says to him, "You men think I am a child whom you can rape and rebuke and then placate with a piece of chocolate!" Indeed, she is not the sort of woman who seeks a husband and no more. Her first lover meets with her again following the break-up of her engagement to our hero (it seems his request to do so was the cause of the break) but she refuses his advances and politely rebuffs him, even though she is now an abandoned fiancée. A year or so passes, and our hero returns to her in a terrible state, begging for her forgiveness and wanting to renew their relationship. His abandoned fiancée has not been spared wagging tongues and provocations, but does she welcome him? Does she seize the chance to recover her man and silence the wagging tongues? Not at all. On the contrary, she tells him, "Listen, my friend. I am not the right person for you. Our life together will not go well. Before you, I feel exposed. I will stand exposed before no man."

I repeat once more, the author's success is dazzlingly impressive. However, we must bear in mind as well that the novel reflects a personal experience and as such is excused the requirements of creativity with regard to both content and characters, although we must point out that a novelist only truly merits the name when he leaves the boundaries of his own self and writes about others. At the same time, there is no doubt that it is his right to treat his own experience, if only once, and it is also his right, if he should do so and do so well, that appropriate witness be borne to the sublimity and mastery of his art.

The Reports of the Islamic Research Academy against *Children of the Alley*

The First Report

1. The story unfolds over 552 large-format pages. It belongs to the genre of symbolic narrative, dealing with the history of humankind starting from Adam and all that befell him and his sons and the mission of the Messengers—Moses, Jesus, and Muhammad—and goes to our present time and all the new daily scientific developments.
2. The writer makes symbolic allusion to every famous event and well-known person, adding from his imagination features that define and identify each, even though these may not be in keeping with their true historical context. Thus God is symbolized by "Gabalawi," Paradise by "the castle garden," Adam by "Adham," Satan, or Iblis, by Idris, Moses by

"Gabal," Jesus by "Rifaa," Muhammad by "Qassem," and so on, including the symbols used to portray events.

3. The writer has failed in his treatment of God and the Messengers:
   a) Regarding God:
   He has incarnated God and described Him with adjectives of a slanderous nature that he has placed in the mouths of either Satan or Qadri (Adam's disobedient son out of the two) or the "bullyboys" and also sometimes in the mouths of the Messengers, with others occurring as part of his depiction of certain situations. He has Satan describe Him as having been a highwayman in the past and say that He will be a criminal lout in the future. He describes the customs of His family as being outrageously foolish and cowardly and says that He changes and substitutes things in His book as His anger and failures dictate. He makes Qadri, son of Adam, say that He is one of the afflictions of the age and is "the biggest thug of all." He also makes one of the bullyboys say He is dead, or as good as dead. He makes the overseer of the estate say that He is confined to His room and only opens His door when the things He needs are brought to him. He makes a disciple of Jesus say that He is impotent and that if He still had His original vigor, things would go the way they were supposed to. And he makes Arafa, the symbol of science, say that He is asleep and unaware of the crimes He has committed. Finally, he concludes the story of the Messengers' missions with the death of Gabalawi. Refer on this to the following pages of the book: 23, 25, 29, 51, 55, 56, 65, 66, 71, 87, 95, 230, 237, 274, 289, 410, 484, 492, 497, 499.
   b) Regarding the Messengers:
   He portrays them all as frequenting hashish dens and taking drugs, and this is the least of the things ascribed to them by the author. Jesus is described by one of the bullyboys as a hermaphrodite: on p. 275, Batikha says, "The bullyboys of the alley meet to talk about a creature that's neither man nor woman!" [*Children of the Alley*, trans. Theroux, 204; slightly amended by the translator of the present work]. He describes himself, as do his disciples, as a drunkard and a hashish addict: on p. 288, Rifaa (Jesus) says, "Wine wakens the demons, but it makes those who have rid themselves of their demons drowsy"; and on p. 291, Karim, one of Rifaa's assistants, asks, "Should I get the brazier ready?" and Rifaa refuses decisively, saying "We need to keep our wits about us." Rifaa is also said to have married a whore, even

though he does not consummate the marriage, not to mention that according to the text of the Qur'an Jesus did not marry. The writer also contradicts himself when he makes some of Jesus's disciples avoid marriage because they want to imitate him and he makes Jesus's birth an outcome of marriage, which is contrary to the text of the Qur'an. Also, the end of what he has to say about Jesus is incompatible with the Qur'an's statement to the effect that he was not killed; the writer has him killed at the end, as per pp. 292–95.

c) Regarding Muhammad, symbolized by Qassem:

1. He describes him as frequenting cafés, smoking a waterpipe, drinking wine, and being fond of women, whom he watches out for in the open at sunset, as per pp. 318, 322, 338. Also p. 341, when he speaks of his marriage to Qamar (Khadija) and says that he approaches her "in his silk gallabiya, his body giving off heat mingled with the smell of liquor until he stood before her, looking down at her" [Theroux, 253], etc.
2. Among the inordinately slanderous sayings the writer puts in the mouth of a thug who is maligning Qassem is that "the son of a whore knew how to sow dissension among us" [Theroux, 328].
3. One of the most atrocious things he says in explaining the reason for Qassem's multiple marriages occurs on p. 443, where he says, "Nothing about him changed, although his marital life expanded, as though it was following the same course of renewal and expansion that the estate took" [Theroux, 332]. Then he goes on to describe the reason for his marrying, saying, "He was looking for something he had lost when he lost his first wife, Qamar," and likewise, "He wanted to strengthen his ties with all the different neighborhoods of the alley," or again, "The fact is they admired his vitality even more than his character," and "In our alley, loving women is a skill in which men lose themselves. They brag about it. It imparts a status that equals that of bullyboydom, in its time, or even surpasses it" [Theroux, 333]. The writer ends his story by saying that the progress and development of science, in the fashion that he imagines it, heralds the end of prophetic missions and removes all traces of them, and that this is one of the signs of God's senescence and ultimate death.

These are the aspects of the story that demand censure, and the fact that real events and characters have been transferred into indicative events and symbolic characters in no way lessens the seriousness of that censure; none of that hides the true face of each event and character. Nor is the seriousness of these charges lessened by the fact that what the writer has given us is—all beliefs and sacred matters aside—an excellent work of art, and that it would have been within the writer's power to keep his work, as art, away from the depths to which it descends. It is therefore recommended that the story not be published in written, audio, or video form.

Success is God's.
12 May 1968

The Second Report

After examining the novel *Children of the Alley* by Naguib Mahfouz, we find it to be a clearly symbolic story that alludes to life and humankind. Despite its symbolic nature, however, it contains a great deal of confusion and is organized according to neither historical context nor any straight symbolic line. Symbolic allusion is made in it to several periods—from the beginning of creation to the mission of Moses, peace be his; from Moses's mission to that of Jesus, peace be his; then Muhammad's mission, may God cherish and keep him; then the period of the decadence of and struggle over the Islamic world, and so on. In the symbolic figure that he names "Gabalawi" he has incarnated God, describing him in slanderous terms that he places in the mouth of either Idris (Iblis) or Qadri (Cain), Adham's (Adam's) disobedient son out of the two, or of the "bullyboys," or even sometimes of the Messengers themselves, or as part of his depiction of certain situations. He makes Iblis say of him, for example, that he had been a highwayman in former times and will be a criminal lout in the future. He describes the customs of His family as being outrageously foolish and cowardly and that He changes and substitutes things in His book as His anger and failures dictate. He makes Cain, son of Adam, say that He is one of the afflictions of the age and is "the biggest thug of all." He also makes one of the bullyboys say He is dead, or as good as dead. He makes the overseer of the estate say that He is confined to His room and only opens His door when the things He needs are brought to him. He makes a disciple of Jesus say that He is impotent and that if He still had His original vigor, things would go the way they were supposed to. And he makes Arafa, symbol of modern science, say that He is asleep and unaware of the crime He has committed. Finally, he concludes the story of the Messengers' missions with the death of Gabalawi at the hand of Arafa. Regarding the Messengers, he portrays them as frequenting hashish dens and taking drugs and he makes one of the bullyboys describe Moses (Gabal) contemptuously as a hermaphrodite, "neither man nor woman." He describes himself, as do his disciples, as a drunkard and a hashish addict. Rifaa is also said to have married a whore, even though he does not consummate the marriage. Later it is said that some of Jesus's disciples avoid marriage because they want to imitate him. He also makes Jesus's birth an outcome of marriage and he ends the story of Jesus by having him be killed.

Regarding Muhammad (Qassem), he describes him as frequenting cafés, smoking a waterpipe, drinking wine, and being fond of women, whom he watches out for in the open at sunset. In maligning him he uses phrases such as the words he makes a thug say, namely, "the son of a whore knew how to sow dissension among us" [*Children of the Alley*, trans. Theroux, 328]. Explaining the reason for Qassem's multiple marriages, he says, "Nothing about him changed, although his marital life expanded, as though it was following the same course of renewal and expansion that the estate took" [Theroux, 332]. Later he says, "He was looking for something he had lost when he lost his first wife, Qamar," and likewise, "he wanted to strengthen his ties with all the different neighborhoods of the alley," or again, "The fact is they admired his vitality even more than his character," and "In our alley, loving women is a skill in which men lose themselves. They brag about it" [Theroux, 333]. The seriousness of these charges is not lessened by the fact that they are presented in symbolic form, because the symbol is accompanied by whatever is needed to identify its intended referent, clearly and unambiguously. Nor is it lessened by the statements sometimes made by certain biased persons, or by those who are devoted to and captivated by these fields, to the effect that the writer was writing art and never intended to write a religious narrative. With regard to this novel, we deal here with the story and its explicit symbols without resort to consideration of the writer's goals or intentions. God Almighty will hold him to account for those. As to the evaluation of the work as a "refined" piece of art, we leave that to those critics whose "refined" tastes find such art easy to stomach.

The Islamic Research Academy has decided that circulation or publication of the work, whether in written, audio, or video form, is dangerous and its import likewise, based on this report and those of the other censorship apparatuses.

Success is God's.
Secretary General, Islamic Research Academy
1 December 1988

Two Letters to Philip Stewart

To Philip Stewart (translator of *Awlad haratina*)

Dear Mr. Philip Stewart,
Greetings and sincere congratulations on the two newborns: 1) Your daughter, and 2) The novel.

Please excuse my late response: I spent the summer and part of the fall in Alexandria for health reasons but my health's not too bad now. I read your introduction and admire the idea behind it. I found that it offers a way of accommodating both those who accuse my novel of atheism and those who describe it as a Sufi work. I am also impressed that you traced it back to its origin in Bernard Shaw, in tune with my own admiration for him and especially for his major work *Back to Methuselah*. Dr. Mandur is probably the only critic to have hinted at such an idea, when he said that I had conveyed a traditional concept of God without alluding to God himself.

You deserve great thanks, first for translating the novel in a style to whose excellence and beauty all its readers have attested and second, for writing this excellent introduction.

Please accept my best wishes.

A Letter to Dr. Muhammad Hasan 'Abdallah

(Author of *al-Islamiya wa-l-ruhiya fi adab Naguib Mahfouz* [Islamic Thought and Spirituality in the Works of Naguib Mahfouz]).

Dear Dr. Muhammad Hasan 'Abdallah,
I received your book *al-Islamiya wa-l-ruhiya fi adab Naguib Mahfouz* and read it with passionate interest and without putting it down. I aver that it is new in its perspective, innovative in its vision, and irrefutable evidence of the independence of your ideas and the exaltedness of your goal. I could find no contradiction between your judgments and the beating of my heart—and perhaps the unease that arises sometimes from readings of my work has its origin in the fact that my heart combines a striving toward God with faith in science and a predilection for socialism. The attempt to link God and socialism excites suspicions of atheism among some and of conservatism among others. I have always been amazed that the philosophy of socialism could be taken as a religion, since I, as a student of philosophy, know that it consists of constructs that are renewed with the

passage of time and can never, in any way, be suitable as an object of worship. What I admire in communism is its absolute social justice, which has yet to be applied in Russia itself. From each according to his ability and to each according to his need: a perfect basis for human interaction that turns humanity into a sublime family. But why should the necessity of my believing in that require that I should first believe in materialism or deny God?

All I can do, my dear sir, is to send you my sincere thanks and gratitude, while beseeching the Lord that He make you a beacon of unsullied belief and enlightening science and make your book a guide for the Arabs in their dire predicament, one that will propel them along the path of culture and progress without abandoning what is immortal in their inherited values.

Sincerely,
Naguib Mahfouz
15 March 1972

Minutes of the Questioning of Naguib Mahfouz Following His Attempted Assassination (1994)

(Mahmud Salah, *Awlad shari'ina: Naguib Mahfouz, muhawalat ightiyal*, 24–26 and 45–47)

Sharif al-Hilwani, president of State Security's Chief Prosecutor's Office removed to Naguib Mahfouz's room at the Police Hospital on 20 October to obtain his statements regarding his attempted assassination.

Your name and personal data:
My name is Naguib Mahfouz 'Abd al-'Aziz Ibrahim, eighty-three years of age, writer for *al-Ahram* newspaper, winner of the State Appreciation Award and the Nobel Prize.

Describe the details of how you came to be injured:
On Friday evenings I usually leave the house at 4:50. My friend Fathi Hashim waits for me with his car and we drive together to Casino Qasr al-Nil to attend the weekly literary discussion group, which convenes from five to seven. At the beginning, I used to go to the group by taxi or sometimes on foot. Later my friend Dr. Fathi Hashim volunteered to take me with him in his private car. The group is every Friday, and last Friday, 14

October 1994, I did indeed leave at about 4:50 and found my friend (Fathi Hashim) standing by the door of the car so that I could get into the seat next to the driver. Usually Dr. Fathi waits till he is sure I've gotten into the car, and then goes around and gets in so that he can drive and we set off. But this time I don't remember if I got in first or he went around so he could get in first. The time I took to go down to the door of the apartment block till I got into the car wasn't more than one or two minutes approximately. The moment I sat down inside the car I was taken aback by a strange impression of something like a wild animal or a German shepherd attacking me and seizing me in its claws. I sat there asking myself, "What's going on? What's a wild animal doing in the car?" Then I felt a body pressing down on me so I looked and there was someone who seemed to be jumping from the car and aiming a dagger that seemed to be pointed and with a piece sticking up. But the moment I saw the person and the knife being aimed by his hand at my body, I knew that it was to do with terrorists and they'd attacked me and that the business I'd heard about six years ago had happened because six years ago, when I won the Nobel Prize and I was sitting in the Scheherazade Café and the correspondent of the Kuwaiti newspaper *al-Anba'*, who used to sit with me sometimes in the café, said, "Sheikh Omar Abdel-Rahman has declared your blood forfeit." It was the first time I'd heard of the sheikh. I remember that. I asked him, "Why did he declare my blood forfeit?" The *al-Anba'* correspondent from Kuwait told me, "The sheikh (Omar Abdel-Rahman) says, 'If we'd killed Naguib Mahfouz thirty years ago, there would have been no Salman Rushdie.'" A few days after this incident, a man from the Egyptian security services phoned me and said, "I advise you to accept a guard to go around with you." I told him, "It's just talk. Omar Abdel-Rahman didn't issue a fatwa for my murder. It was a conditional sentence. He is saying, '*If* we had killed Naguib Mahfouz thirty years ago, there would have been no Salman Rushdie.'" He said, "I know, but Omar Abdel-Rahman has followers and they're wackos and any of them might understand what he said as a signal or a fatwa to have you murdered." I told him that my circumstances and way of life would make it difficult to have a personal guard with me, because I walk for hours almost every day and have literary circles and meetings and it would be torture for the guard who had to accompany me. I told him, "The guard might get fed up with me and kill me himself!" He wrote up a report of our conversation and persuaded me to have a guard appointed to stand at the door of the building and he always used to come but on the day of the incident he wasn't there, although his absence on that day isn't strange because I'd often find that he wasn't there in front of the building. So things moved along and I was completely reassured because I couldn't believe that a novel written and published in 1959 and banned from publication in Egypt *(Children of the Alley)* just because I won the Nobel Prize could cause all these terrible things.

Going back to the day of the incident, after I was stabbed I heard Fathi screaming and gesturing toward someone who was running away—I saw his back—and saying, "Catch the killer!" Then, God bless him, he remembered me and came running back and covered me with his jacket and rushed me in the car to the Police Hospital, which saved my life, because, as I see it, if he'd delayed even a little I would have lost all my blood and died. Clearly, the Lord cleared the path for us. Even the people standing at the door of the hospital opened it for us immediately without detaining us or asking all the questions they usually do. I received excellent care at the hospital. They took me to the operations room and I was in a state of complete shock and wasn't even in any pain. Even Fathi, after they'd carried out the operation and I'd come around, asked me, "Did you scream?" and I said, "I don't remember." And after I'd come around, I asked for my wife and told her, "They're going to operate on me," and she told me, "It's over, the operation's been done." I've remained in the hospital under intensive care until now and that's all I remember and I'm prepared to answer any questions. I'd like to clarify one important thing concerning *Children of the Alley*, which the terrorists have taken as a justification, or evidence, for declaring my blood forfeit or that I'm an apostate, as they claim: I had written many novels before that that were printed as novels and *Children of the Alley* was my first contact with the press. It was published as a serial in *al-Ahram* newspaper and, to begin with, it's illogical to suppose that I would choose a novel that was risky intellectually or contained anything audacious about the Divine Being to publish in the headlines of the newspapers.

That aside, *Children of the Alley* is like *Kalila wa Dimna*: it creates an imaginary world for the purpose of revealing another world beyond it. We find ourselves among animals living in a forest, but you know, and the ordinary reader knows, that we mean a critique of the human world with its forms of government, individual relationships, the wisdom of the wise, the stupidity of the stupid. However, so long as we maintain that we are in a forest, our heroes have to be animals and we are not to be held to account for dealing with them as we would with animals because we are dealing with something that is represented symbolically by animals. I used the same principle in *Children of the Alley*. I present Egyptians living in an alley, with their way of life and its injustices in all their detail. Then come the people whom I represented symbolically as the Messengers and others to defend the alley and make sure that Gabalawi's will is executed, so that these symbolic figures could help the alley in the conflict with the villains there, who plunder the estate and oppress the humans, so that right shall triumph in the end as a symbol of the triumph of any of the religions. Contrariwise, the novel supposes that religion has played a role in the evolution of humankind and in defending its members in the name of divine principles. In the same story, someone called Arafa comes along who is very cocksure and claims that he is the one who can set the alley to rights, not Gabalawi or anyone else. He claims too that Gabalawi has died and disappeared. But it turns out that Arafa has fallen under the control of the overseer of the estate and has placed all his knowledge at the service of the master and not of the alley; as a result, even he says that Gabalawi has to be brought back to life. The death and revival of Gabalawi are a symbol of nonbelief and a return to faith. I'm trying to say that this novel, from my standpoint as a writer, is the first proclamation of the need to weld science to faith, that the novel says, very plainly, that religion has rescued humankind from injustice, and that science is also capable of elevating and improving the lot of humankind, provided it does not turn aside from the principles of religion. There is further proof that this novel does not contain apostasy, nonbelief, or an attack on the Prophets or Messengers. This novel was written in 1959, when it was published and then subsequently banned from publication. The punishment for it, however, has come after all this time and after I was awarded the Nobel Prize. This indicates that the intention behind the hostility toward me is not to hold me to account for what is in the novel; they have, rather, taken the novel as a means, or an excuse, for killing me for no reason.

What do you have to say in response to the statement of the two accused (Muhammad al-Mahallawi and Muhammad Nagi) during questioning that the novel (Children of the Alley) *that you wrote concerns itself, in brief, with the story of the universe and creation and that you portray the Divine Being in this novel in the person of Gabalawi and that you conclude in this novel that the expulsion of Gabalawi from the hospice led to its being repaired and that in fact it was the sole solution for its repair, meaning that people should live without a god and without religion?*

First, those who believe this do not read works of literature with a literary or humanistic eye that seeks to know the truth and to understand the battle between good and evil. What matters in their eyes is that the novel should conform, literally, to the teachings of religion, and they go too far even in that, because religion itself has presented the story of good and evil and the story of rebellion (Satan's) against the Divine Being. All my novels turn on clear concepts that cannot in any way be interpreted as intended to oppose themselves to or show contempt for any revealed religion. To say that I am an apostate or an unbeliever is a slander. In fact, in my opinion, it is made by persons who do not know their religion well, because, if they did, they would not pass judgment on a man like me on the basis of one novel. I have numerous novels and other works and no one has said of them that they deny the Divine Being or expose religion to disrespect. Suppose, even, that in *Children of the Alley* I opposed the Divine Being or proved myself an unbeliever, as they claim, how would they know whether I had not returned to my senses and had not, in the course of a long life after the writing of this novel, changed my position? This is if we accept the soundness of their claim, for the sake of argument. And why, if they have the ability to converse and understand and arrive at meanings and intentions, have they not come to me to discuss what I have written, so that their death sentence against me should be delivered after at least hearing the arguments instead of taking me by treachery and assassination? To conclude, I thank God, who is my sufficiency and the best of advocates.

Do you have any other statements to make?
No.

Naguib Mahfouz put his thumbprint to his statement, as he was no longer able to write.

Confession of the Individual Charged with the Attempted Assassination of Naguib Mahfouz

What is your name and why did you join the organization that participated in the attempted assassination of Naguib Mahfouz?
My name is Muhammad Nagi Muhammad Mustafa, electronic equipment repair technician with a vocational diploma from the technical institute at Madinat al-Salam, living in 'Ayn Shams, which I moved to from Mallawi,

Minya governorate. I began my religious commitment four years ago through a friend. I frequented mosques belonging to al-Gama'a al-Islamiya in 'Ayn Shams including al-Safa Mosque and I read lots of books covering the Gama'a and I read its writings, including those of Sheikh Omar Abdel-Rahman, 'Abbud al-Ramz, Nagih Ibrahim, and so on. Our objective as it was taught to me is to make God's Book the government. We have lots of objectives that we carry out, including assassinating writers, celebrities, and the police.

How do you intend to apply God's law using arms? And does Islam permit murder?
It is a method we resort to to terrorize anyone who tries to stop us from carrying out the mission of the group's stated goals. The end justifies the means and on Judgment Day we shall be judged according to our intentions and it doesn't matter if innocent people fall victim to the implementation of our goals.

On whose behalf was the attempted assassination carried out? Who made the plan and what were the details, insofar as you were personally involved in them?
First, there was a religious obligation to assassinate Naguib Mahfouz on the grounds that he had attacked the Islamic religion in his book *Children of the Alley*. We don't discuss such things. All that's asked of us is to obey and carry out orders that are transmitted to us by Basim Mahmud Khalil. The fatwas, so far as I know, came from Omar Abdel-Rahman and the Gama'a's leadership in prison. It was they who declared his blood forfeit, the same as they did with Dr. Farag Foda. These operations are aimed at serving the Gama'a and implementing their plans that they set for the different cells. Also, Basim was killed in a battle with police forces in 'Ayn Shams. It was Basim's task to find out the address of the writer Naguib Mahfouz. I did surveillance with him and we fixed the execution of the operation on the Thursday preceding the event.

What was your plan?
The operation was to be carried out with a knife in view of the nature of the area and the wide security presence that we had observed. Basim and I went to his house on Thursday evening to cut Naguib Mahfouz's throat in his house. I was carrying a knife and a revolver that I'd hidden under my clothes (shirt and pants). Basim was wearing Gulf Arab clothes and our goal was to kill Mahfouz. We were carrying a bouquet of flowers and chocolates so it would look as though we were going to give them to the writer as a

present. We went up to his apartment and knocked on the door. A lady (his wife) opened it and we conveyed to her our desire to meet with the professor but she told us that wouldn't be possible because he wasn't there and she informed us that we could meet him at the Casino Qasr al-Nil tomorrow, Friday, at 5:00 pm. So the Lord didn't facilitate things and the operation didn't take place and we went down.

You went to cut the writer's throat in front of his family?
Yes. Our goal was to cut his throat in his home. I carried the revolver with me to frighten the members of his family and stop any attempt at calling for help. That was our plan. On Friday morning, the five members of the group met and we agreed together that we would kill him on Friday afternoon, God willing. So I went, along with 'Amr Muhammad Ibrahim, to his home and the three others were going to meet us with a car so as to carry out the operation either in front of the house or at the Casino. Either way, we weren't going to come back without Naguib Mahfouz's head. At approximately a quarter to five, the writer came down with another person and stood next to me for a few moments, which seemed like an eternity to me. My hand was inside my clothes, fingering the knife. I waited until he was in his seat in the car, then I went and stabbed him in the neck with all my strength, in a particular spot so as to end his life, and I let go of the knife and ran. I took a taxi to Tahrir Square, then went to 'Ayn Shams to meet the other members of the group at an agreed-upon time to study the situation following the execution of the operation. At the start of the meeting, we all hugged one another and the slogan of the day was "Congratulations!"

The position of Islam on the killing of old people and so on is well known. What religion would consent to what you did?
The fatwa was for him to be killed and we carried out what was asked of us. It would be an honor for any Muslim to kill Naguib Mahfouz and I attained that honor. Indeed, I wanted to kill him, and if I am destined to leave prison alive, I will not hesitate to kill him again. True, it is God who determines how long a person lives but I stabbed him and buried the knife in his neck and I told my colleagues he was dead and they'd better believe it, but God, glory be to Him, had fated him to live a long life. I was steady as I carried out my crime and I wasn't shaken as I saw the knife and the blood pouring from him and heard the man moan at the force of the blow. I expected him to die, like Farag Foda.

Children of the Alley *and the other writings and books of our great writer, have you read them?*
I haven't read *Children of the Alley* but I have read four books by him but I've forgotten their titles. I don't know exactly what the novel says but according to Sheikh Omar Abdel-Rahman's fatwa and other fatwas I've read, Mahfouz is against the Islamic religion in his novel.

But that is not true.
I have no knowledge of the novel. I carry out what we've agreed to do.

What were the expectations of the terrorist group between the event and the moment of its downfall?
Unfortunately we did not expect to be caught, especially after we'd fled from the area of the incident, in Agouza. We'd agreed to meet up the next day at a café in 'Ayn Shams. We were surprised to see a car pull up close to us and a group of people get out. Immediately, we got up out of our seats and whispered to each other that they were police and a few seconds later we opened fire and they fired back. I was hit and so was Basim, who died in the hospital. 'Amr Ibrahim was hit and hasn't recovered yet. That the State Security Service was able to get to us so fast confirms how strong it is. The thing that really worries our organizations now is the extent to which security services have infiltrated our organizations. This operation caused great confusion in the ranks of the Gama'a, especially its military wings. The killing of high-ranking member Tal'at Hammam came as further confirmation of the power of Security to get to the Gama'a's leadership. It's enough to remember that I and a number of other members of our group weren't even on the books as security threats but Security got to us all the same. I mention this as a testimonial, despite our differences with Security and our war against them.

What is your relationship with Omar Abdel-Rahman and the fugitive elements here and abroad?
Omar Abdel-Rahman is the scholar of al-Gama'a al-Islamiya and its main legal authority. He is highly regarded by its members. He has written lots of books and writings that enrich jihadist action. The second man is Sheikh 'Abd al-Akhar Hammad, a fugitive overseas who is in second place because of his standing as an educated and cultured young member of the Gama'a now. He has a book called *Jawaz taghyir al-munkar wa-hadd al-ra'iya* (The Permissibility of Changing What Is Forbidden and of Punishing God's

Subjects), where he explains the dangers facing us and the legal proofs on which we rest our actions against the regime. There are other groups too, including those of 'Abbud al-Ramz, 'Isam Dirbala, Nagih Ibrahim, and 'Asim 'Abd al-Magid, all of whom are in prison now following the events of 1981. They have writings that talk about different things to do with the actions of the organizations and their positions and that include their fatwas and rulings and these are useful to us in our action. These writings are the foundation for action within the Gama'a, alongside *Mithaq al-'amal al-islami* (The Islamic Action Charter), which defines the objectives we are calling for.

What is the nature of your relationship with the Islamic Gihad *organization?*
We both fight in the same trench, but the Gihad is concerned to keep its action secret, unlike al-Gama'a al-Islamiya. That is where we disagree, because they always want action to be covert and we work in the open. That said, the military wings of the Gama'a have now adopted the Gihad's secret approach for their action, such as shaving their beards and wearing ordinary clothes—jeans and so on.

And the Muslim Brotherhood? How do you view them?
It is clear that this organization's public discourse is very different from the truth it keeps hidden under wraps. They work covertly for a certain objective they have set themselves, which is to govern the country. It is certain—and this is no secret—that the Brotherhood is happy when operations occur that cause a big stir in Egypt. They aspire to light fires everywhere without any charges sticking to them.

How do you see the role of mosques, speaking as an organization member who has carried out a major terrorist crime?
Unfortunately, the government mosques have no preachers capable of attracting worshipers. The mosques are in need of total proselytization and the training of cadres if they are to convey their message—unlike the organizations, which attracted me and were able in a very short time to convince me of their ideas, so that I carried out the first crime of my life.

Were you and your partners aware of the reverberations that would result from the attempt on the life of the great writer Naguib Mahfouz?
Of course. That's what we were planning for. It's one of the major goals the Gama'a seeks to achieve through its operations.

On 10 January 1995, after twelve sessions, the Higher Military Court passed sentence of execution on Muhammad Nagi (first accused) and Muhammad al-Mahallawi (second accused). The court declared in its opinion that "These organizations wished to bring harm, by the agency of their members, to the security and safety of their country, although it would have been better had they been the ones who were harmed. Likewise, the contents of the papers submitted in evidence show that the miserable remnants of this army of terror strive unceasingly to reassemble and form new groups seeking to assassinate the symbols of our intellectual life, and what is Naguib Mahfouz if not such a symbol? Their bellies thus took fire with the idea that to slay him would be tantamount to slaying all intellectuals. The incident with Naguib Mahfouz was only the start of a series of crimes. We also find that the leaders of these terrorist organizations carefully trained the accused Muhammad Khudayr al-Mahallawi on how to manufacture explosives from raw materials, which he then took pains to bring into one of their dens. Likewise, members of the organization used forged identity cards, as they do in most of their planned operations, and adopted false names to hide their identities. Firearms and printed materials indicating their erroneous ideas were seized in their possession, as were explosives, which they had intended to employ in the service of dastardly terrorism."

GLOSSARY

'Abbas al-'Aqqad	1889–1964; prolific public intellectual, journalist, poet, critic, and writer on a wide variety of topics.
'Abd al-'Aziz al-Islambuli	1905–64; founder of *al-Ma'rifa* magazine (1931 to 1934) in which Naguib Mahfouz published many of his first articles.
'Abd al-Hakim 'Amir	1919–67; leading member of the Free Officers movement that overthrew the monarchy and of the Revolutionary Leadership Council; Chief of General Staff of the Egyptian army from 1953 and vice-president from 1964 until his death.
'Abd al-Halim Hafiz	1929–77; highly popular Egyptian singer.
'Abd al-Hamid Guda al-Sahhar	1913–74; prolific novelist and short-story writer.
'Abd al-Karim Qasim	first prime minister of Iraq following the overthrow of the monarchy in 1958. He was executed on 9 February 1963 after a show trial that lasted only minutes.
'Abd al-Qadir Hatim	1918–2015; politician and journalist, sometime minister of culture, founder of *Sawt al-'Arab* (The Voice of the Arabs) radio channel and of the Middle East News Agency.
'Abd al-Rahman al-Sharqawi	1921–87; journalist, poet, and novelist writing on rural themes.

'Abd al-Sabur Shahin 1929–2010; Islamist thinker and writer, and a member of the faculty of Cairo University's Dar al-'Ulum (Faculty of Arabic Language).

'Abd al-Wahhab Mutawi' 1940–2004; journalist and writer, editor of *al-Ahram* newspaper's Readers' Letters column from 1982 until his death.

Abu Zayd al-Hilali hero of a popular folk epic and an icon of valor and chivalry.

Adel Kamel 1916–2005; one of the foremost writers of the first generation of Arab novelists; among his most important works are *Mallim al-akbar (The Magnificent Conman of Cairo)* and *Malik min shu'a'* (The Ray King).

Age of Barbarism in Islamic historiography, the period before the arrival of Islam.

Ahmad 'Abbas Salih 1926–2006; journalist and screenwriter, best known for his book *al-Yamin wa-l-yasar fi al-Islam* (Right and Left in Islam); adapted a number of Naguib Mahfouz's novels for the screen; managing editor of *al-Katib* magazine.

Ahmad 'Abd al-Mu'ti Higazi 1935– ; poet, translator, and journalist.

Ahmad Badrakhan 1909–69; film director and screenwriter.

Ahmad Baha' al-Din 1927–96; liberal journalist and editor.

Ahmad Hamrush 1921–2011; a member of the Free Officers movement and historian of the July revolution, journalist, and writer of plays and short stories.

Ahmad Kamal Abu al-Magd 1930–2019; politician, jurist, and Islamic thinker.

Ahmad Rushdi Salih 1920–80; journalist, critic, and academic working on Egyptian popular literature; founded the leftist magazine *al-Fajr al-jadid* (The New Dawn) in the 1940s; taught at the Higher Institute for the Theater Arts.

Ahmad Shawqi 1870–1932; perhaps the most important poet of early twentieth-century Egypt; also a playwright.

al-Akhbar — *The News*, a daily newspaper, published by the Akhbar al-Yawm Establishment.

Akhbar al-adab — *The Literary News*; a weekly newspaper, published by the Akhbar al-Yawm Establishment.

Akhbar al-yawm — *The News of the Day*, a weekly newspaper, published by the Akhbar al-Yawm Establishment.

'Ali Sabri — 1917–91; member of the Free Officers movement, founder of the intelligence apparatus, and head of the Arab Socialist Union.

Amina Rizq — 1910–2003; actress whose career spanned from 1928 to 1996.

'Amr ibn al-'As — c. 573–664; leader of the Muslim conquest of Egypt and its first Muslim governor.

Anis Mansur — 1924–2011; influential columnist, editor, and author.

'Antar ibn Shaddad — poet of the pre-Islamic era in Arabia and subject of popular romances, in which he is portrayed as a paragon of chivalry.

Anton al-Gumayyil — 1887–1948; Egypto-Lebanese journalist and novelist; managing editor of *al-Ahram* newspaper in the 1930s.

al-Baquri — Ahmad Hasan al-Baquri, 1907–85; member of the Muslim Brotherhood and eventually of its Guidance Office. After the 1952 revolution, Abd al-Nasser appointed him minister of religious endowments, and the Brotherhood forced him to resign from the group; he remained minister until 1959.

al-Barudi — Mahmud Sami al-Barudi, 1839–1904; prominent poet and politician; briefly prime minister during the 'Urabi uprising.

Casino Opera — a large open-air café and restaurant, since disappeared, on Opera Square in downtown Cairo.

The Charter	Arabic: *al-Mithaq*; a document issued in 1962 for consideration by a popular congress in which Gamal Abd al-Nasser put forward a blueprint for Egypt's future following the 1952 revolution as a socialist Arab-nationalist state led by a new body, the Arab Socialist Union, and on whose basis the 1964 constitution was drawn up.
ḍād	a letter considered unique to Arabic, whose speakers sometimes refer to themselves as "the people of the *ḍād*."
Farag Foda	1946–92; prominent columnist and human rights advocate, assassinated by the Gama'a Islamiya for alleged apostasy.
Fathi al-'Ashri	translator and theater and film critic; secretary to Naguib Mahfouz following the Nobel Prize award and author of *Ayyam ma'a Naguib Mahfouz* (Days with Naguib Mahfouz).
Fathi Ghanim	1924–99; journalist and novelist.
Fathi Radwan	1911–88; politician and journalist; founded the New National Party in 1944 (disbanded 1953); minister of national guidance (information) from 1952 to 1958.
Fikrun wa-fann	Arabic-language magazine, founded by the German government in 1963 as a public diplomacy tool.
Gabir 'Asfur	1944– ; critic, academic, and literary journalist.
the Gama'a Islamiya	"the Islamic Group"; an armed fundamentalist group that emerged in the 1970s and carried out a campaign of attacks and assassinations during the 1990s under the spiritual guidance of Omar Abdel-Rahman.
Gamal al-Ghitani	1945–2015; prominent novelist and literary journalist, editor-in-chief of the literary journal *Akhbar al-adab* from 1993 to 2011, and author of several books recording his conversations with and memories of Naguib Mahfouz.
Ghali Shukri	1935–98; literary critic and historian; editor-in-chief of *al-Qahira* magazine.

Hafiz Hafiz Ibrahim, 1871–1932; a leading poet, known for his revival of a "classical" style. Not to be confused with the fourteenth-century Shirazi poet of the same name.

Hasan 'Abbas Zaki (1917–2014); twice minister of the economy (1958–62, 1965–71); later, a member of the Islamic Academy.

Hasan al-Banna 1906–49; founder of the Muslim Brotherhood.

Hasan Sabri al-Kholi held numerous political posts including, at the time of publication of *Children of the Alley*, head of print censorship; later personal representative to Gamal Abd al-Nasser.

Hilmi Sallam journalist associated with 'Abd al-Hakim 'Amir, who appointed him editor-in-chief of *al-Gumhuriya* in July 1964. He was relieved of the post after ten months for revealing information specifically embargoed by Abd al-Nasser.

Hoda Shaarawi 1879–1947: campaigner for women's education and suffrage, and leader of the Egyptian Feminist Union from 1923 until her death.

the Hoodlums Arabic: *al-Harafish*; the name given by Naguib Mahfouz to an inner circle of friends, including writers such as Adel Kamel and Muhammad 'Afifi, with whom he met regularly throughout his life.

Husayn Fawzi 1918–2003; historian, political scientist, and scholar of Islam.

al-Husayn Fawzi 1905–99; pioneer graphic artist and the first Egyptian artist to draw for a newspaper, when he started his journalistic career with *Youth (al-Shabab)* magazine in 1924 while a student. Fawzi studied in Paris and, on his return, saw his mission as being to free Egyptian engraving from the influence of foreigners and to discover within it the elements of Islamic art.

Ibrahim 'Abd al-Qadir al-Mazini 1889?–1949; poet, novelist, journalist, and translator; a member of the Diwan school of poets.

Ibrahim Kamil 1941– ; businessman who attended Naguib Mahfouz's discussion groups.

Ihsan Abdel Kouddous 1919–90; Egyptian writer, novelist, and journalist, and editor at Egypt's *al-Akhbar* and *al-Ahram* newspapers.

Inji Rushdi 1925–2011; journalist at *al-Ahram*.

Kamal Abu al-Magd 1930–2019; lawyer and Islamic thinker.

Kamal al-Din Husayn 1921–99; member of the Free Officers movement and of the Revolutionary Leadership Council, who held numerous posts under subsequent governments, including president of the Executive Council, general supervisor of the National Union, minister of local government, president of the Higher Council for the Sciences, president of the Higher Council for the Arts and Literature, president of the National Research Council, head of the Teachers' Syndicate, president of the Higher Council for the Universities, president of the National Institutes, president of the Egyptian Olympic Committee, president of the Center for Pedagogical and Psychological Research, and president of the Atomic Energy Committee.

Kamal al-Mallakh 1918–87; journalist, archaeologist, and writer.

Kamil al-Shinnawi Mustafa Kamil al-Shinnawi, 1908–61; journalist, poet, and writer of musicals.

Khaled Abd al-Nasser 1949–2011; eldest son of President Gamal Abd al-Nasser, implicated in the activities of the Thawrat Misr (Egypt's Revolution) secret organization but eventually found innocent.

Khamis and al-Baqari Mustafa Khamis and Muhammad al-Baqari, executed on 7 September 1952 for organizing a strike for an independent labor union at a factory in Kafr al-Dawwar in the Delta.

Khutt nickname of a certain Muhammad Muhammad Mansur, leader of a band of desperadoes involved in murders and robberies in Upper Egypt's Asyut area in the 1940s.

Louis Awad 1915–90; public intellectual with an anti-traditionalist and reformist stance, prose and poetry writer, and journalist; literary editor at *al-Ahram* newspaper.

Mahmud Amin al-'Alim 1922–2009; leftist intellectual and writer.

Mahmud Nur al-Din 1940–98; an intelligence officer who founded Thawrat Misr (Egypt's Revolution), an armed group dedicated to the assassination of Israeli intelligence officers working in Egypt under diplomatic cover following the country's normalization of relations with Israel.

Mahmud Taymur 1894–1973; short-story writer.

Mikhayil Nu'ayma 1889–1988; Lebanese poet, novelist, and philosopher.

Misr al-Fatah a political party with a paramilitary wing formed in 1933 to promote a nationalist agenda with religious elements.

Mohamed Salmawy 1945– ; academic, journalist, and writer; a confidant of Naguib Mahfouz.

Muhamad Fayiq 1929– ; minister of national guidance 1966 to 1970.

Muhammad 'Abd al-Wahhab 1902(?)–91; singer, composer, producer, and actor, sometimes called the Father of Modern Egyptian Music.

Muhammad Gabril born 1938; journalist and prolific novelist, short-story writer, and critic.

Muhammad Hasan 'Abdallah 1935– ; critic and academic, author of numerous works on Arabic literature, including two on Naguib Mahfouz.

Muhammad Hasanayn Haykal 1923–2016; prominent journalist and confidant of Gamal Abd al-Nasser; editor-in-chief of *al-Ahram* newspaper from 1957 to 1974.

Muhammad Husayn Haykal 1888–1956; writer, journalist, and politician; author of *Zaynab*, according to some the first Egyptian novel.

Muhammad Mandur 1907–65; critic and translator.

the Muslim Brotherhood official name: The Society of the Muslim Brothers. One of the earliest and most widespread Islamic revivalist, or Islamist, movements, founded in Egypt in 1928 by Hasan al-Banna; it is run by its top executive arm, the Guidance Office.

Mustafa Mahmud 1921–2009; physician and later journalist, Islamic reformer, and prolific writer on science, philosophy, religion, politics, and society.

Mutran Khalil Mutran, 1872–1949; Lebanese poet, translator, and journalist who lived most of his life in Egypt; a member of the Apollo literary group.

al-Nahhas Basha Mustafa al-Nahhas, 1879–1965; politician, leader of the Wafd Party from 1927 to 1952, minister and prime minister under the Wafd.

al-Naksa "the Setback"; euphemism for the defeat of the Arabs by Israel in the June 1967 war.

Nasir al-Din al-Nashashibi 1902 or 1921–2013; Palestinian historian and journalist who worked in Egypt for some part of his career.

Nasr (Hamid) Abu Zayd 1943–2010; leading liberal academic theologian who argued that the Qur'an, while divinely inspired, was also a "cultural product"; in March 1993, his promotion to a full professorship at Cairo University was denied; later, he was declared an apostate by an Egyptian court and required to divorce his wife, leading to his going into self-exile in the Netherlands in 1995.

National Union a political organization formed by Abd al-Nasser under the 1956 constitution that replaced all pre-existing political parties in Egypt and, following the 1958 creation of the United Arab Republic (UAR), in Syria; abolished in 1961 following Syria's secession from the UAR and replaced in Egypt by the Arab Socialist Union.

Near East Broadcasting Station aka "the Voice of Britain"; controlled by the British secret services, the station broadcast propaganda to the Arab World from 1941 or 1943 until 1957.

Night of Power a night during the month of Ramadan (generally said to be the 27th) when it is popularly believed that all prayers are answered.

Nizar Qabbani 1923–98; Syrian poet and diplomat, best known for his love poetry.

Per Gahrton 1943– ; Swedish politician, since 1981 a member of the Green Party.

Raga' al-Naqqash 1934–2008; literary critic and editor on many literary journals.

Rakha Muhammad 'Abd al-Mun'im Rakha, 1910–89, regarded as the founding father of the newspaper cartoon in Egypt.

Saad Zaghloul 1859–1927; prominent nationalist politician and leader of the movement for independence from Britain; founder of the Wafd Party.

Sabri Hafiz 1939– : critic and academic at the School of Oriental and African Studies, University of London.

Sa'd al-Din Wahba 1925–97; journalist, playwright, and screenwriter.

Sa'd **Ardash** 1924–2008; actor, first director of the Cairo International Festival for Experimental Theater.

Sa'id Guda al-Sahhar 1909–2005; publisher, who in 1932 founded Maktabat Misr publishing house. He also founded, in partnership with his brother, novelist 'Abd al-Hamid Guda al-Sahhar, Lajnat al-Nashr li-l-Jami'iyyin (the Committee for Graduate Publishing) publishing house, which published works by young writers, among them Naguib Mahfouz.

Salah al-Bitar 1912–80; Syrian, a leader of the Socialist Arab Ba'th Party and minister of culture of the Central Government during the period of Egyptian–Syrian unification (1958–61).

Salah Jahin 1930–86; iconic colloquial poet, songwriter, playwright, and cartoonist.

Salama Musa	1887–1958; journalist and public intellectual who promoted secularism and Fabian socialism and was instrumental in introducing the works of Darwin, Nietzsche, and Freud to Egyptians.
Salih Gawdat	1912–76; poet, writer, and journalist.
Sami Khashaba	1939–2008; theater critic and translator.
Sarwat 'Ukasha	1921–2012; member of the Free Officers movement, journalist and translator; several times minister of culture under Gamal Abd al-Nasser.
al-Sayyid al-Shurbagi	journalist, screenwriter, and author of works on art and culture.
Sayyid Qutb	1903–66; key Islamist thinker and writer; best known for his call for action against secularism *Ma'alim fi al-tariq* (Signposts on the Road) and from circa 1953 a high-ranking member of the Muslim Brotherhood; executed for treason.
al-Sayyid Yasin	1933–2007; social scientist, director of the Al-Ahram Center for Political and Strategic Studies from 1975 to 1994.
Sharif Yunus	1961– ; academic, teacher of modern and contemporary history at the University of Helwan, author of works on Sayyid Qutb and Egyptian politics and society.
Shawwaf Uprising	short-lived uprising led from Mosul, Iraq, in March 1959 by army commander 'Abd al-Wahhab al-Shawwaf against the regime of 'Abd al-Karim Qasim and 'Abd al-Salam 'Arif.
Sheikh Ahmad al-Sharabasi	1918–80; cleric, preacher, and writer on religion.
Sheikh Muhammad al-Ghazali	1917–96; cleric and prolific writer and speaker on Islamic issues whose influence was felt deeply within the Islamist movement in Egypt and outside.

Sheikh Mustafa 'Abd al-Raziq 1885–1947; an Islamic philosopher and rector of al-Azhar who strove to prove the compatibility of traditional Islamic philosophy with the rationalism of modern thought.

Sheikh Sayyid Sabiq 1915–2000; cleric and writer on Islam.

Socialist Union the Arab Socialist Union, Egypt's sole political party from 1962 to 1977; replaced by the National Democratic Party.

State Prize a long-established prize different from the State Prize established in 1958. It had a monetary value of around two thousand Egyptian pounds and was awarded in 1957 to both Ihsan Abdel Kouddous and Muhammad Kamil Husayn for his novel *Qarya zalima* (Dark Village).

Su'ad Husni 1943–2001; popular actress and singer.

Suhayl Idris 1925–2008; Lebanese novelist, short-story writer, journalist, translator, and founder of the literary journal *al-Adab* in 1953 and the publishing house Dar al-Adab in 1956.

Sulayman Fayyad 1929–2015; journalist, editor of several journals, short-story writer, biographer, and lexicographer.

Surat Maryam the nineteenth chapter of the Qur'an.

Tagammu' Party "the Rally Party," officially named in English the National Progressive Unionist Party.

Taha Hussein 1889–1973; hugely influential novelist, short-story writer, journalist, translator, critic, editor, and minister of education (1950–52). Known as "the dean of Arabic letters."

Tahiya Halim 1919–2003; painter.

Tariq al-Bishri 1933– ; prominent lawyer and writer on Islamic society and history.

Tawfiq al-Hakim 1898–1987; a pioneer of the Arabic novel and drama, much of whose work deals with social and philosophical issues.

Thawrat Misr "Egypt's Revolution"; an armed group dedicated to the assassination of Israeli spies, active in Egypt in the 1980s.

'Umar ibn al-Khattab c. 584–644; second caliph of Islam, regarded as a paragon of piety and justice.

Umm Hashim a name by which al-Sayyida Zaynab, daughter of the Prophet Muhammad, is known; her tomb is housed in a large mosque in Cairo and she is the object of intense popular veneration.

Umm Kulthum 1904(?)–71; celebrated Egyptian diva, probably the best known female singer in the Arab world; Naguib Mahfouz named one of his daughters after her.

Yusuf al-Qa'id 1944– ; novelist.

Yusuf al-Siba'i 1917–78; former army officer who held numerous official and semi-official cultural and media posts and wrote many novels, a number of which have been made into films; assassinated in Cyprus by opponents of Egypt's 1978 peace treaty with Israel.

REFERENCES

Works by Naguib Mahfouz Referred to in the Text

All quotations from Naguib Mahfouz's work are taken from published translations.

'Abath al-aqdar. [First published in Arabic in 1939] (English translation: Raymond Stock. *Khufu's Wisdom*. Cairo: The American University in Cairo Press, 2003).

Asatidhati. Edited and with an introduction by Ibrahim 'Abd al-'Aziz. Cairo: Dar Merit, 2002.

Asda' al-sira al-dhatiya. [Serialized in *al-Ahram*, 1994] (English translation: Denys Johnson-Davies. *Echoes of an Autobiography*. Cairo: The American University in Cairo Press, 1996).

Awlad haratina. Beirut: Dar al-Adab al-Bayrutiya. 2nd ed. 1986 (English translation: Philip Stewart. *The Children of Gebelawi*. London, Heinemann, 1981; Peter Theroux. *Children of the Alley*. Cairo: The American University in Cairo Press, 1996, 2015). Page citations refer to the 2015 edition.

Bidaya wa nihaya. [First published in Arabic in 1949] (English translation: Ramses Awad. Ed. Mason Rossiter Smith. *The Beginning and the End*. Cairo: The American University in Cairo Press, 1989).

Hadith al-sabah wa-l-masa'. [First published in Arabic in 1987] Cairo: Maktabat Misr, 1987 (English translation: Christina Phillips. *Morning and Evening Talk*. Cairo: The American University in Cairo Press, 2007).

al-Hubb taht al-matar [First published in Arabic in 1973] (English translation: Nancy Roberts. *Love in the Rain*. Cairo: The American University in Cairo Press, 2011).

al-Karnak [First published in Arabic in 1974] (English translation: Roger Allen. *Karnak Café*. Cairo: The American University in Cairo Press, 2007).

Khan al-Khalili [First published in Arabic in 1946] (English translation: Roger Allen. Cairo: The American University in Cairo Press, 2008).

Kifah Tiba [First published in Arabic in 1944] (English translation: Humphrey Davies. *Thebes at War*. Cairo: The American University in Cairo Press, 2003).

al-Liss wa-l-kilab. [First published in Arabic in 1961] Cairo: Dar El Shorouk, 2006. (English translation: Trevor Le Gassick and M.M. Badawi. *The Thief and the Dogs*. Cairo: The American University in Cairo Press, 1984, 2013). Page citations refer to the 2013 edition.

Malhamat al-Harafish [First published in Arabic in 1977] (English translation: Catherine Cobham. *The Harafish*. Cairo: The American University in Cairo Press, 1994).

al-Maraya [First published in Arabic in 1972] (English translation: Roger Allen. *Mirrors*. Cairo: The American University in Cairo Press, 1977).

Miramar [First published in Arabic in 1967] (English translation: Fatma Moussa Mahmoud. Edited and revised by Maged el Kommos and John Rodenbeck. *Miramar*. Cairo: The American University in Cairo Press, 1978, 2016). Page citations refer to the 2016 edition.

al-Qahira al-jadida. [First published in Arabic in 1945] Cairo: Dar El Shorouk, 2006. (English translation: William M. Hutchins. *Cairo Modern*. Cairo: The American University in Cairo Press, 2008, 2013.) Page citations refer to the 2013 edition.

Radubis [First published in Arabic in 1943] (English translation: Anthony Calderbank. *Radophis of Nubia*. Cairo: The American University in Cairo Press, 2003).

al-Sarab [First published in Arabic in 1948] (English translation: Nancy Roberts. *The Mirage*. Cairo: The American University in Cairo Press, 2009).

al-Shahhadh. [First published in Arabic in 1965] (English translation: Kristin Walker Henry and Nariman Khales Naili al-Warraki. *The Beggar*. Cairo: The American University in Cairo Press, 1986, 2020. Page citations refer to the 2020 edition.

al-Summan wa-l-kharif. [First published in Arabic in 1962] Cairo: Dar El Shorouk, 2006 (English translation: Roger Allen. *Autumn Quail*. Cairo: The American University in Cairo Press, 1985, 2018). Page citations refer to the 2018 edition.

al-Tariq. [First published in Arabic in 1964] (English translation: Mohamed Islam. Ed. Magdi Wahba. *The Search*. Cairo: The American University in Cairo Press, 1987).

Tharthara fawq al-Nil. [First published in Arabic in 1966] (English translation: Frances Liardet. *Adrift on the Nile*. Cairo: The American University in Cairo Press, 1993).

al-Thulathiya—Bayn al-qasrayn, Qasr al-shawq, al-Sukkariya. 1st ed. Cairo: Dar El Shorouk, 2006. [First published in Arabic in 1956, 1957, and 1957 respectively] (English translation: William Maynard Hutchins, Olive E. Kenny, Lorne M.

Kenny, and Angela Boutros. *The Cairo Trilogy—Palace Walk, Palace of Desire, Sugar Street*. Cairo: The American University in Cairo Press, 2001).

Zuqaq al-midaq. [First published in Arabic in 1947] (English translation: Trevor Le Gassick. *Midaq Alley*. London and Washington, DC: Heinemann & Three Continents, 1977; Trevor Le Gassick. *Midaq* Alley. Cairo: The American University in Cairo Press, 1985; Humphrey Davies, *Midaq Alley*. Cairo: The American University in Cairo Press, 2011, 2015). Page citations refer to the 2015 edition.

Other Books and Articles

Abaza, Nabil, ed. *Hikayat Awlad haratina* (articles by 'Abd al-Galil Shalabi, Samir Sirhan, Mahmud Amin al-'Alim). Kitab al-Yawm book series. Cairo: Mu'assasat Akhbar al-Yawm, 1995.

'Abd al-'Aziz, Ibrahim. *Ana Naguib Mahfouz*. Cairo: al-Hay'a al-Misriya al-'Amma li-l-Kitab, 2012.

———. *Layali Naguib Mahfouz fi Shibard*. Cairo: Battana, 2017.

'Abd al-Hayy, 'Abd al-Tawwab. *'Asir hayati*. Cairo: al-Dar al-Qawmiya li-Tiba'a wa-l-Nashr, 1966.

'Abd al-Qadir, Faruq. *Fi al-riwaya al-'arabiya al-mu'asira*. Kitab al-Hilal monthly book series. Cairo: Dar al-Hilal, September 2003.

'Abdallah, Muhammad Hasan. *al-Islamiya wa-l-ruhiya fi adab Naguib Mahfouz*. 1st ed. Kuwait: Maktabat al-Amal, 1972.

Abu al-'Aynayn, Sa'id. *Rakha: faris al-karikatur*. Cairo: Mu'assasat Akhbar al-Yawm, 1990.

Abu Zayd, Nasr Hamid. *al-Qawl al-mufid fi qadiyat Abu Zayd*. Cairo: Maktabat Madbuli, 1996.

al-'Aqqad, 'Abbas. *Jawa'iz al-adab al-'alamiya*. Beirut: Dar al-Qalam, 1964. Reprint, Cairo: Hindawi, 2014, https://www.hindawi.org/books/19725020/. Citations refer to the free online Hindawi edition.

'Asfur, Gabir. *Naguib Mahfouz: al-ramz wa-l-qima*. 2nd ed. Cairo: al-Majlis al-A'la li-l-Thaqafa, 2010.

'Awadayn, Ahmad al-Sayyid. *Muhakamat Awlad haratina*. Cairo: Dar al-Ma'arif, 2014.

Darwish, Bakr. *al-Saffah: qadiyyat Amin Sulayman*. Cairo: Dar al-Tiba'a al-Haditha, 1972.

Dawwara, Fu'ad. *Naguib Mahfouz min al-qawmiya ila al-'alamiya*. Cairo: al-Hay'a al-Misriya al-'Amma li-l-Kitab, 1989.

Eid, Husayn. *Naguib Mahfouz: sira dhatiya wa-adabiya*. Cairo: al-Dar al-Misriya al-Lubnaniya, 2006.

Gabril, Muhammad. *Naguib Mahfouz: sadaqat jilayn*. Cairo: al-Hay'a al-'Amma li-Qusur al-Thaqafa, 1993.

al-Ghitani, Gamal. *al-Majalis al-mahfuziya*. Cairo: Dar El Shorouk, 2006. Published in English translation as *The Mahfouz Dialogs*, trans. Humphrey Davies. Cairo: The American University in Cairo Press, 2007.

———. *Naguib Mahfouz yatadhakkar*. 1st ed. Beirut: Dar al-Masira, 1980.

Gohar, Sami. *al-Samitun yatakallamun*. 6th ed. Cairo: al-Maktab al-Misri al-Hadith, 1976.

Hakki, Yahya. *'Itr al-ahbab*. 1st ed. Cairo: Dar al-Kitab al-Jadid, 1971.

——. *Zahrat al-'umr*. Cairo: al-Hay'a al-Misriya al-'Amma li-l-Kitab, 1998.

Hannura, Masri. *Naguib Mahfouz wa-fann sina'at al-'abqariya*. Cairo: Dar El Shorouk, 2008.

Hussein, Taha. *Hafiz wa Shawqi*. Cairo: Dar Hindawi, 2014 [1st ed. published in 1933].

Ibn Tamim, 'Ali. *al-Nuqqad wa-Naguib Mahfouz*. Abu Dhabi: al-Majma' al-Thaqafi, 2008.

'Isa, Salah. *Shakhsiyat laha al-'ajab*. Cairo: Dar Nahdat Misr, 2010.

Johnson-Davies, Denys. *Memories in Translation: A Life between the Lines of Arabic Literature*. Cairo: The American University in Cairo Press, 2006.

Mahfouz, Naguib. *Misr al-qadima*. 3rd ed. Cairo: Dar El Shorouk, 2016. Arabic translation of: James Baikie, *Ancient Egypt* (London: A&C Black, 1912).

———. *Atahaddath ilaykum*. Beirut: Dar al-'Awda, 1977.

Muwafi, Wahid, ed. *Qissat Nubil Mahfouz*. Cairo: Maktabat Madbuli, 2013.

al-Naqqash, Raga'. *Naguib Mahfouz: safahat min mudhakkaratihi wa-adwa' jadida 'ala adabihi wa-hayatihi*. Cairo: Markaz al-Ahram li-l-Tarjama wa-l-Nashr, 1998.

———. *Fi hubb Naguib Mahfouz*. Cairo: Dar El Shorouk, 1995.

Nigm, Ahmad Fu'ad. *al-Fagumi: al-sira al-dhatiya al-kamila*. Cairo: Jazirat al-Ward, 2009.

al-Qa'id, Yusuf. *Naguib Mahfouz in haka*. Cairo: al-Hay'a al-Misriya al-'Amma li-l-Kitab, 2015.

Said, Edward W. *Beginnings: Intention and Method*. New York: Basic Books, 1975.

Salah, Mahmud. *Awlad shari'ina: Naguib Mahfouz, muhawalat ightiyal*. Cairo: Akhbar al-Yawm, 1997.

Salmawy, Mohamed. *Naguib Mahfouz, watani misri: hiwarat ma'a Mohamed Salmawy*. Cairo: Dar El Shorouk, 1997.

El Shabrawy, Charlotte. "Naguib Mahfouz, The Art of Fiction No. 129." *The Paris Review*, issue no. 123, Summer 1992.

al-Sharif, Ahmad Hashim. *Naguib Mahfouz: muhawarat ma qabl Nubil*. Cairo: Rose al-Yusuf, 1989.

Shaw, Bernard. *The Complete Plays of Bernard Shaw*. London: Constable and Co, 1931. Also: Project Gutenberg eBook of *Back to Methuselah*, http://www.gutenberg.org/files/13084/13084-h/13084-h.htm

Shukri, Ghali. *al-Muntami: dirasa fi adab Naguib Mahfouz*. 4th ed. Beirut: Dar al-Afaq al-Jadida, 1987.

———. *Naguib Mahfouz: min al-Jamaliya ila Nubil.* Beirut: Dar al-Farabi, 1991.

———. *al-Arshif al-sirri li-l-thaqafa al-misriya.* Maktabat al-Usra. Cairo: al-Hay'a al-Misriya al-'Amma li-l-Kitab, 2015.

Stagh, Marina. *The Limits of Freedom of Speech: Prose Literature and Prose Writers in Egypt under Nasser and Sadat.* Stockholm: Almqvist & Wiksell International, 1993.

Yunus, Sharif. *Nida' al-sha'b: tarikh naqdi li-l-idiyulujiya al-nasiriya.* Cairo: Dar El Shorouk, 2012.

Personal Meetings and Telephone Calls

Muhammad Husayn Haykal, Sami Sharaf, Sulayman Fayyad, Muhammad Fa'iq, Philip Stewart, Gabir 'Asfur, Farouk Hosny, Mohamed Salmawy, Yusuf al-Qa'id.

CPSIA information can be obtained
at www.ICGtesting.com
Printed in the USA
LVHW052139230322
714151LV00002B/3/J

9 781649 030856